By the Waters of Babylon

By the Waters of Babylon

Meditations on the Psalms for the
Solace and Renewal of the Soul

Benjamin W. Farley

Foreword by
Luther H. Rickenbaker III

WIPF & STOCK · Eugene, Oregon

BY THE WATERS OF BABYLON
Meditations on the Psalms For the Solace and Renewal of the Soul

Copyright © 2014 Benjamin W. Farley. All rights reserved. Except for brief quotations in critical publications or reviews, no part of this book may be reproduced in any manner without prior written permission from the publisher. Write: Permissions. Wipf and Stock Publishers, 199 W. 8th Ave., Suite 3, Eugene, OR 97401.

Wipf and Stock
An Imprint of Wipf and Stock Publishers
199 W. 8th Ave., Suite 3
Eugene, OR 97401

www.wipfandstock.com

ISBN 13: 978-1-62564-927-0

Manufactured in the U.S.A.   07/21/2014

Unless otherwise noted, Scripture quotations are from the Oxford Annotated Bible: Revised Standard Version Bible, Copyright © 1962 by Oxford University Press, Inc.; Old Testament Section, Copyright 1952; New Testament Section, Copyright 1946, by Division of Christian Education of the National Council of Churches of Christ in the United States of America. Reprinted with permission. All rights reserved.

Dedicated to
Jack and Kitty, Betty and Ward,
Marilyn and Ken

Contents

Foreword by
Luther H. Rickenbaker III | ix

Acknowledgements | xi

Introduction | xiii

Book One **Psalms 1–41**

1 From the Aspect of Eternity | 3
2 Under the Shadow of God's Wings | 20
3 Our Light and Refuge | 36
4 Remorse and Redemption | 47

Book Two **Psalms 42–72**

5 Songs of the Temple Singers | 67
6 A Broken and a Contrite Heart | 85
7 Solace for Times of *Storm and Stress* | 98

Book Three **Psalms 73–89**

8 Plight and Deliverance: Hymns of
   the Levite, Asaph | 119
9 God's Steadfast Love | 134

Book Four **Psalms 90–106**

10 Obtaining a Heart of Wisdom | 149
11 The Right Hand of God | 166

Book Five **Psalms 107–150**

12 Psalms of Encouragement and Gratitude | 183
13 The Quintessential Grace of God | 198
14 Israel's Songs of Ascents | 206
15 By the Waters of Babylon | 223
16 The Unsearchable and Immeasurable
   Depths of God | 229
17 An Epilogue of Praise | 239
18 Postscript: Poetry, Time, and Eternity | 249

Selected Bibliography | 251

Foreword

IN THIS VOLUME, BENJAMIN Farley gives rise to a flood of unique and compassionate interpretations of the Psalms. The message he brings to light in each chosen Psalm is complemented by references to classical and modern literature, philosophical, theological, musical, and autobiographical reflection. For the reader, the erudite combination of these sources lifts these biblical masterpieces to high levels of personal and spiritual meaning.

The author's clear thinking is expressed in beautiful lyrical prose. The book's title is poetic, along with narratives such as the following: "The Psalms are a mirror, as well as a channel of blessing. They summon us to come to God, just as we are. To hide our guilt is not an option. It is the last thing we need to do. God knows us for what we are, and whose we are – his! . . . Even the most hermetic monk or devout nun cannot escape a restless past, or shattered hopes they bring to a monastic life. Not even David could, to whom the Psalmist attributes this piece (Psalm 138:3,7). That is why grace is essential, because it 'preserves' our life in spite of Babylon's mournful streams that bring to surface remembered woes."

These provocative and engaging meditations will serve well those who are seeking a thoughtful challenge and resolve to their faith. They will be encouraged to read the Psalms in light of what the finest thinkers and people of faith have struggled with through the centuries in order to establish a worldview that is neither local nor provincial; where a personal God of love is always faithful to his people regardless of what happens in their lives.

In 1983, when William Sloane Coffin preached on the death of his son, Alexander, he quoted biblical passages throughout the Bible that often give comfort to people in troubled times. He quoted one passage twice. It was Jesus' cry from the cross where he quoted Psalm 22:1: "My

God, my God, why hast thou forsaken me?" He made the point that the Psalm only begins that way; it doesn't end that way. In an effort to encourage hope for people of faith, this is exactly the way Benjamin Farley approaches the Psalms. He does it in an intellectual, artistic, and personal manner in an effort to foster hope for people of faith in the present day.

With reference to the solitude of pain, the author goes on to suggest that, like the people of Israel, we all experience God's abandonment at some time in our lives. But the salient feature of God's character, demonstrated in the Psalms, is that he is always present at the broken places in our hearts, and especially there, where we are made strong through his unmerited favor.

One overriding feature of this book is that the meditations do not have to be read from the first page to the last. As a treasury of devotions, they may be read as personal needs for joy, comfort, forgiveness, grace, and healing arise in the life of the reader.

Luther H. Rickenbaker III

Minister Emeritus
Central United Methodist Church
Spartanburg, South Carolina

Acknowledgments

I WISH TO ACKNOWLEDGE my gratitude to the many bookstores across the South and elsewhere that have carried my books, along with the many readers who greeted *Fairest Lord Jesus* with gracious compliments. *By the Waters of Babylon* is its sequel, thanks in part to the readership and encouragement of those who found the former meditations helpful. I am especially grateful to the SC Commission of the Arts and its annual Book Festival, which provides support for authors of varied venues. So also to Theresa Wallace, Randy Akers, and other staff members. I am equally grateful to Jill Hendrix of Fiction Addiction of Greenville, SC; The Book Dispensary of Columbia, SC; High Noon of Ballentine, SC; Ed's Books of West Columbia, McCaslans of Greenwood, SC; and booksellers scattered across Georgia, North Carolina, and Virginia. Thanks also to Dr. Ben Sloan, Dr. Gale and Carol Coston, Libby Case, Drs Ellen and Eric Skidmore, Dr. Mike Bragan, Lynda Bouchard, the Rev. Luther Rickenbaker, Dr. Elizabeth Gressette, Drs. Anne Matthews, Mack Braham, and Richard Kenan of Rotary International, as well as Jennifer Pender, MD, and numerous others whose support has never waned.

Above all, I wish to thank Dr. Norma Kirkland for her editorial assistance and painstaking labor devoted to each chapter. So also, I am indebted to Catherine Johnson, Attorney-At-Law, who committed hours of time to proofing the work and whose vital suggestions have been instrumental in improving the text.

Finally, in addition, I wish to thank my wife, Alice Anne, for proofing the book and catching last minute errors.

Introduction

FEW BOOKS OF SACRED literature have inspired the human heart as The Psalms. With poetic majesty and unconditional depth, the Psalms console and edify the restless heart. They have done so for millennia. One hardly needs to ask why. Within its pages we encounter no one less than the living God, whose Spirit overflows with love and redemption for each of us. Equally, we meet ourselves, at our best and worst, in our anguish and longing, solitude and desperation, so much so that the Reformer John Calvin labeled the Psalms a "mirror" of the soul.

> I have been accustomed to call this book, I think not inappropriately, "An Anatomy of all Parts of the Soul;" for there is not an emotion of which any one can be conscious that is not here represented as in a mirror.[1]

Martin Luther dubbed it "the little Bible," since it contains the essential teachings of the Bible.[2] In his mind, "no books of moral tales or legends" are as "noble" as the Psalms.[3]

To meet the Eternal within the bounds of time humbles and fulfills our existence. And existence it is! The Psalms hold nothing back. In its metaphors of praise, thanksgiving, and lament we are enjoined to be ourselves with God. This is true even in cases of faith's collapse, when out of frustration we question the very character of God. "Why have you turned your face from me? Why are you so slow to answer my prayer, or silent when I cry for help?"

It is a human book, an all-so-human book, and yet God's unbounded haven for souls that seek the truth. We cannot be healed if we deny

---

1. *Preface to Calvin's Psalms*, Dillenberger, 23.
2. Luther's *Preface to the Psalms*, Dillenberger, 38.
3. Ibid., 36.

the truth, or mask the underlying symptoms of our disquietude. Thus the Psalter brings us to God's secret place, where we experience anew his ineffable presence and, unafraid and hopeful, find solace and encouragement for the soul.

Historically, the form in which we possess the Psalms today represents the collected hymns and lyrical verses employed by the priests and choir directors during the period of the Second Temple, i.e., 500 BCE or later. Many reflect an earlier period, even before the time of David. Some suggest familiarity with Egyptian hymns, dating to the time of the pharaohs, while others to the Mesopotamian worship of Ishtar and the gods and goddesses of the Euphrates River Basin. This fact should alarm no one. All God's children—whatever their time and culture—have and still hunger for the living God. Their voices also rise to sing God's praises and claim his forbearance. No culture exists in a vacuum, therefore, that Israel drew spiritual insight from neighboring societies, or amended their religious traditions to suit its own, should come as no surprise, nor pose cause for alarm.

Numerous commentaries exist that detail the time and place, the period and setting of the Psalms. Overall, the Psalms conform to specific types, which have been collected under the Five Books of the Psalter. Scholars classify these principally under three headings: hymns of praise, thanksgiving, and lament. In turn scholars break the collection down into additional sub-types, namely: enthronement hymns, royal psalms, songs of trust, songs of Zion, sacred history hymns, as well as songs of ascent and wisdom psalms. Many of the laments are personal pleas for mercy and assurance, while others witness to Israel's national crises in times of upheaval.

Underlying all the psalms, however, is the inescapable relationship between time and eternity that the Psalms offer. That relationship alone redeems life and floods humankind with grace and meaning. It is to that end that the meditations that follow are devoted. Herein, where time is caught up by the Eternal, and the individual encounters the Unconditional, we are blessed with the fulfillment of our existence. As the late Paul Tillich explained throughout his works, because we are finite and mortal, we feel threatened in three ways: by a fear of nonbeing, by a sense of guilt due to unavoidable doubt, and by an anxiety that life is meaningless. In the final analysis, only God, the Ground of all Being, can save us from our guilt and anxiety and provide us with the love and courage we require to fulfill our individual destinies.

In further interpreting the Psalms for their meaning today, it is useful to keep in mind the ancient hermeneutical methods employed by the Early Church up, until, and partly through the Reformation. Four levels of meaning were attributed to each text—the literal or *historical*, the *allegorical* or metaphorical, the *tropological* or moral, and the *anagogic*. The allegorical purports to discern a meaning beyond and/or behind the literal and historical text; whereas the anagogic investigates a passage's typological or eschatological sense—a text that anticipates the salvific events of the Messianic Era. Augustine's interpretation of the Psalms draws widely on the allegorical and anagogic. Calvin limits himself to the historical and immediate plain sense of the Word, emphasizing its moral level essentially. Luther loves to test the spiritual and mystical/allegorical limits of a text, as did Augustine.

In the meditations that follow, I strive to clarify the historical setting, if and where it is needed, though preferring a combination of an existential and spiritual approach. By existential, I mean what Paul Tillich explains in his many works: a divine answer to the threat of nonbeing, doubt, and meaninglessness. I also attempt to preserve something of the original intent of the Psalms. After all, the Psalms constitute a pinnacle work of the Jewish faith. To Christianize them thoroughly, as Luther does, is understandable, but not at the expense of denigrating Israel's own witness to God, which she achieved at the time Judaism produced this masterpiece. In so many respects, the Psalter is a Prayer Book for all religious persons. Here, too, they are invited to encounter Israel's Eternal God of steadfast love [*hesed*] and righteous longing [*zedek*]. If there is one underlying theme, it is this *hesed* love, inseparable from God's enlightening will for all mankind to claim. Even as Luther knew, a "righteousness of grace" dominates its prayers and poems. That they are couched in the language of a people, hard-pressed to survive, need not dismay us. Theirs was a time, subject to the will of the most powerful nations of the Ancient Near East—from the waters of Babylon and Persia to the Upper Nile of Egypt.

Also of merit is the Hebrew word for the Psalms: *tehillim* (plural), The word means "praise" and is closely associated with the word *tephillah* or prayer—that indispensable element of faith without which we can neither sound the self nor communicate with God. It is more than mere contemplation or an escape from our beleaguered subconscious. It is where God awaits us in our harrowing humanity. Prayer and praise constitute the means by which God woos our hearts to embrace the mystery and joy of life, rather than curse the darkness and its toilsome road of sorrow.

By way of footnote, an additional comment is necessary. Frequently I refer to the Centre de Villemétrie, a Protestant Monastic Community that existed in the 1950–70s just south of Paris. I was a novice monk in its community in the early 1960s. André de Robert was its director, a man of genuine spiritual devotion and an exemplar of Christ's kindness and spirit. André's name and the community appear from time to time in the text. He was an ordained minister of the Reformed Church of France, and, after many years as an itinerant evangelist, was asked to direct the Centre and its program of Christian engagement in a secular world. On weekends, Christian friends and secular enquirers alike arrived from Paris to study at the Centre and draw renewed inspiration from André's commitment to the Gospel and the Christian faith.

Book One
Psalms 1–41

1

From the Aspect of Eternity

> [But] his delight is in the law of the LORD, and on his law he meditates day and night.
>
> Psalm 1:2

It was the philosopher Benedict Spinoza who proposed that it is only under the aspect of eternity (*sub quandam aeternitatis specie*) that we come to understand anything. Until then, we are blinded by our emotions and the limitations of our time. The Apostle Paul held a similar view: "For now we see through a glass, darkly; but then face-to-face: now I know in part; but then shall I know even as also I am known" (1 Cor 13:12 KJV). Long before Paul, the Psalmist had adopted a parallel view. It is only when we see the world from God's perspective, that we begin to realize *who we are* and *what our role* in the universe can be.

For the Psalmist, it was God's divine word, contained in the Torah that revealed that sacred perspective. It became his focal point of delight and meditation. Note, also, his emphasis on time: "day and night." Our time is fragile and finite, compared with God's time; ours brief and mortal, while God's endures from eternity to eternity. For the Psalmist, the portal to God's time was the Torah, alone replete with grace and wisdom to keep souls nourished and alive—like the trees in his metaphors. However, he also knew how important *time itself* is. For apart from a life immersed in the Eternal, we become like the chaff that the wind blows away.

As Abraham Heschel put it so aptly: "God is not in things of space, but in moments of time." In context he was writing about the Sabbath, but his insight applies here. If we want to experience God's "perspective" of all that is good and sacred, then time spent with God allows time for God to lift us into his holiness, where wisdom and healing abound.[1] Clearly, the Psalmist invites us to experience that perspective today and every day for the rest of life.

∽ ∽ ∽

> Why do the nations conspire, and the peoples plot in vain?
>
> Psalm 2:1

In truth, we know why. Neither the kings of the earth, nor the rulers in their counsel treasure the LORD'S perspective. Nor, in the Psalmist's mind, do they meditate on his grace and wisdom, either by day or night. Their "delight" lies in something else: economic competition, trade alliances, treaties of mutual advancement, spying, containment, and war. Little wonder that they have "set themselves . . . together, against the LORD and his anointed, saying, 'Let us burst their bonds asunder, and cast their cords from us.'" They are too embedded in their geo-political enclosures to consider the saving wisdom of God's "bonds" and "cords." They wish none of it. Not even slogans declaring, "In God We Trust," or belt buckles engraved with "*Gott Mit Uns*," can save us from our noble intentions when our heart's treasure lies somewhere else.

Let us leap forward, so to speak, under God's aspect of eternity. Do you remember who said these words? "Enter by the narrow gate; for the gate is wide and the way is easy, that leads to destruction, and those who enter by it are many. For the gate is narrow and the way is hard, that leads to life, and those who find it are few" (Matt. 7:13–14). As for God's "bonds" and "cords," "Take my yoke upon you and learn of me," he added, "for my yoke is easy and my burden is light." That is why God, "who sits in the heavens," smiles, and in his heart of hearts struggles against the temptation to hold mankind in "derision." God is love, John reminds us. The Psalmist, for all his humility, knew God primarily from his post-Exilic side of time. How Israel learned it all the hard way! Still, he captures

---

1. Heschel, *Sabbath*, xiv–xv.

the essence of God's promise of salvation: "I will tell of the decree of the LORD: He said to me: 'You are my son, today I have begotten you.'"

If only we could see *sub quandam aeternitatis specie*. That is why Luther defined us as "justified, yet sinful." Why Paul explained: "That while we were yet sinners, Christ died for the ungodly." And why the Psalmist concludes his coronation tribute with redemptive words of grace and forbearance: "Blessed are all who take refuge in him" (Ps 2:11).

∽ ∽ ∽

Many are rising against me; many are saying of me, there is no help for him in God.

Psalm 3:1-2

Tradition ascribes Psalm 3 to David. He penned it while fleeing Jerusalem in the year of Absalom's rebellion. The northern tribes had united with David's restless son to overthrow the aging king. David's Court Historian, as he is known, captures the event in all its sordid and heartbreaking details. The revolt sent David scurrying across the Kidron Brook and across the Mt. of Olives, protected only by a handful of faithful guards and his life-long companion, Jo'ab, the commander of his army. Somewhere in the pitiful entourage, his favorite wives struggled to keep up, no doubt Bathsheba among them, and possibly Absalom's mother, Ma'acah. Sometime that night, David crept into a cave and composed this first of the Psalmist's laments. As such it is brief, scarcely seven verses in length, with an eighth added by the Psalmist. Was David able to see Zion in the starlight, aglow with the glory of all that he loved? "O LORD, how many are my foes! Arise, O LORD! Deliver me, O my God! I cry aloud to the LORD, and he answers me from his holy hill" (Ps 3:4 & 7).

We know the fate of Absalom. How David wept: "O my son Absalom, my son, my son Absalom!" (2 Sam 18:33) Neither David nor Israel ever got over it. Yet David loved God too much to fault anyone but himself. He rent his clothes, sobbed with remorse with all his heart; then, with painful sadness, endured Jo'ab's deserved rebuke. Finally, he lifted his soul to God, and, as the historian continues, "arose, and took his seat in the gate" (2 Sam 19:8). To which the Psalmist adds: "Deliverance belongs to the LORD; thy blessing be upon thy people! Selah!" (Ps 3:8)

Historians and novelists have long recorded the story of humankind's familial failures, tales of betrayal and discontent. One needs only recall Dostoevsky's *The Brothers Karamazov*, or Turgenev's *Of Fathers and Sons*, or Pearl S. Buck's *The Good Earth* to realize how universal the story is. We, the readers, know only too well of the skeletons in our own closets. It is not for us to judge either David or Absalom, or fault others for the same; nor to fail to seek forgiveness for ourselves. How honest of the Psalmist to place this Davidic "mirror" before us, immediately following the First and Second Psalms. In doing so, the Psalmist provides us with a Prelude of God's consolation and redemption for all fallen souls. Indeed, "deliverance" belongs to God.

"O God, hear our prayer, too, and grant us thy consolation today. Lift us into thy presence once more and into thy holy arms of grace."

∽ ∽ ∽

> Answer me when I call, O God of my right! Thou hast given me room when I was in distress. Be gracious to me, and hear my prayer.
>
> Psalm 4:1

Who among us has not prayed as above? Calling on God to answer in our time of distress? Reminding God that he alone is the redeemer of righteousness? Even hinting that we are innocent, if not wholly, at least somewhat, and surely deserving of his attention? It is a universal prayer, attributed to David, our human mirror. In translation we miss the beauty of it, however, as well as its flowing quality. In its opening verse, the Psalmist fills each line with words of alliteration. "Right," or "righteousness," in Hebrew is *zedek*, and "distress," *zarah*. Perhaps we might translate it, "O God of *arbitration*, thou mender of *ailing* hearts, thou *advocate* of every soul."

In the New Testament, the word for "righteousness" is *dikaiosuné*. In Classical Greek it meant "well-being," though often it was translated as "justice." What is required of man and society in order to achieve a well-ordered and just world? The Greeks had their Psalmists, too, whom they called "playwrights." Yet even the greatest of these—Aeschylus, Sophocles, and Euripides—could not provide an answer. It remained

from the aspect of eternity 7

for Plato to venture a definition of "righteousness," both for individuals and the state. Only when the state is ruled wisely, and its guardians act with courage, and its citizens pursue their crafts with integrity, can justice prevail. The same of individuals: only when one's life is ruled by *wisdom, courage,* and *restraint*, can the "well-being" of the soul become a reality. So Plato proposed in his Dialogue of the Republic.

The Psalmist and Paul found themselves forced to question such idealism. O, not that wisdom, courage, and restraint are not of the highest value. Far to the contrary! But from the aspect of eternity, it is only God who can take our broken efforts and restore our hearts to "wellness." He is the true Advocate of all redress. Then, in "peace," may we "lie down and sleep . . . [and] dwell in safety" (Ps 4:8). Or as Paul put it for the ages to savor: "For I am not ashamed of the gospel; it is the power of God for salvation to every one who has faith . . . For in it the righteousness of God is . . . revealed" (Rom 1:16–17).

"O living God, we lift our hearts to thee, for thou alone canst do for us what our hearts cannot do, and that is to make us whole with thy all-surpassing peace."

∽ ∽ ∽

Give ear to my words, O LORD; give heed to my groaning.
Hearken to the sound of my cry, my King and my God, for
to thee do I pray. O LORD, in the morning thou dost hear
my voice; in the morning, I prepare a sacrifice for
thee, and watch

Psalm 5:1–3

Beauty and sadness, tenderness and grief offer us their balm in this prayer of lament. Robed in his gown of blue, purple, and crimson linen—the holy fabric of Moses' time[2]—the Psalmist, if not David, awaited the dawn. With faith in God, he scans the sky for daybreak's orb to crest the rise on the Mount of Olives, still a slumber in its dark-green groves. The individual before the Eternal! It heralds the call of God in our solitude to

---

2. The reference is to Exodus 26:31; 27:16.

begin each day anew with God. If not, life falters and fills our hearts with remorse for what might have been.

The Psalm continues. God foresees the brokenness that will overcome all "who delight in wickedness," whose sojourn is marred by "evil, lies, brutality, and deceit" (Ps 4:4–6). God grieves for them, for he knows the regret they shall one day bear. But for those who await his glory, God's "steadfast love" [*hesed*] and righteous presence [*zedek*] will never fail (Ps 5:7–8).

As something of an aside, note how the Psalmist requests the choirmaster to accompany his prayer with a melody of "flutes." Think of that! Even Native Americans carried their flutes into the woods, and, finding a grassy slope, sat down to play their willow reeds for the Spirit of God to hear.

"O ye who sang for shepherds at Jesus' birth! In your tender mercy, bear our prayers to God's heart, as his glory fills our own with joy and love."

∽ ∽ ∽

> O LORD, rebuke me not in thy anger,
> nor chasten me in thy wrath.
>
> Psalm 6:1

It was the year 428 CE. Genseric's Vandals surrounded Hippo. Only Count Boniface's weakened legions protected the city. It was August, and Augustine of Hippo lay dying in his monastic cell. He knew he could not live much longer. He feared his library of Neo-Platonic literature and own works would soon be consigned to the flames. Knowing the end was near, he asked his faithful monks to inscribe the Penitential Psalms on his cell's walls, that he might contemplate God's grace and mercy before his demise. He was not afraid to die, nor did he fear death. Rather, he wanted only for his heart to be prepared to meet God.

In the tradition of the Ancient Church, Psalm 6 is the first of seven Psalms, known as the Penitentials.[3] To this day they remain the Psalter's most exquisite prayers for reflection and self-examination. Verse by

---

3. The Seven Penitential Psalms are designated as 6; 32; 38; 51; 102, 130; and 143.

verse, they grant our hearts the joy and pain of confiding in God and finding in him the courage to love and embrace whatever life brings. Here is the true realism of the soul: the recognition of life's grand yet mortal span. Words like "sorely troubled," "languishing," "tears," and "moaning" catalog the frequent woes of mankind's common journey. That God cares to hear them, indeed, invites and welcomes them, empowers us to commit our lives to him with hope and gratitude.

In the Psalmist's time, life after death was not an option. Israel had yet to discover that Eternity with God is an aspect of God's mercy and love. As the Psalmist looked to God with longing, he could only pray: "For in death there is no remembrance of thee; in Sheol who can give thee praise?" (6:5). It required the period of the Maccabees before the realization of resurrection emerged. Nonetheless, Israel found consolation in experiencing God's goodness *now* and in trusting in God, no matter what lay ahead.

Augustine drew on that strength, too, though well cognizant of the Resurrection. Now the Psalmist puts us to the question. Are we, too, willing to trust in God, no matter what? This first of the Penitentials invites us to do so. For it assures us that the LORD does hear "the sound of our weeping" and "accepts our prayers." He will never leave or forsake us, or fail to remember us, however brief our days this side of his *aeternitatis* may be. That being the case, can we not trust the other side of God's *aeternitatis* to be filled equally with his goodness, mercy, and love?

∽ ∽ ∽

> [He] has bent and strung his bow; he has prepared his deadly weapons, making his arrows fiery shafts.
>
> Psalm 7:12–13

According to the Psalmist, David authored Psalm 7 as a cry of innocence in rebuff of accusations brought against him by a mysterious figure, known only as "Cush, the Benjaminite." In his lament, David implores God to intervene on his behalf. He begs the God of righteousness to favor his appeal and uphold the righteousness of his cause.

Of especial beauty is the rich imagery David employs in his self-defense, as well as the emboldened imagery with which he describes the

God of righteousness. The "bent bow," the "deadly weapons," the "arrows" of "fiery shafts"—all weapons of the late Bronze and Early Iron Age. Their images are still preserved in murals of Egypt's mighty pharaohs, riding fearlessly on their swift chariots, sending deadly arrows into Nubian lions, or cowardly, fleeing, bearded Asians. Such a godly Avenger, with crook in one hand and flail in the other! Christ as Shepherd and Temple Cleanser comes to mind as we yearn with the Psalmist for commensurate moments of divine aid.

Can we have God's presence without the arrows, the bent bow, and the fiery shafts? Are not the bow, the arrows, and the shafts metaphors of our own awareness of the price of Pride? Of the unrighteous envy that brings man down? Do we want to be part of that mindset, knowing that the bent bow and quiver of arrows will bring us down? Whose side are we on? The God of love and righteousness, or the gods of spite and wrong? Who is this "Cush, the Benjaminite?" we ask. Is he not that lesser side of ourselves, whenever we choose unrighteousness over God's mercy and love?

"O God we know how steeped in unrighteousness we are. That we can never be the principal agent of our own redemption! That alone belongs to thee—O Father of mercy and God of grace. Now flood our hearts anew with thy perfect goodness and unsearchable peace. And to thee, O LORD, may all praise be given, now and evermore."

∽ ∽ ∽

> When I look at thy heavens, the work of thy fingers, the moon and the stars which thou has established, what is man that thou are mindful of him?
>
> Psalm 8:3–4

Few verses of Scripture capture the soul's inimitable essence as powerfully as the above. Immanuel Kant, the most punctilious German philosopher of the Enlightenment was forced to conclude the same. Having read David Hume's *Essay on Human Understanding*, which shocked him out of his "dogmatic slumbers," he turned his restless attention to writing the most astute *Critique of Reason* that mankind had heretofore read. Observing the identical phenomenon of the Psalmist's night sky and pondering its meaning for his interior life, he felt compelled to write: "two things ever and anon inspire me to awe: the infinite starry heavens above and the moral law within."

In that statement, nothing less than the Universal without, and its claim on the Individual within, resides. It is there in both the Psalmist and Kant's texts: the stars above and life's mystery within! Both capture our souls' restive searching while mending our mortal hearts. "What is man that thou are mindful of him and the son of man that thou dost care? Lo, thou has made him a little lower than thyself, and crowned him with honor and glory." In truth, the Psalmist's insight provides critical depth for understanding the findings of contemporary astrophysicists and biological scientists alike. Granted that the Big Bang and man's long, evolutionary ascendancy are accepted theories beyond doubt; nonetheless, the Psalmist reminds us that, first and foremost, we belong to God. We are more than mere stuff, however sparkling it might be, whether of stardust or galactic debris. Even this side of eternity we belong to God. God calls us to enjoy his shining stars, his bright night of twinkling infinity. So also he elicits the deep and mysterious wonder of our minds to ask questions that he alone can answer. In doing so, he draws us closer to his love and majesty, to himself and the depth of his being. Kant was fond of the term "Universal." But God transcends the Universal, which itself is abstract and impersonal, just as he longs for us to relate to him as personal and beyond all sterile stereotypes.

~ ~ ~

> Be gracious to me, O LORD! . . . O thou who liftest me
> up from the gates of death, that I may recount all thy
> praises, that in the gates of the daughter of Zion
> I may rejoice in thy deliverance.
>
> Psalm 9:13–14

It would be interesting to know the etymology of the "gates of the daughter of Zion!" To know of its eponymous trail, linking the heart of Israel with man's quenchless thirst for God would be a boon to savor, to say the least. It must surely have a long and hidden story behind it! Israel was not the only culture to long so, or to express it in "female form." Ancient

Greece traced no less than seven daughters to the paternal throne of Zeus, among them Athena, Aphrodite, Persephone, and Artimus, to name but a few. The Acropolis of Athens opened its gates to all in honor of the city's namesake. One can only image the thrill of ascending its marble steps, at the top of which awaited the open arms of the Winged Victory of Samothrace. In Egypt, the focus shifted to Isis and her many shrines along the Nile. In Mesopotamia, it was Ishtar, the morning star, who blessed her devotees with love and happiness, while in India it was Dawn who greeted her beloved with the warm and blinding radiance of the rising sun.

But let us return to the Psalm. Is it not possible that Israel retained the feminine symbolism to accentuate the parental and gentle side of God? Even Calvin was fond of referring to the Church as "our mother" and to God's injunctions as the "cooing of a wet nurse," cradling her baby. O for the gates of the daughter of Zion! Are they not Israel's doorway that leads to the heart of God, where all mankind are welcome in love? Yes! "Open thy gates, dear LORD, even to us, as we struggle to swing open the gates of our hearts to thee."

∼ ∼ ∼

> "God has forgotten, he has hidden his face,
> he will never see it."
>
> Psalm 10:11

So think the proud and the biblical "wicked," the greedy, the callous and the "man . . . of the earth [who] strikes terror" (Ps 10:2–3, 11). Not much has changed, has it? We too live in a similar age, even in a time such as ours. Yes, we may be protected by laws and Bills of Right, yet we are anxious and frightful everywhere. How the Psalmist's description of Israel's tormentors describes our own! As the Psalmist laments: "[who] in the pride of their countenance" have ceased to seek God, and chant the age-old mantra to their own despair: "There is no God." Or, should God exist, "he will never see" (Ps 10:4). Sadly, in the mind of many, this is still true, for what does it matter if God should exist or even "see?" In the end, they argue, history is blind. No divine keeper records human crime, or if he does, no retribution will occur. It is the plague of our era this side of

God's *aeternitatis*. We can get away with whatever. Each individual is free to affirm or deny the role of the Infinite in his life.

Oddly enough, history does record the fall of the mighty. The ruins of Rome, the columns of Persepolis, along with the sands of Libya, Egypt, Nabataea, and Syria bear witness to the quarried rubble and scattered debris of yesteryear's empires and, now, silent civilizations. Not to mention the crumbling temples and vine-covered mounds of Mesoamerica, India, and the Great Wall of China—Meccas of today's tourists and wanderlust spirits. Yes, crime and terror continue to daunt us. Such is the human story. Nevertheless, the power of God for good endures. It has never waned over the years. Yea, "thou *dost* see," writes the Psalmist; yea, "thou *dost note* trouble and vexation . . . [and carest for] the hapless [who] commits himself to thee" (Ps 10:14). Our temptation is to demur, to hang our harps on life's willows and balk with the Psalmist: "Why dost thou stand afar off, O LORD?" Yet, as the men and women of biblical faith came to realize—regardless of how high and mighty the sons of men may rise—God never forgets the individual in his or her hour of desperation or lonely solitariness when forced to cry: "Arise, O LORD; O God, lift up thy hand; forget not the afflicted" (Ps 10:12).

Who is that biblical man of faith today, that daughter of Zion, who stands at the gates of mercy and justice, if not God's believers? Are we not "the light of the world," said Jesus? The "salt of the earth," to preserve what is good and sound for all? In the final analysis, the cry for the God of righteousness to prevail begins in our hearts—however frightened, sinful, or anxious we may be. God calls us to commit ourselves in love to him. That has always been the truth.

"O LORD, for all our fear, strengthen us, dear God, that we may serve thy common good and cast our lives on thee."

> In the Lord I take refuge; how can you say
> to me, "Flee like a bird."
>
> 11:1

It was a desperate time in David's life, a time of stress and of mounting disorder. His kingdom appeared in peril; so also his kingship. He was old and tired. What was he to do? "Flee like a bird!" his advisers counseled. "Consider your few remaining years. Forget your past and its comforting notions. They are a ruse. It is time to dump them. For Heaven's sake, David, take our advice, before you lose everything."

Have we not received similar advice in the hour of our desperation? What to do? Whose counsel to trust? In whose voice to take refuge? Even Buddhists have had to wrestle with the question, "To whom do we go?" Their answer: "We take refuge in the Buddha. We take refuge in his teachings. We take refuge in his Order." Preceding them by four long centuries, David faced the same. His answer was as firm as theirs: "I take refuge in the LORD. I take refuge in his teachings. I take refuge in the House of His Holy Tabernacle."

Faith requires courage; a risk in the greatness and goodness of God, no matter how terrifying life's excoriations may be. One thinks of the young David, squaring off before Goliath, in a time of Israel's tribal paralysis. With courage, he committed his way to God and raced toward the giant with nothing but a sling in his hand. So also in the case of the blinded Samson, who, in the last breaths of his regret, recommitted his life to God, knowing full well the consequences of his action. With his feet shackled in iron claws, he groped with swollen hands for the rough columns of the Philistines' temple. Then with a mighty prayer he cried aloud: "For the LORD and love of Israel!" He bent his back; he stretched out his arms; he looked to God, and brought its mighty stones down on their pagan heads.

Philosophically, the theologian Paul Tillich reminds us that faith will forever involve risk, inasmuch as risk is an inseparable facet of our human condition. Tillich identifies three aspects of existence: 1) the threat of nonbeing, 2) the inescapability of existential doubt, and 3) the fear of meaninglessness. The poet Rilke often addressed all three, especially nonbeing. It lies at the heart of much of his work: *Einmal und nicht mehr.* "Just once and never again"[4] appears thematically throughout his verse. As for existential doubt, it is the precondition that underlies every effort and every thought we venture. And who among us has not questioned the meaningfulness, or meaninglessness, of his life? "In whom shall we take refuge to override the human angst?" the Psalmist asks.

"No!" said David. "I will not flee like a bird. I will not take flight from the power and kindness of God. I will never cease to cling to him and his everlasting love." Can that not be our prayer, too, for ourselves and our families, and all that we cherish?

∼ ∼ ∼

> The fool says in his heart, "There is no God."
>
> Psalm 14:1

Few passages of Scripture cut to the quick so swiftly as Psalm 14:1. An immediacy hovers about it, with the Psalmist refusing to mince a single word. Had he finally seen enough corruption, enough disbelief, so as to break his meditative quietude with his thunderous denouncement? "The Lord looks down from heaven upon the children of men . . . They have all gone astray, . . . there is none that does good" (Ps 14:2–3). Let us be clear. He is speaking about you and me, of the "fool in our heart" that would sever its ties with God. That's impossible to pull off, the Psalmist is arguing. There is no refuge for the "fool in our heart," save in the Greatness of God.

It is what Anselm labored with intensity to enable Gaunilo (a fellow monk) to see. In the former's *Proslogion,* the eleventh-century abbot stated and restated his position for Gaunilo to grasp. The fact that the "fool" maintains in his heart "there is no God" proves ontologically that God is already *in his thoughts.* Think about that! However if God is the being than which none greater can be thought, God must exist outside our thoughts as well, else he is not the being than which none greater can be thought. For a being outside ourselves is greater than one confined to our thoughts only. Today his argument is referred to as the *ontological* argument for the existence of God. It is based on the Greek word

---

4. Rilke, *Duino Elegies,* 80.

ontos, which has to do with being, with what is real, and not merely with thought alone. It is ontological, because the idea of God exists both as an inescapable reality *within our* thoughts as well as in the grandeur of the universe before our eyes. God is present, like it or not.

Still, the question remains. Is the God in your heart the God of your *refuge*, or merely the God of your *thoughts*? Is God real to you, or to me, or just an idea in our mind?

"O that deliverance for Israel would come out of Zion!" the Psalmist opined. "When the LORD restores the fortunes of his people, Jacob shall rejoice, Israel shall be glad" (14:7b). Then shall the ontological without become the ontological within. "For God sent the Son into the world, not to condemn the world, but that the world might be saved through him" (John 3:17).

∼ ∼ ∼

> O LORD, who shall sojourn in thy tent?
> Who shall dwell on thy holy hill?
>
> Psalm 15:1

Every culture has an answer for the Psalmist's question. The Psalmist reserved a unique one for Israel. It was the way of the righteous servant: "He who walks blamelessly, and does what is right, and speaks truth from his heart" (Ps 15:2). In ancient China, the answer was the Chün-tzu, or the way of the Superior Man. His secret lay in following Confucius' Five Constant Virtues: self-respect, magnanimity, sincerity, earnestness, and benevolence. In India, the *Code of Manu* prescribed one's conduct for each of the four stages of life. For Buddhists, the answer remains allegiance to the Eightfold Path; for Islam, a complex union of Quran, Hadith, and Consensus.

Still the question persists and haunts us upon further exploration. Note the Psalmist's emphasis on "sojourn" and "dwell" [*shakhan*, or *yashab*]. Neither is an accidental verb, thrown in for language enrichment. Rather, they hint at the very theology of the soul. We are here on earth as sojourners and indwell our finitude by the grace of God. It is an all-too-brief passage when viewed from life's end. Upon whose holy hill and under whose sacred tent shall we dwell during this passage? For the

Psalmist and David, it was Zion's holy heights, crowned by Mt. Moriah, and the sacred tent of the Ark, which housed YHWH's Mercy Seat. This was the metaphorical destination that nurtured their life's pilgrimage. The Psalmist recommends the same to us. Remember that Mt. Moriah was the scared site where Abraham was summoned to journey. On its hard, granite face he was instructed to offer his son Isaac as a sacrifice to God. But far from taking his son, God gave his son back, as a sign of divine grace until the day that God should send his own Son. As for the "tent," it represented the Holy of Holies, where the very heart of God's mercy "dwelt," accompanied by his cherubim. Who among us today would not long for God's cherubim to guard and accompany us as they did the Ark of old? "Come!" Says the Psalmist. "Dwell with God in the shadow of his holy tent and entrust your life to God."

There is still more. We are not to make light of the Psalmist's "blameless man." Recall that in Psalm 14 there is none that does good. Thus "the righteousness of the law," as Luther was fond of identifying it, had its place in Israel's existence. We live in two kingdoms, Luther surmised: on the one hand, an earthly society that needs God's restraint, and on the other hand, God's heavenly kingdom that saves us by grace. We live in both at the same time. We cannot survive without either. So too Calvin extolled what he called the threefold use of the Law, as 1) a tutor until Christ should come, 2) as God's means of piquing our consciences as a call to repentance, and 3) as a guide for our conduct in our efforts to create a just society. This does not make the law greater than grace, nor justify our being self-righteous or smug. No, we need God's grace as well as his love to make society as livable as possible. As for being "blameless," we know we can never be that.

In the end, we live by grace, which even the Psalmist knew, as he cast his heart on God's righteousness and mercy, calling us to cast our hearts on both, too.

∼ ∼ ∼

> "Full of merit, and yet poetically,
> dwells man on this earth."
>
> Friedrich Hölderlin[5]

During the past century, the philosopher Martin Heidegger could never let go of Hölderlin's line above. He built an entire school of philosophy about the poet's insight. We are here only as dwellers, and at that, only for a brief, determinate time. The idea of dwelling *poetically* especially captured Heidegger's imagination. Ever since the departure of antiquity's hero-gods (Dionysus, Heracles, and Christ) the world has been drifting toward the night of its decline. Now man is left alone to name the universe, define himself, and act in the absence of the gods. Heidegger refers to the latter as the default of the gods, inasmuch as man's savior-heroes have failed to return. Only the poets remain to sing the gods' songs, reminding mankind of his lonely task of acting in the absence of God. Heidegger would go on to define man under his concept of *Dasein*, meaning a beingness that is here and now, a concept he based on Edmund Husserl's phenomenology. *Da* or *das* means here, there, that, or now. *Sein* means being, with all its awareness, possibilities, and consciousness, indeed, the whole of it, past, present, and future. Unfortunately, however, in Heidegger's mind, man's *Das* and *Sein* have undergone forfeiture, or fallenness; thus, humanity suffers from a blind unwillingness to accept one's actual condition, along with the brevity of one's life. Hence, we live in a "destitute time," void of a clear perception of God, or any meaning or anchorage at all, dwelling poetically upon the earth as sojourners without God. Only the poets understand and, thus, sing their vigil songs, while awaiting God's return, or searching the heavens for a new god.

    Heidegger's assessment is not to be lightly brushed aside. His analysis of mankind's present predicament strikes too closely home to be ignored. Ours is a destitute time, with a loss of direction and hope. Indeed, we search the skies for the gods to return, but beyond the Big Bang, what do we see? If anything, only the quiet demise of faith, with the roar of divine hope slipping into an agnostic sea.

---

5. See Martin Heidegger, *Existence and Being*, 270–287.

Religion is a form of poetry, so too the idea of God, but it is so much more. For as in the case of the Psalmist, only faith can restore our fallen hopes; and only the "poetry" of grace mend our brokenness. The God of faith and holy grace has never gone away. The same yesterday, today, and tomorrow, God is always here. The Eternal present is an ineffable part of God's own *Dasein*. The idea of default is no more than an echo of the emptiness in our hearts that only God can fill. For the poetry by which man dwells on earth is the reality of God's grace. Yes, poetically dwells man on this earth, but dwells best only when his heart and hopes are open to the Spirit and Grace of the living God.

2

Under the Shadow of His Wings

The Lord is my chosen portion and my cup; thou holdest my lot. The lines have fallen for me in pleasant places; yea, I have a goodly heritage.

Psalm 16:5–6

SOMETIMES IN THE EVENING at Villemétrie, we would listen to music, to recordings selected most often by André or Pierre—our brother secretary. The latter's favorite composer was Dvorak and his *New World Symphony*. Pierre could only imagine what America was like, from its Great Plains to the Old South, or how it had inspired the Czech composer to create his lyrical and enduring masterpiece. Its Second Movement always filled me with loneliness, while awakening memories of my childhood on my grandmother's farm in Virginia. Nonetheless, we would laugh together, share jokes, recite poetry, or simply gather before the glowing fireplace and quietly read a book or assemble a puzzle, stored in a cabinet in the grand salon. André enjoyed perusing Rudolf Bultmann's New Testament theology, and would sit with his penknife in lap, reaching up occasionally to slice open an uncut page as he read through the theologian's text. Indeed, all the lines had fallen in pleasant places, and our heritage, though varied, was as rock-solid as God's everlasting love. It was a year of the LORD's chosen portion and cup.

Now, the Psalmist invites us, too, to seize God's portion and cup, each laden with redemptive symbolism of its own! "Take, eat, this is my body, broken for you . . . Behold, the cup of the New Covenant, shed for the remission of sins. Drink of it, all of you" (Mark 14:22).

What is the bread of hope on which we nourish our hearts? What is the cup of promise we raise to our lips? The choices are legion, the portions unlimited; they have always been so, but only one satisfies the heart. Only one guides us toward the path that leads to life's "pleasant places," wherein God abides in mercy and love.

~ ~ ~

> Hear a just cause, O LORD; attend to my cry! . . . O Savior of those who seek refuge . . . Keep me as the apple of the eye; hide me in the shadow of thy wings, . . . when I awake, I shall be satisfied with beholding thy form.
>
> Psalm 17:1, 7–8, 15

There is so much in this Psalm! The cry of lament! The refuge of the Savior! The apple of God's eye! The shadow of His wings! The ineffable form we behold in the hour of our wakefulness! It is a poem about God, in which only metaphor, symbol, and image can capture the depths of God. Even more, it is a poem about you and me. It is about us, and our longing for redemption and forgiveness; about our need for the love of a caring Father and the comfort of a mother's arms. And all of it knowing full well that we can never behold God as he is, even though we experience his presence as an indelible reality in our hearts. We are driven to remember what Paul said about Christ, "who, though he was in the form of God . . . emptied himself, taking the form of a servant, being born in the likeness of men" (Phil 2:6–8). If there is a secret about God and the form alone under which God may be found, perhaps it is here. Yes, in beholding his Son: "who for us men and our salvation, came down from heaven, and was incarnate by the Holy Ghost of the Virgin Mary, and was made man; and was crucified also for us under Pontius Pilate, who suffered and was buried; and on the third day rose again?" (Nicene Creed) Is that not where God has always been found? Incarnate in the form of a servant, who loves and cares and gathers the broken and contrite under the shadow of his wings? Whether Jewish or Christian, Buddhist or Moslem, grace and kindness are never out of style. As in Hinduism, they are the karma of today's joy and tomorrow's bright new future.

> The cords of death encompassed me, the torrents of perdition assailed me; the cords of Sheol entangled me, the snares of death confronted me. In my distress I called upon the LORD; to my God I cried for help. From his temple he heard my voice, and my cry to him reached his ears.
>
> Psalm 18:4–6; 2 Sam 22:5–7

Many years ago, while serving on a Kibbutz in Israel, our group was given a tour of the Negev. I shall never forget descending past the desert's bright corol faults into the cool shadows of the passageway that opened onto Adullam's Pool. According to tradition, it was here that David hid from the jealous Saul before his own rise to power. Shafts of soft sunlight filtered through the Negev's dust to bathe the hideout in a miasma of ocher haze. Shimmering on the silent pool, images of David's plight came to mind. "I called upon the LORD and my cry reached his ears."

We have all experienced our seasons of perdition, torrents, and struggles with Sheol's entangling cords. According to the *Gilgamesh Epic*, it was in the watery depths of Akkad's marshes that Gilgamesh wrestled with the slithering serpent, groping for the tree of life to save his friend Enkidu. But just as he held its branch fast in his grip, the serpent stole the slippery reed from his hands. Not so with YHWH. "From his temple he heard my cry . . . He reached from on high, he took me, he drew me out of many waters [and] delivered me" (Ps 18:6, 16–17).

In context, David's rescue followed only after a wrenching storm. The earth reeled, its foundations trembled, and heaven's clouds burned red with glowing coals. God was on the move. He bowed the heavens and came down; riding on a cherub, flying swiftly upon the wings of the wind (Ps 18:7–10). Through these metaphors, the Psalmist depicts God himself as dwelling poetically on the earth. He will not forsake his servants who turn to him.

That is our hope, to tell the truth. Sometimes it takes a raging storm to bend our knees, a failed and unrequited dream, or broken life for which we are at fault. The somber cloud, the darkening night, the cry from deep within! It is we who are entangled in the marshy coils of Sheol.

"Thank heavens, dear God, that you come down and lift us from the pit! May we never cease to praise thee, or ever flee from thee, but rather hallow and love thy name, day by day!"

∼ ∼ ∼

> The LORD rewarded me according to my righteousness; . . . For all his ordinances were before me, and his statutes I did not put away from me. I was blameless before him, and I kept myself from guilt. . . . Yea, thou dost light my lamp; . . . Yea, by thee I can crush a troop; and by my God I can leap over a wall.
>
> Psalm 18:20–29

The Psalmist's love for David knew no bounds, nor does his verse discount our hope. Blameless we may never be. Even the Israelite could not keep all of God's Covenant Law. For that reason, the Psalmist reminds us that God alone is mankind's redeemer, the hope of every contrite heart: "For thou dost deliver a humble people" (Ps 18:27).

Contrary to Luther's bias, the writers of the Wisdom Literature acknowledged God's grace. They attributed their personal and national survival solely to God's providential care, though they did so principally from the post-Exilic side of Judah's fall. Pride had led their nation into weakness and division; lethargy into a syncretistic fragmentation of their soul. Then came the rise of Assyria and Babylon and the brief resurgence of the pharaohs. Israel was the first to fall, then Judah. It was only after Cyrus' Edict of Liberation that Judah's exiles were allowed to return home. Soon afterward the foundations of the Second Temple were laid, Jerusalem's walls rebuilt; and, by 450 BCE, Ezra's revised Torah became the heart of Judah's conscience. Slowly the little kingdom rose from its rubble of hopelessness to become a beacon of spiritual light, thanks to God's enduring grace and Judah's rekindled faith. O to be faithful again! A lover of God's *hesed* and *zedek*, devoted to his everlasting mercy, his righteousness and peace! That is what the Psalmist is trying to say.

We do not measure God's love today based on our blamelessness, or purity of heart. Nor do we offer sacrifices to appease "God the void" or "God the Enemy," as the philosopher Whitehead depicted an earlier era's religious plight. Rather, it is upon the mercy of God's love that we are called to lay the foundations of our temple-hearts. It is God's gift of grace that assuages our souls and provides the sacred oil that replenishes our lamps. As for "crushing a troop" or "leaping over a wall," we must surmise that the Psalmist's metaphors were selected to embolden his time with courage and fortitude. As Sidney Lanier captured it in *The Marshes of Glynn*:

> As the marsh-hen secretly builds on the watery sod,
> Behold I will build me a nest on the greatness of God.

~ ~ ~

> The heavens [*ha-shamayim*] are telling the glory of God; and the firmament proclaims his handiwork. Day to day [*yom*] pours forth speech, and night to night [*lilah*] declares knowledge . . . In them he has set a tent for the sun, which comes forth like a bridegroom . . . and like a strong man runs its course with joy. Its rising is from the end of the heavens, and its circuit to the end of them; and there is nothing hid from its heat. . . . The law of the LORD is perfect, reviving the soul. . . . But who can discern his errors? Clear thou me from hidden faults.
>
> Psalm 19:1, 4c, 5–7, and 12

From the earliest archives of the Hebrew language, the Psalmist selects the richest of ancient texts and reworks them to his favor. *Ha-shamayim* in Hebrew means *the heavens!* But the word itself was as a derivative of a still more ancient word from the Sumerian culture of Mesopotamian religion. *Shamash* was the supreme Sumerian god, mirrored in the blazing sun; while his daughter, Sin, represented the moon [queen of *lilah*] and the light of the night. In Egypt, it was the god Ra or Re who daily ferried his boat of reeds across the sky, to cruise the underworld at night, before returning through morning mists the next day. In Homeric Greece, it was Apollo who mounted his chariot before dawn's silver light, and, gripping the reins of his wild steeds, steered his sphere of blinding fire, up and out of its gates and across the Hellespont, to ride full sky above the Aegean Sea. In each of the cultures above, God was identified with the golden orb and the piercing eye of the sun. God of light and God of justice, each ruled his own. But the Psalmist takes us to the highest sphere possible, to the God of gods himself, whose glory transcends the fullness of heavens (the *ha-shamayim*), along with the moon and the sun and all God's starry hosts, and in doing so subsumes the myths of the ancient world under the watchful eye of God's grace and all-sufficiency. Beyond the reification of nature, the Psalmist lifts us to the regal home of God; and from the empty hopes of polytheism, to the realm of mercy and righteous love.

Even more, viewing the shimmering stars and searing sun, the Psalmist is reminded of God's perfect law, the Torah itself—in all its "soul reviving" and "enlightening" power. How perfect it is, yet "who can discern his errors?" Can you or I? Who can save us from our "presumptuous sins?" he humbly asks. Thanks be to God, whose grace alone makes us whole!

～ ～ ～

> The LORD answer you in the day of trouble! . . . May he send you help from the sanctuary, . . . May he grant you your heart's desire, . . . May the LORD fulfill all your petitions! . . . Some boast of chariots, and some of horses; but we boast of the name of the LORD our God.
>
> Psalm 20:1–2, 4–5, 7

Scholars categorize the above Psalm as a "prayer for the king's victory in battle." Since it refers to the sanctuary and Zion, it no doubt dates from a post-Davidic period. But having said that, it is our time that is in question, our time that is the trouble. After all "the day of trouble" and the "heart's desire" often occur concurrently. Why can't we have what we desire, as long as it is good? Especially if we work for it, and our aims and methods are noble?

There was a gracious family that loved de Robert. They spent hours of time with our brotherhood. Without hesitation, they helped clean the chateau's wavy glass windows, polish the brass and the silver in the *grand maison*, and scrub the hardwood floors. They did the latter in that arduous European manner—by sliding steel-wool pads back and forth under foot, until one's calves and quads ached with pain. Then followed the mopping with wax and oil. They gave and gave and gave. It was their "heart's desire." And then "the day of trouble" came like Kipling's "thunder out of China 'cross the bay." Their financial world collapsed, and they withdrew, silently with embarrassment and shame, though we loved them and struggled to reassure them that they were dearer to us now than ever. I can still see the refined gentleman and his lovely wife of Huguenot-Scottish descent. He wore a vest and spectacles, cravat and French cuffs, creased trousers and polished shoes; while Madame sported a white bandana about her red hair as she scooted about in her long skirts of red-and-black plaid.

In his poem, "Voices from Lemnos," Seamus Heaney hits us hard with his iron cold analysis of our virtues and vices. Often the two are intermingled, and, in his mind, sadly, too often, we exult in both, displaying our self-pity and mistakes, as if they were medals of the highest-regard.[1] Bad things happen to good people, in spite of their virtues and blameless character. There was no shame in the couple's financial collapse on the day of their trouble. Unfortunately they took it so in quiet Gallic fashion. They had no boast in steeds or chariots, nor need to. Their only boast was love for André and the good of the équipe, and, of course, their devotion to God. Would that they had borne their sorrow with open pride, for André and even God to see! Certainly the LORD would have heard their petitions and granted their hearts peace and resolve.

Psalm 20 celebrates a victory and the king's triumph o'er his foes. But not all of Israel or Judah's kings were as fortunate as David, or the Psalmist's monarch in this particular verse. In good or bad seasons, troubled or happy times, Psalm 20 reminds us that God's love surrounds all whose hearts are joined to his. Under the shadow of his wings, neither self-pity nor self-regard ultimately matters. What matters is the happy

---

1. Heaney, *Poems*, 303.

degree to which we let God rule our lives. Then neither victory nor loss can separate us from God.

∾ ∾ ∾

He asked life of thee; thou gavest it to him, length of days for ever and ever [*l'olam va'ed*].

Psalm 21:4

The phrase "for ever and ever" [*l'olam va'ed*] is a measure of time and distance. "A very distant time," is what it means. As "far out as the horizon stretches and beyond that" equally captures its meaning. Eternity is a different concept and pertains only to God. Only God is eternal. That God should grant us life [*ha-yah-im*] at all is a miracle; that it should endure "as far out as the horizon and far beyond" constitutes a double miracle. Time belongs to God. Remember, we live in space, as Heschel stated. We know what to do with space, but sadly, we don't always know what to do with time. God, on the other hand, occupies time, from its creation to its end. That is why time is so precious. God comes to us "in moments of time," as Heschel assessed it. God comes to us in the hours of all our time—sacred and mundane—if we are but open to him. That is what makes time precious, as well as our life and length of days. Therein lie hope and joy, whatever sorrows or gains we may face. It is a beautiful gift, as far out on the horizon as our sojourns may take us. Though we may not see what lies beyond in distance or time, God is still with us. Such knowledge brought comfort to the Psalmist and to the king whose victory they celebrated with harp and song. Can it not be the case equally for us? As one of my closest professional friends once put it: "We must press on and just keep our wits about us until we step into the great white light."

Until then, we can join the Psalmist in praise and thanksgiving. "Thank you God for our length of days. For however far out and for however long thou dost grant us space and time. Take our hearts and fill them with joy. Enable us to give thee our days and our nights, that thou mayest fill them with thy holy presence and sacred peace, thy mercy and goodness. And humble us, dear God, that we may share our portion and cup with all thy children everywhere. May all praise be to thee, O God, until our journeys bring us into thine eternal light."

∽ ∽ ∽

> My God, my God, why hast thou forsaken me? I cry by day, but thou dost not answer; Yet thou art holy . . . In thee our fathers trusted; . . . and thou didst deliver them.
>
> Psalm 22:1–4

We have all prayed the first two verses of this distressing psalm. Jesus prayed it from the cross with a broken heart. How could his Father have willed this hour, only to abandon him on the eve of the Sabbath at the pinnacle of his horrific pain? "My God, my God, why hast thou forsaken me?" As I write these words, a wooden crucifix with Christ's outstretched arms catches my attention. It is a gift from a Catholic charity in gratitude for the small donations I have mailed them over the years. Though I am not a Catholic, my heart has been blessed to do so. So little to be reminded of so much that God has done! Of a love that never ends and shatters our notion of sacrifice! I have given so little; he gave his life. Well did Jesus cry from his cross! "My God, my God!"

The truth is, there shall always be times when Christ's prayer will be appropriate. Times when we shall truly sense God's abandonment, as well as the rejection of those we have most trusted and loved. It is a facet of life, inseparable from our choices as individuals and as a society—a residuum of our existentiality. The Psalmist's prayer rightfully mirrors our soul's fragile condition and weeps at the consequence of our choices, good and bad. After all, it cost God the pain of watching his own Son die. As C.S. Lewis couched it in his *The Problem of Pain*: "pain shatters the illusion that all is well . . . and that what we have is our own and enough for us." Above all, Christ's "Trial and Sacrifice" exemplifies the true form of "self-sufficiency which really ought to be ours."[2] No wonder Jesus felt forsaken as he bore that pain.

---

2. Lewis, *Problem of Pain*, 77–97.

Nevertheless, how hopeful and redemptive rises the Psalmist's conclusion! "Yet thou art Holy. In thee our fathers trusted and thou didst deliver them."

∼ ∼ ∼

All the ends of the earth shall remember and turn to the LORD; . . . Yea, to him shall all the proud of the earth bow down; before him shall bow all who go down to the dust, and he who cannot keep himself alive.

Psalm 22:27–29

Once again, the Psalmist is addressing us. He is encouraging us to bow down before God, "O proud of the earth!" Israel never lost hope in that Messianic time when God would gather all the earth's people and bind them as one to himself. Such utopian dreams have come and gone and scattered like wind-driven chaff along the pathways of mankind's highest ideals. Isms to end all isms have a way of perishing, long before their designers bow their knees to accept their demise. O might the "proud of the earth bow down!" We are all numbered to "go down to the dust." How silly our pride to think that we can do it without God! It is a form of twisted wickedness, of *forfeiture*, as the philosopher Heidegger dubbed it.

Yet, the Psalmist's plea is worthy of championing. To dream one day of a globally just society, bound by equity and compassion for all, has been mankind's elusive pursuit for ages. We must not surrender that vision. Plato sought it; so also the Five Books of Confucius, the *Code of Manu*, the scrolls of the Talmud, along with John Locke and Rousseau's egalitarian theories. Covenants among people worldwide are essential to mercy and equity, however unreliable or promising. Of such is the nature of man. Of such is our hunger for justice and goodness. Still, under the shadow of God's wings, we are called to pursue the highest and noblest of ends. In keeping with the Davidic promise, we are summoned to fashion the fairest and finest constitutions we are capable of producing. And that to be done while recalling the wisdom of Augustine and Luther: that so long as we dwell on earth, we dwell best when our eyes and our hearts are allegiant to the City of God and his righteousness and grace.

> Thy rod and thy staff they comfort me. Thou anointest my head with oil; my cup runneth over.
>
> Psalm 23:4–5 KJV

Neither the Valley of the Shadow of Death, nor the enemy encamped within sight of his fire's glow, ever discouraged the young David. He was the apple of God's eye. The hero of a thousand songs, closer to Jonathan than even to his own sons, except perhaps Absalom! He was the Old Testament's equivalent of the Apostle Paul who finally learned how to be abased and how to abound, discovering, in whatever state he was, "the secret of facing plenty and hunger, abundance and want," since God was on his side (Phil 4:12).

There is an optimism about the Psalms that refuses to let us linger in our seasons of self-pity and despair. No! God's rod and God's staff are not empty metaphors. Like the pharaoh's flail that drove back the enemy, and his shepherd's crook that gathered in the lambs, God's rod and staff remind us of his abiding providence and everlasting promise to comfort us in life and in death! Yes, and even more, goad, chastise, and reprimand us when necessary. That too is part of his love as God the Companion. His rod and his staff represent his presence with us now, not just in the past or in some time to come. With the oil of his love, he anoints our hearts and heads that our cups might overflow with his mercy, as far out in the future as we can see.

> My cup runneth over.
>
> Psalm 23:5 KJV

David's turn of phrases and metaphors speak directly to our hearts. From his "green pastures," to his "beside the still waters," down to his "cup that runneth over," in the "presence of his enemies," we are mesmerized by his story and drawn to his path. His phrases celebrate the goodness of God, as well as the miracle of life, even when darkened by death's long shadow and fears that never subside. "In the world you have tribulation," said Jesus, "but be of good cheer for I have overcome the world" (John 16:33).

Over the centuries, the "cup that runneth over" has remained a symbol of variant blessings, but of two in particular. One is the sacramental cup of forgiveness and mercy, of sacrifice and offering, known to cultures worldwide as an aspect of their specific religion. The other is the exuberant cup of life itself, of one's unique destiny, seized and lifted with gladness and thanksgiving. In truth, we need both. Not just the sacramental cup of redemption, but the cup of existence and gratitude as well. Long faces and sepulchral spirits reflect an absence of both. No! God has given each of us a cup to enjoy, running it over with goodness and joy, if we but hold it close to his fountain.

Today's pop culture is big on the "attitude of gratitude." If the mantra appears disingenuous at times, smile and forbear. It requires faith and hope, along with love and grace to lift us beyond life's dark shadows. It takes someone to love us, as well as our loving someone else, to sit at that sacred table in the presence of enemies and reflect on the goodness of life. Even poets know how perilous it is not to love the life you're given.[3] How compelling Burns' lines still ring in our hearts:

> Should auld acquaintance be forgot,
>   And never brought to mind?
> Should auld acquaintance be forgot,
>   And auld lang syne!
>
> For auld lang syne, my dear,
>   For auld lang syne,
> We'll take a cup o' kindness yet
>   For auld lang syne!

At the heart of this Psalm, God invites each of us to renew our trust in him. On the eve of our hearts' descent into the night of our culture's decline, God descends to light our lamps again. Once more he tilts his heart toward us to overflow our cups with faith, hope, and love.

---

3. Heaney, *Poems*, 152.

∽ ∽ ∽

> The earth is the LORD's and the fullness thereof, the world and those who dwell therein; for he has founded it upon the seas, and established it upon the rivers. . . . Lift up-your heads, O gates! and be lifted up, O ancient doors! that the King of glory may come in.
>
> Psalm 24:1–2, 7

Not even God will let us forget that poetically we dwell on the earth. We are all dependent on God. Even his vast creation is reliant on his miraculous grace. The earth, the seas, the rivers—all share the sparkling debris of the Big Bang, drifting gloriously in the palm of God's hand! And we, too, our own *Dasein*, dwelling in a space and time reserved and blessed by YHWH alone.

Perhaps Heidegger had it right—this dwelling in the palm of God's hand, however destitute the time. We are dwellers on the earth, the *ha-eretz* that God established on the restless waters of the primeval seas, which he nourished with rivers and myriad seed. Bending over its shoals, he scooped up a handful of clay, moist and nutrient-rich, and, with his divine *ru'ah*, transformed it into living souls.

We belong to God, along with his stars, his rivers and seas, and all that dwell on the orbiting earth. Sojourners, we are. Dwellers of tents, though now constructed of mortar and steel. "O ye gates of concrete, of sweat and toil! Lift up your heads, ye mighty doors! Lift up your gates, O cities of asphalt, cable, and tile! Of lonely streets and lamplight at night. We belong to God. Rejoice, rejoice! We belong to God."

> For thy name's sake, O LORD, pardon my guilt, for it is great.... Turn thou to me, and be gracious ... for I am lonely and afflicted. Relieve the troubles of my heart, and bring me out of my distresses.
>
> Psalm 25:21, 16–17

Clearly David, along with the Psalter's staff of unknown writers, knew the secret of abasement and bounty, of a humble heart and a joyful spirit. Their secret rested in trusting God, the living God, both in their hearts and in the history of God's loyalty to their people.

Who among us has not sought God's pardon for the angst of guilt and the dishonor of wrong? Inevitably it swells in our conscience to resurface as shame, and then later as remorse. As the Psalmist so well knew, only God's love can lift us to wholeness again. As he or a successor would later write, "If God shouldst mark iniquities, who could stand?" (Psalm 130)

The Psalms are a mirror, as well as a channel of blessing. They summon us to come to God, just as we are. To hide our guilt is not an option. It is the last thing we need to do. God knows us for what we are, and whose we are—his!

It was André's custom, once a quarter, to invite each brother to meet in his office for counsel and prayer. André needed the meetings for himself as much as for each of us. I still remember the winter meeting when he asked me to share my thoughts as a young theology student. He was especially curious as to why I had come to Villemétrie. He sat forward and listened as I poured out my doubts about God as well as myself. He listened for well over an hour. Then he smiled. "The gifts of the Spirit are many, and the gift of faith is only one. God never leaves anyone giftless, and God's gift to you, *c'est son don de doute*, his gift of doubt." I knelt as he prayed and, with something in the way of numb shock, accepted God's gift of doubt, never to worry about God's existence again. Indeed, I felt a little like Jacob, staring up into the angel's face, in the middle of the Jabbok Brook.

Are we not all "lonely and afflicted," at one time or other? What is God's gift to you? Who is your André with whom you pray? For whom do we pray as well? We all need a brother/sister sojourner with whom to share our loneliest loneliness and troublesome afflictions. But most of all, we need that restful silence that awaits the soul in its secret meeting with God!

∽ ∽ ∽

> Vindicate me, O LORD, for . . . I have walked in my integrity, and . . . trusted in the LORD without wavering. Prove me, O LORD, and try me; test my heart and my mind. For thy steadfast love is before my eyes, and I walk in faithfulness to thee. . . . Sweep me not away with sinners, nor my life with bloodthirsty men.
>
> Psalm 26:1–2, 8

Echoes of the temple drift through this Psalm, as the supplicant makes his rounds to declare his innocence. "I wash my hands . . . and go about thy altar, . . . singing aloud a song of thanksgiving" (Ps 26:6–7). It is not our place to question his "integrity" or doubt his "love of the habitation" in God's house. It was a different era, a time of solemn perambulations about sacred precincts, accompanied by rituals of cleansing and the singing of songs. Do we not participate in rituals of the same? Bearing the cross and the Bible before us, wearing bright robes and singing loud songs? Traversing the transept in processional order, before ascending to choir, or lectern and pulpit? Or, if Roman Catholic, kneeling in prayer with rosary in hand, to pause later in silence before each treasured Station of the Cross?

There is a beauty to holiness not to be distained. It came in a vision to the prophet Isaiah when he saw the LORD, seated on his "throne, high and lifted up," in the year that King Uzziah died (Isa 6:1). "Holy, holy, holy is the LORD of hosts; the whole earth is full of his glory," sang the seraphim that evening on the occasion of the young Ahaz' coronation. They sang in praise of God and for the young king to hear, too. But the scion's proud eyes were closed to the coals, the ascending pale smoke, and the muffled wings of the glowing seraphim, with which they covered their faces before the Glory of the LORD (Isa 6:2–4).

We need the realm of the Holy, with its quiet echoes of angels' wings, bearing our sorrows and broken hearts up through life's spectral smoke to the throne of God. The "righteousness of the law" was a form of God's grace in the time of David and his successors' era. Still, David well knew of salvation by grace. "For thou hast no delight in sacrifice; . . . The sacrifice acceptable to God is a broken . . . spirit and contrite heart" (Ps 51:16–17). Whatever innocence we shall ever have belongs solely to God, to grant and bequeath, to justify and bestow.

"Thank you, dear God, for the beauty of your holiness and the gift of your grace that makes us whole."

3
Our Light and Refuge

> The LORD is my light and my salvation; . . . of whom
> shall I be afraid? . . . Though a host encamp against me,
> my heart shall not fear; . . . Thou hast said, "Seek ye my
> face." "Thy face LORD, do I seek." Hide not thy
> face from me.
>
> Psalm 27:1, 3, 8–9

The Psalmist knew how to pack a prayer with every venue of our human condition. Nothing slips his mind, neither by way of need, anguish, or salvation, nor belief, trust and confidence in God. All of it is here.

What we find specifically in this Psalm is the truth about ourselves, as well as our quest for God. Life is difficult and filled with uncertainty, ambiguity, and the threat of meaninglessness. Our enemies may not be as openly arrayed against us as they were against David, nor as readily identifiable. Yet, their persistence in conniving forms surfaces as a daily reminder of evil's residuum. Jealousy, revenge, spite take no holiday. Whether at home or in the workplace, people who want to hurt others know how to find ways to unsettle them. So do thieves, gangs, cartels, criminals and plotters of graft and corruption. They delight in encamping about one's heart, particularly when we are most vulnerable. How we long for God—the stronghold of protection—to vindicate our plight and come to our rescue!

In the rural Knobs of Virginia, where I was reared as a boy, one had to be ever vigilant. Times were hard. Thieves lurked about. They knew whose smoke houses were ill guarded and springhouses easy to rob. It was during the War, and many men were far from home, fighting in the Pacific theatre, or in North Africa, or flying sorties over Germany.

Night encased the farmhouse. The red embers in the hearth glowed low, the kerosene lamplight on the table but a glimmer. "Shhhhh!" whispered my grandmother. "Someone's outside." Huddled between my mother and sister, along with Pauline—a farm girl—I watched as my grandmother tiptoed to her bedroom and returned with a pistol. It looked huge to me. With its 9-inch barrel and bulging cylinder of bullets, it wavered in her right hand as she approached the room's side door. In her gruff commanding voice, she said aloud for all to hear. "You step through this door, and I'll shoot you dead! I will, as surely as my name is Katherine White." She was an expert marksman, as the county knew. And so must the would-be intruder have surmised. A hush enveloped our tiny parlor. From outside a faint rustling stirred, followed by a dull thump of something tumbling to the ground. Then, silence! "Come now," chortled my grandmother, "time to go to bed." The next morning Pauline found a pair of brass knuckles, as large as an iron, by the door. We took turns trying it on. It slipped past my wrist up to my elbow. It would have sliced the flesh from any temple the intruder might have struck.

> The LORD of hosts was with us.
> The God of Jacob was our refuge.

Not all our adversaries come to us in such direct ways. Nonetheless, life's adversaries are there. Faith is fortunate to have the God of Jacob as its shelter and its eternal stronghold, its retreat and asylum from life's woes. So, too, are we. "O God, be our safe haven, our citadel in time of need, our shelter and our stronghold in time of trouble. Enable us, through trust in Thee, to face with courage all life's foes!"

∾ ∾ ∾

> One thing have I asked of the LORD, that I will seek after; that I may dwell in the house of the LORD all the days of my life, to behold the beauty of the LORD, and to inquire in his temple.
>
> Psalm 27:4

One could devote a book to this Psalm, if not a full-length theological dissertation, or an extended exegesis on Israel's history and the spiritual depth of the Hebrew language. A "Little Bible!" Indeed!

It is hard to escape the Psalmist's word, "dwell." Or the idea of "all the days of my life." Once again we are plunged into a metaphysical trinity, such as Husserl's phenomenology, Heidegger's analysis of our human condition as *Dasein*, and Hölderlin's imagery of our existence as dwelling poetically upon the earth. The Psalmist would have understood these three men; nonetheless, he would have added, that any genuine phenomenology of the self must ultimately rest upon the power and grace of God—and that for as far out in the distant future as one can see.

To make it all the more concrete, the Psalmist evokes the images of "the house of the LORD," the "beauty of the LORD," and inquiring in God's "temple," where Torah studies are provided to perfect the living of a human life. Anyone who has ever entered a Gothic cathedral, like Notre Dame de Paris, or its sister, the Cathedral of Chartres, will forever remember its magnificent stained-glass windows, patterned after the petals of a rose. With entranceways guarded by portals of saints and angels staring down upon you, you enter with curiosity and awe. As you pass through the nave into the sanctuary, the magenta reds and royal blues, emerald greens and-golden beams of the windows begin to glow with a light that seeps into your soul. Your eyes adjust to the dark, and, ever so slowly overhead the vaulted columns of the hushed cathedral come into view. To sit before the votive candles, if not light one, and stare into those vibrant windows inspires you to linger as long as possible in such magnificent cathedrals, designed and constructed by masters of glass and stone. Far from idolatrous, the windows adumbrate the beauty and glory of God. That generations of artisans and townspeople were marshaled to achieve these monuments speaks volumes of an Age of Faith that our present time seems helpless to imagine today.

The beauty of the LORD, as well as his house, and the study hall of his Torah, is as accessible today as it was in the time of Israel or the Gothic era. Look within your heart, the Psalmist directs. Call upon God's name, and let him fill your soul with his presence and glory. "For he will hide thee in the day of trouble; he will conceal thee under the cover of his tent, and set thee high upon a rock" (Ps 27:5).

If God is willing to do that for you and me, might he not be willing to do it also for others, if we would but invite them to come with us to our houses of worship, and there in the courts of God's holiness, inquire and learn?

~ ~ ~

Thou hast said, "Seek ye my face." My heart says to thee, "Thy face, LORD, do I seek." Hide not thy face from me.

Psalm 27:8–9a

The hiddenness of God is a phenomenon that spans all time, from the period of the Greeks to our own era. Imagine yourself in Athens, at the time of the Eleusinian mysteries, as you sit huddled with others while listening to Euripides' Chorus sing these verses of *Hecuba*:

> God! O God of mercy! . . . Nay:
> Why call I on the Gods? They know, they know,
> My prayers, and would not hear them long ago.[1]

From the heart of Matthew Arnold rises a similar cry at a time when modern skepticism was eroding Europe's faith:

> But now I only hear
> [Faith's] . . . long, withdrawing roar,
> Retreating . . . down the vast edges drear
> And naked shingles of the world.[2]

Many others have added to Arnold's cry since the 1850s: Nietzsche, Unamuno, Ortega y Gasset, Sartre, and Camus. Each believed and maintained that we *do dwell* poetically on the earth—however we define "poetic." We are still searching the skies for the Savior-God to return.

Why does God seem to be hidden, if not absent, in our time? Why has he withdrawn his face and left us devoid of his presence? If the truth be known, his hiddenness is a consequence of *our* withdrawal from God, not his from us. It is we who have cloyed to be the center of all values, as Nietzsche's Zarathustra might put it, or have become our own measurer of all things, "of things that are and of things that are not," as Protagoras claimed. Would God not have to hide his face from all that, lest God be

---

1. Jones. *Western Philosophy*, 21
2. From Arnold's poem, "Dover Beach."

blamed for the godless world that mankind have chosen to create and indwell?

Martin Buber, last century's greatest Jewish writer, offered his own analysis in his *The Eclipse of God*. For Buber, the preceding centuries of the great philosophers, from Descartes through Kant and Hegel, had turned *the living God* of Abraham, Isaac, and Jacob into *a concept* of pure consciousness and abstract being. In doing so, they preempted God's confrontational task as judge and, consequently, compromised his redemptive role as savior. As a result, they weakened his transcendence and immanence, from which we can never flee. That Nietzsche would pronounce this eclipse as the "Death of God," whom we have killed with our own knives, follows as swiftly as night swallows dusk. Thus ensued the modern autopsy of mankind's fate, with his unfortunate destiny to be lamented as Unamuno offered in his *Tragic Sense of Life*, and later by Camus in his phrase: "the absurd man," who longs for meaning though he cannot find it.

What the Psalmist knew is still valid. Without God, life limps between hope and desperation, longing and despair. "Thy face, LORD, do I seek," is the cry of every person come of age. Man, woman, or child. It is ours. It is we who need God. To seek his face once more! The God of dread and holiness, as well as Whitehead's "God the companion." The wisest counsel to conclude is, that whenever dread or fear appears in our hearts, lo, they come as God's descending angels to draw us to himself again. "Thy face, LORD, do I seek," is the prayer of Everyman and Everywoman.

∽ ∽ ∽

> To Thee, O LORD, I call; . . . if thou be silent to me, I become like those who go down to the Pit.
>
> Psalm 28:1–2

The Hebrew word *te-hah-rash* means more than just "deaf," or "silent." It means to turn away, to refuse to speak at all. That is what fills the Psalmist's heart with alarm—that God should turn away, look aside, not even glance at him, or deign to reply. What recourse is left then, for the Psalmist or any of us, if God turns away? Have you ever implored someone for help, only to observe them withdraw in silence, if not glance condescendingly at you, or close their eyes and not even speak? I have known colleagues in high places like that: ministers, physicians, bankers, scholars, professors, and even a few friends now and then. Yes, even friends! It hurts, no matter the person or occasion or the cause. "To thee, O LORD, do I call! If thou be silent, what recourse do I have? If thou dost turn away, what remains for me to do?" Once, when I questioned a surgeon's invasive plan, he drew back in his chair, closed his eyes, and turned away in complete silence. Fortunately, there were other physicians to whom I could turn. But when the hurt is existential and the dread of emptiness stares you in the face, there is only one Physician to whom we can repair, and that is God!

In the 1940s as a child, I caught all the illnesses of childhood to which children succumb: scarlet fever, whooping cough, chicken pox, mumps, and measles. My grandmother would crank up the wall phone and call the doctor in town. In an hour or so, he'd drive out to the farm, ford the creek in his shiny Packard, with its running boards glistening wet. After parking, he'd come inside and apply whatever remedy he deemed appropriate. Whatever the case, I always improved. While at Villemétrie during the winter of 1960, I grew considerably ill with a temperature that shot up into the high numbers. André came by my room with a cup of hot red wine, sweetened with sugar and a squeeze of lemon. He smiled as he pulled up the room's only chair, sat down, and held the cup for me to drink. "*Voici, mon frère; bois le tous.*" The next morning I awoke in a sweat, but the fever had broken.

We are vulnerable to life's ills, as well as the vicissitudes of the soul. Moments of dread and guilt, remorse and sorrow partner with us as long as we live. For we, too, have turned our face away from friends and foes alike, closed our eyes and kept silent in their times of remorse and trouble. We are not as innocent as we wish we were. The Psalmist knew God would hear his prayer, in spite of his "sickness unto death," as Kierkegaard calls it. It is good to come before God, knowing that if he should choose to turn away and close his eyes, we fully deserve it. But the biblical God of the Psalms does better than that. True. "There is none that does good, no, not one" (Ps 14:3). Still, what makes the God of the Psalms our Redeemer is that knowing our frame, God, nonetheless, binds his heart to ours. As our Psalm ends: "The LORD is the strength of his people, he is the saving refuge of his anointed," who saves his people and carries them, as "their shepherd, . . . forever" (Ps 28:8–9). That is what inspired Luther and

Calvin's own love of the Psalms, finding within its verses the grace of the living God unto salvation.

~ ~ ~

> Ascribe to the LORD, O heavenly beings, ascribe to the LORD glory and strength.... The voice of the LORD is upon the waters; the God of glory thunders,... The voice of the LORD breaks the cedars,... He makes Lebanon to skip like a calf,... The voice of the LORD flashes forth flames of fire.... The voice of the LORD makes the oaks to whirl, and strips the forest bare.
>
> Psalm 29:1, 3, 5–7, 9

Anyone who has ever weathered the eye of a storm—whether a hurricane, tornado, tsunami, or flood—can identify with the Psalmist's description of Nature's wrath. True to his passion, he depicts it in poetic form. But when caught in the terror of one, it's not its "poetic" dalliance that seizes the mind. It's one's life itself, or spouse's, or one's children's fate! It's their safety that fills one with horror and distress.

In the dusk of that evening long ago, Pauline and I had completed our last farm chores, when we noticed the murky, lemon cloud that suddenly formed and began creeping slowly across the horizon toward Abingdon—two miles away. Like a drunken demon, it licked its inflamed tongue back and forth across the town's dwellings, crushing them between its teeth. Then, with a sudden lurch, the dragon roared and swept down upon the hills about us, frolicking in fury along the way. The cedars on the farm bowed their heads; the broom sedge rippled like froth on a brackish sea, and the breath of the monster's passing pelted us with stinging grit, picked up from the narrow lane that led to my grandmother's house. The sky turned black, then a horrifying sallow hue, as the tornado's peals filled the night with crackling bolts of white-hot lightning. We ran to the house, to my grandmother's arms. And just in time, just ahead of the hail that ripped off the roof of the granary and roared headlong for the barn. We survived, but it took weeks to clean up the debris across the farm and in Abingdon.

our light and refuge 43

No poetic thoughts filled our mind on that evening, but the storm's savage wrath and destructive path have remained in my memory. Lingering with it poses an even larger question. How could the Psalmist write such metrically pleasing poetry in the midst of a storm? What was he thinking? If he were living today, would he still be writing poetry, especially in the light of the heartbreaking darkness that swept across Europe in the form of the Holocaust? I think we must answer, "Yes," as shocking as that may seem. Storms are a product of Nature, which God created to rule the earth and sweep the heavens clean with their fierce winds and torrential rains; the other is a product of human nature, whenever mankind chooses to replace God with a godless blind will. That fury requires recording and exposure, too. That is why God is so needed, which enables us to dwell poetically upon the earth.

Psychologists are wont to advance that the best predictor of future behavior is a study of one's past conduct. In the spirit of that wisdom, the Psalmist took up his quill and papyrus to write poetry. Who among Judah's exiles could not recount YHWH's hand in saving Israel countless times? The LORD had shown them loyalty in the past. In faith they knew God would do so again. As the Psalmist's last quatrain proclaims with joy "The LORD sits enthroned over the flood; . . . May the LORD give strength to his people! May the LORD bless his people with peace!" (Ps 29:10–11)

~ ~ ~

> To Thee, O LORD, I cried; . . . What profit is there in my death, if I go down to the Pit? Will the dust praise thee? Will it tell of thy faithfulness? Hear, O LORD, and be gracious to me! . . . Thou hast turned . . . my mourning into dancing; . . . and girded me with gladness, that my soul may praise thee and not be silent.
>
> Psalm 30:8–12

Death, Sheol, Dust, and Silence! Even in translation the Psalmist's words cut straight through the soul. As finite and mortal, we shall go back to death, dust, Sheol, and silence. It is a given, the fate of all mankind—"our mortal coil," as Shakespeare put it. It does prompt an awkward question, if not an embarrassing and personal one. At least it did for the Psalmist! "Of what value are we to God if our end is death?" From whom will God derive "praise" and "faithfulness," once we are silent and in the grave? Will the praise of his angels and those "heavenly beings" of Psalm 29:1—those mythological sons of gods—will their praise suffice? No doubt the latter were holdovers from the period of the Sumerians! Would God be so preoccupied with his own glory as not even to miss mankind? The Psalmist is almost taunting God, if not teasing him, while pleading his innocence. "Of what value am I to you dead?" The Psalmist did not want to die without feeling vindicated, or at least have his life recognized by God as having been worthwhile, regardless of his sorrows. He wanted to know whether God cared, however brief his life might be. It is a fair question, and one we also raise, each in our own way.

We should love this man for being so humble and candid. After all, didn't God create us in his image to dwell on the earth, to enjoy it, and have dominion over it? What, then, is the purpose of life, if silence is its end? What joy can God derive from a soul that returns to dust? Can we not bargain here? Undoubtedly, the Psalmist wanted to. The Psalmist struggled with this anxiety as all humans do. It is a facet of our existential doubt, as Tillich phrased it. It surfaces whenever we meditate on our lives and ponder the threat of meaninglessness and its twin, nonbeing.

Most of us probably never consider the angst above. But it is worth considering. If we should stop thinking about God—however far out on the horizon our future may extend—then we risk losing sight of God *in the present, now,* at this very moment. Without loving and praising God now, or seeking God's kingdom and his righteousness first, of what value is any moment, *now or in the future*? Without God's living presence in our souls, we *are* nothing but *dust*. Yes, nothing but dust, destined to die, and slip forever into time's silent Pit. Even Socrates taught that the unexamined life is unworthy of human beings.

For all the Psalmist's angst, God lifted his soul upward. To believe in God and trust in his goodness *now* transforms a heart's "mourning into dancing, girded with . . . gladness." It transformed David from a shepherd boy into a king; Paul from a Pharisee into Christianity's founding theologian; Augustine of Hippo from an orator of the Roman courts into faith's greatest champion during the fall of Rome. We could go on. We could list others. But what the Psalmist wants to know is whether he can include us. Are we willing to love and trust God *now*, and let God take care of our angst, whatever its form, now and in the future?

~ ~ ~

> In thee, O LORD, do I seek refuge; let me not be put to shame; . . . I trust in thee, O LORD, I say, "Thou art my God." My times are in thy hand; . . . Be strong, and let your heart take courage, all you who wait for the LORD!
>
> Psalm 31:1, 14–15, 24

Who among us does not find peace in those words: "My times are in thy hand"? What would our lives be like if they were not in God's hands? There are many examples, aren't there? Cain, the pharaohs who oppressed Abraham's descendants, Saul in his declining years, massacred with his sons on Mt. Gilboa. Or what of Absalom or Judas? The list grows on and on, even into our own time: Hitler, Mussolini, Stalin, and misguided terrorists who betray the deepest beliefs of their faith.

It is spiritually reassuring to know that our times are in God's hand, even in the worst of times. It is consoling to know that God is present and that the phrase "the providential hand of God" is not just a theological presumption. Rather, it is a reality we can claim and experience. Little did I know as a boy, reared on a farm, that one day I would become a professor, and of all things, philosophy! I was content with the Knobs and the wooded hills around us to have remained loyal to the seasons of the earth. But college, Church, and serving with André opened other paths to pursue. Looking back, my youthful journey was in another's hands, waiting for me to grasp.

We have all thought about the same. When you consider your own life, has there ever been a time when you were not in God's hands, even when you took your life out of God's hands? Maybe you tried it alone for a while, like the Prodigal. But it doesn't always work that way. Some of us never wake up, and we just die like that, like a wounded bird in God's hands. Yet when we do wake up, we glance about, hoping somehow that God is still there, watching over our shoulder, waiting for us to stir and open our eyes again.

Notice that the Psalmist says "times," not just "a time," or "once in a while." The seasons of life come and go. The rites of passage never cease. From birth to old age, we are always in passage, always in pilgrimage, each step of the sojourn an adventure in which we need God. That each of these times falls under God's scrutiny is a gift of grace, a *don de Dieu*, to be cherished.

How directly God comes to us in this Psalm! "Do you want your life to be guided by my hand," he asks, "or are you determined to go it your own way? If so, I will be there, nonetheless, as I was for Jacob, Samson, even Saul, and that wanderlust boy, that slept with hogs until he came to his senses, longed for his Father, and found his way home."

"O God, help us to search our hearts, and to want forever to be guided by thy hand!"

4
Remorse and Redemption

> Blessed is he whose transgression is forgiven, whose sin is covered. . . . Thou art a hiding place for me, thou preservest me from trouble; thou dost encompass me with deliverance.
>
> Psalm 32:1, 7

This is quite a tall order! Plus a remarkable *don de Dieu*! To be forgiven, to have one's sins covered, and to be hidden, protected, and encompassed about by God! But should we be surprised? This is the second now in the series of the Church's treasured Penitential Psalms—God's gift to cleanse our hearts anew. God has always loved this way. That is why Anselm's definition of God still remains a treasure: as "that than which none greater can be conceived."

How close were the Vandals now, as Augustine knelt before the psalms attached to his cell's walls? What were his thoughts, what were his words, if not those of David's or of the Psalmist's? "Blessed is he whose transgression is forgiven." In an earlier work on the Psalms, Augustine found himself drawn to verse four: "For days and nights thy hand was heavy upon me; my strength was dried up as by the heat of summer." Thus in response he wrote: "I was made miserable by my own misery."[1] Note that he did not blame God for the emptiness that burned in his heart; rather, he accepted full accountability for the misery he had brought on himself. In Calvin's own commentary on the Psalms, he highlights the

---

1. Schaff, *Augustine*, 71.

phrase: "thy hand was heavy upon me," in order to remind readers of the price that God paid for man's salvation, lest he forget Jesus' passion and death.[2]

All in all, God comes to us in these prayerful verses to cover our darkest thoughts and to wipe away our tears of sin. If ever we were hunted beasts, God offers himself as a hiding place for our preservation and mending, encompassing our livelong days with his salvation and love. It is a hymn of praise, calling us to confession and thanksgiving, a prayer which God makes available for each of us to pray.

~ ~ ~

> Rejoice in the LORD, O you righteous! Praise befits the upright. For the word of the LORD is upright; and all his work is done in faithfulness. He loves righteousness and justice; . . . Let all the earth fear the LORD, let all the inhabitants of the world stand in awe of him!
>
> Psalm 33:1, 4–5, 8

As I type these words, the nation is celebrating the 50th anniversary of Martin Luther King, Jr.'s speech: "I Have A Dream." Hearing it again is as stirring as hearing it the first time. "I have a dream that one day this nation will rise up and live out the true meaning of its creed: 'We hold these truths to be self-evident, that all men are created equal.'" It was his dream and is still the dream that America strives to achieve.

It was David's dream too, though at a different time, in a different world, and in a different manner. Since the time of Moses, Israel knew what God's dream for his holy people contained: "To do justice, to show mercy, and to walk humbly with God!" (Mic 6:8). It was seared in their hearts, though era after era and king after king ignored it, until Babylon razed their walls and trampled their dream under its boots. It is difficult, however, to kill a dream, a vision of what is right and merciful. In the final analysis, the beauty of the Psalter lies not simply in ministering to our hearts, but also in ministering to our consciences. Righteousness and justice transcend barriers of race and creed, nationality and culture. They

---

2. Calvin, *Psalms*, Vol. 1, 529.

are as ancient as Plato's philosopher-king's state, founded on wisdom and courage. Or Aristotle's idea of the "golden mean," or Kant's concept of the "Categorical Imperative," or Rawls' "theory of justice," in which he deferred to the "least advantaged." Now it is we who are asked to take this Psalm to heart, that all the inhabitants of the world might stand in awe of God; and all the inhabitants of the earth care for justice, show mercy, and walk humbly before God!

～～～

> Blessed is the nation whose God is the LORD, the people whom he has chosen as his heritage! The LORD looks down from heaven, he sees all the sons of men; from where he sits enthroned he looks forth on all the inhabitants of the earth, he who fashions the hearts of them all, and observes all their deeds.
>
> Psalm 33:12–14

In a world such as ours, God's oversight is as needed as ever. The belief in the Providence of God both comforts and challenges us to be strong and faithful. We may not know how history will end, or when or where we shall be called upon to lie down one last time on the pallet of life's journey, but we know whose we are—now and at the hour of that inevitable time.

Scholars label Psalm 33 an "enthronement psalm." It was recited to flute and lyre at each king's enthronement, as well as on the anniversary of his ascension to power. Its purpose was to remind him that he and his people belonged to God; they were the LORD'S, endowed with heart and soul and will and purpose, to be faithful to his Covenant, first made with Abraham and later with all Israel. So also, the hymn celebrated God as the sole Creator of heaven and earth and of all that breathes within. It is very likely that the Psalmist was drawing upon the old Mesopotamian myth of the *Enuma Elish*, in which the god Marduk creates the heavens and the earth from the glittering entrails of the watery monster Tiamat, or goddess Rahab, as she is also known. With a swing of his sword he vivisected her and flung her carcass into the sky. In fact, an echo of the latter's name appears in Genesis in the Hebrew word *te-hom*—that darkness that hovered over the waters of chaos and over which God spoke: "Let there be light," and it was so. "And God saw that the light was good."

It is this goodness that the Psalmist wishes to celebrate. God's creative and sustaining presence are still operative in the world. Instead of chaos and instability ruling the nations of the earth, it is the LORD himself who stands at the helm. It is he who "sits on high," who "loves righteousness and justice," and whose "work is done in faithfulness," on the basis of his "steadfast love." That is why Israel can rejoice and deem herself blessed. In doing so, the Psalmist promotes once again the themes of *hesed* and *zedek*, mercy and justice, by means of which God guides and redeems individuals and nations.

There is comfort and courage in knowing that when chaos and evil stalk the earth, God calls us to himself again. In the hindsight of history, faith can trace God's hand nudging a valiant servant here, a nation there, to rise to the occasion; and, in the name of faith and righteousness, best the evil of the hour. Second Isaiah certainly did as much when he singled out Cyrus as God's Anointed, who brought the Babylonians to bay. It takes faith and courage to do that and in the doing of which to give the glory to God and not to ourselves. It is through our choices and efforts that moral good is advanced and violence and hatred silenced. That is why the Psalmist reminds us of God's love, justice, mercy, and equity, for they shine like beacons, guiding us through the darkest of times. That is why the might of kings, horses, and chariots wanes in the light of God's goodness and care.

Theologically, the providence of God acknowledges that all of life falls under God's sway. As Creator, Sustainer, and Redeemer, God governs man by his gracious will, setting bounds over his freedom—both physically and morally—as well over nations, yet redeeming and renewing man whenever he cries to God. However violent and disastrous a time may appear, its crimes and woe never fall beyond the range of God's steadfast love and enduring mercy. What Joseph's brothers meant for ill, God was able to use for good. It lies behind Paul's learning how to be abased and how to abound, of Abraham Lincoln's commitment to preserve America's Union, and of the Allies refusal to permit Nazi Germany and the Empire of Japan to crush the world under their boots, and eliminate with impunity whole classes of people in grizzly gas chambers. That evil was brought to an end.

At a personal level, the oversight of God has the power to lift our hearts when sad, to experience strength in the face of sorrow, peace in the midst of pain, hope in the midst of despair, courage in the midst of fear. Psalm 33 heralds the good news that we belong to God. It champions the conviction that his purposes do endure, and that a life invested in him, however great or prolonged its sufferings might be, is never an investment in vain. Even the existentialist Sartre had to acknowledge that during the Resistance, France's victors were still unable to conquer the French spirit and its capacity to say: *"Non!"* There are limits to evil's power. Indeed, blessed is the nation whose God is the LORD.

Our challenge is to cling in faith to the same. To believe and so strive that good may vanquish evil, right conquer wrong, and justice and mercy, kindness and love inform and guide our every step and every breath. May it so be, dear LORD!

~ ~ ~

A king is not saved by his great army; a warrior is not delivered by his great strength. The war horse is a vain hope for victory, and by its great might it cannot save.

Psalm 33:16–17

One of the sadder chapters of the American West is the story of the slaughter of the Comanche Nation's horses on September 28, 1874. Under the command of Col. Ranald Slidell Mackenzie, the Comanche people were surprised in a place called Palo Duro Canyon and driven away before their warriors could mount their horses to counter-attack. Knowing that without their horses their marauding days would be over, Mackenzie ordered his men to corral and shoot the captured animals. Willingly or unwillingly, his troopers obeyed, killing 1,084, by count. Less than a year later, the Army rounded up another 6–8,000 horses, and shot them, too. This sorrowful end to a great "equestrian empire" has never been forgotten by either the Comanche people or by the historians who comb the records and chronicle the cruel details. David Quammen, writing for the March 2014 issue of the *National Geographic* spares none of the ugly facts as he retells the story and the Comanche People's revival of their former magnificent steeds.

The Psalmist looked upon the "war horse" as a king's vain attempt to build, expand, and maintain an empire. Commitment to the Covenant and YHWH's will was a king's first priority—not trust in troops or warriors, chariots or horses. The Psalmist refers to "war horses" only three times (Pss 20, 33, and 147). In none of the passages does he find justification for their usage. Yet, in Psalm 149 he pauses long enough to recognize the legitimate role that armies play and did play in Israel's road of ascendency, decline, and survival. To that extent, he was not a pacifist. Rather, he was a realist. Amassing chariots and horses hinted of war. Perhaps he had access to the Annals of the Kings of Judah and Israel before they became finalized in the Books of Kings and Chronicles. If he had access to Isaiah's scroll or Jeremiah's, he knew they scoffed equally at the practice of buying horses from Egypt and, even as far away as Cyprus. The mobilization of armies and the amassing of war materiel have always saddened the parents of sons and daughters who fight their nation's conflicts. We no longer ride horses into battle; instead, our sons and daughters are hurled at the enemy in much more costly, sophisticated, and state-of-the art killing machines. In the American West, horses are still rounded up and shot, much to everyone's despair. Yet, we understand the Psalmist's intention. Aside from God's steadfast love and justice, we will always be writing "Odes to an Unknown Horse," to an "Unknown Soldier, Sailor, Marine, or Airman." This is not to disdain a nation's right of self-defense or the decision to declare war when its institutions and its people are threatened. It is to ponder with the Psalmist the truth that makes for peace in which to place our heart's highest hopes and confidence. It is to come before God first before rushing off to war.

"O LORD, search our hearts and mend our spirits as we contemplate the joy of thy salvation and thy goodness that endures from generation to generation. Amen."

～ ～ ～

> I sought the LORD, and he answered me, and delivered me from all my fears. . . . The LORD is near to the brokenhearted, and saves the crushed in spirit. Many are the afflictions of the righteous; but the LORD delivers him out of them all.
>
> Psalm 34:4, 18–19

remorse and redemption

Whoever arranged the Psalms knew how to weave together the myriad hopes and woes that define us as human beings. Call it "inspired" if you wish, but the Wisdom Writers made no such claim. They saw their task and call as simply to praise God as he is—in all his glory and righteous love—and to portray themselves precisely as they were and we are: as finite human beings, as fragile as Pascal's tenuous reed, fraught with the knowledge of our perishable nature:

> Man is but a reed, the most feeble thing in nature; but he is a thinking reed. The entire universe need not arm itself to crush him . . . But, if the universe were to crush him, man would still be more noble than that which killed him, because he knows that he dies and the advantage which the universe has over him; the universe knows nothing of this.[3]

The Psalmist would have concurred with Pascal's lines, if not seized upon them as his own, for many are the afflictions of the righteous and equally many pass through life with broken hearts and crushed spirits.

In a letter to a notary in *Calvin's Ecclesiastical Advice*, the Reformer responds to an official who is concerned with respect to a divorce request. According to the report, a young woman was married to a man, against her consent. Quickly, the marriage became abusive and crushing to the girl's heart. The notary is moved by her plight, but "the law is the law," and he is reluctant to grant a divorce. Among non-Reformed denominations, Calvin's legacy has often been perceived as inflexible and rigid. But not so in this case! Weighing her circumstances, Calvin casts aside all misgivings and advises the notary to nullify the marriage at once, since, in his estimation, without her consent, no marriage took place.[4] Indeed, she had suffered enough.

"The LORD is near to the brokenhearted and saves the crushed in spirit." We love these words and cling to them rightly. Who among us has not felt desolate at times, or nursed a crushed spirit and trammeled hope, or felt betrayed and rebuffed when least deserved? In those moments, we are closer to God than we may realize, the Psalmist hints. Take heart! Take courage, for God is present to lift up your soul. Remember, "God's power is made perfect in weakness" (2 Cor 12:9c). The all sufficiency of the self may be a Stoic principle, even admired, but the Gospels know better. Yes, we are to be as strong as we can, but God's power is made

---

3. Pascal, *Pensées*, 116.
4. Calvin, *Ecclesiastical Advice*, 129–131.

perfect in our weakness in order to redeem us from our insufficiency when we need him most. "Three times I besought the LORD about this [Paul's thorn in the flesh]; . . . but he said to me: 'My grace is sufficient for you'" (vs. 9b). "O LORD, may we find strength in those words, too!"

∼ ∼ ∼

> Contend, O LORD, with those who contend with me; fight against those who fight against me! . . . O LORD; be not silent! . . . Bestir thyself, and awake for my right.
>
> Psalm 34:1, 22–23

Although this psalm is categorized as a "lament," in reality, it is a cry for God's help. More than that, it is cry for God to take sides; indeed, for God to wreak havoc against our enemies. It is a natural cry, an all-so-human wail from the deepest recesses of our consciousness as well as our subconscious. It rises out of the depths of our hearts, especially when we are fearful, sore bestead, or crushed by life's unfairness. "For Heaven's sake, dear LORD! Bestir thyself! For thy name's sake! Hear my case, O LORD, and come to my rescue!" It's a good prayer, an honest prayer—straight from the heart.

Rather than be embarrassed, we can celebrate the Psalmist's desperation, for his desperation mirrors our own. The joy of his lament, if we may call it "joy," is the immediate access before God that it makes available. Jesus refused to take sides when asked by a brother to intervene against another brother. But Jesus seized upon the occasion to ease the brother's mind with a parable about values that is far more worth cherishing.

The joy of the Old Testament is its blistering humanness, its revelation of the soul's authenticity before God. "Here I am LORD, in all my hurt and humanity, pain and pity, a misery unto myself." The LORD heard the Psalmist's prayer as he hears ours. There is no shame to pray for God's help, even in a wretched moment tainted with a vengeful spirit. God understands; he is not deaf to the woes and inequities of life's drama, or to the evil that men heap on one another. It is all right to pray when hurt, to let God know how desperate, depressed, and distraught you are. It is good prayer. There is no embarrassment in claiming it for the self.

The converse would result in the suppression of any form of anger, thus leading to despair and passive-aggressive behavior. "Out with it!" the Psalmist urges. "Let God know." A cry to God never goes unheard when a soul requires repair and healing. If only Achilles had understood the above, he would never have dragged Hector's corpse behind his chariot as he circled the walls of Troy to avenge the death of his kinsman, Patroclus. The saddest part of all, however, is the role that Zeus and Apollo played, for each god favored Hector's spear over Patroclus' armor. They took sides and willed the brave youth's death. No wonder Achilles whipped his steeds in maddening chase, as he dragged Hector's body about the city's sun-bleached walls. A cry for vengeance is often justified, though all too frequently it goes too far. For that reason, the *lex talionis* came into existence, not to exact revenge, but to limit retaliation to "an eye-for-an-eye" and "a tooth-for-a-tooth," and nothing more. Unlike the gods, Homer grieved for the dying Hector: "Life left his limbs and took wings for the house of Hades, bewailing its lot and the youth and the manhood it had left behind."[5] In the end, all anger is tragic.

When confronted with evil, pray to God, the Psalmist advises, and do so without shame. Or, in the spirit of Christ, as the Gospels rejoin, return evil with good. "O God, help us each ever to seek thy will, and never, never just our own!"

∽ ∽ ∽

> Transgression speaks of the wicked deep in his heart; there is no fear of God before his eyes. . . . He plots mischief while on his bed; . . . he spurns not evil. . . . How precious is thy steadfast love, O God! The children of men take refuge in the shadow of thy wings. . . . For with thee is the fountain of life; in thy light do we see light.
>
> Psalm 36:1, 4, 7, 9

Most of us are spared the machinations of the wicked, at least, directly. One Christmas season, a thief ripped my mother's gifts from her elderly arms. She sought an officer to report the incident. "He just shook his

---

5. Homer, *Iliad*, 296, Book 16, 866–868.

head," Mom said; then added: "'I'm sorry, Ma'am, but in this throng, things like that happen.'" As a child one night, I awakened to the shattering of glass. Creeping out into the hall, I beheld my favorite aunt—inebriated and staggering—pointing a gun at my father. "It's OK," he addressed her softly. "We understand," as he extended his hand toward her pistol. She turned and saw me in the hall light—her eyes filled with tears. Then slowly, though drunkenly, she placed the pistol in his hand. Dusk had settled in the narrow streets about the French hotel. We were touring Samur, on the banks of the Loire. Suddenly, we heard a woman's scream. I raced to the door and into the hallway. A masculine figure sped down the stairwell, inches from me. With a surge of adrenaline, I plunged after him, only to lose him in the crowded street and its pale lamplight outside. He had tried to rape the frightened woman, but her scream saved her. I shall never forget my favorite uncle, a deputy sheriff of Washington County, who, night after night, checked his revolver before tightening his holster about his hips; then he would smile before stepping out into the night. It was during the War, and bootleggers, thieves, bank robbers, and worse prowled the county. He was tall, lean, red of hair, and as true a marksmen as his inimitable mother, the indomitable Kate White.

Few of us actually witness a murder. My father, who was reared in Oklahoma Territory, watched with his grandfather as a posse of lawmen cornered and killed cattle rustlers on a ranch near their home. Later he counted their bodies—all six—in the back of a buckboard where they had been thrown and brought into town. You, the reader, have likely witnessed far worse, or been robbed or abused, threatened or sued by the greedy, the brutal, and the ugly. Our modern era is no less susceptible to crime and terror than David's, or Israel's, or the huddled bands of returning Exiles who came home to the broken and blackened walls of Jerusalem.

Evil is real. But so is God's love. So also his counsel, his laws of equity, righteousness, and justice. We are tempted to forget, to retreat from the public squares of common suffering, but God needs us to be bold, to champion what is right, while rendering no one evil for evil. In the long run, it is only in God's light that we see light at all, and protected under the mighty shadow of his wings that our spirits are renewed and sustained by his grace. "O LORD, hear our prayers and fill us with insight and gratitude for the living of our days with you!"

> Fret not yourself because of the wicked, be not envious of wrongdoers! For they will soon fade like the grass, and wither like the green herb.... I have seen a wicked man overbearing, and towering like a cedar of Lebanon. Again I passed by, and, lo, he was no more; though I sought him, he could not be found.
>
> Psalm 37:1, 35–36

All the old farms are gone now. Where once cattle roamed, tobacco and corn flourished, and wheat and barley sheaves bowed in the warmth of a summer breeze, now burgeoning developments, gated communities, and tree-lined golf courses dominate the landscape. Not that the latter are representative of the rich and haughty, or vain and arrogant, but gone are the humble who tended their livestock, toiled from before dawn to dusk, and tilled the soil of the land's farms that bordered creeks and hills.

Change is inevitable, and time sweeps away careers and landmarks that generated hope and happiness for its proud and hardy residents. How they lived poetically in a world of their own! Even conquering generals of mighty Rome were required to endure a servant whispering in their ear, "*Sic transit Gloria mundi!*" as they rode in triumphal procession. The glory of this world passes, for both the humble and the proud, the rich and famous, as well as the poor and lowly. The Wisdom Writers of the Psalms were well aware of these disparities. Thus they praised God for the virtues that edify, warning against the vices of the callous and the wicked, who never seem to care.

It is not ours to fault their spiritual vision, or longing for a stable society that embraces hope and promise, wealth and prosperity—for rich and poor alike. The dream for such a commonwealth still inspires social philosophers and political scientists in their quest for a modern state with a thriving economy. Far from being utopian, to achieve a modest compromise would be a reasonable goal.

The haughty and the mighty, along with despots and swindlers, will always be with us. In that respect our world is little different from that of the Wisdom Writers'. It is refreshing to remember the latter's plea for propriety and character, no matter how burdened we may be from past regrets or remorse. God's grace and forgiveness have erased all that. We will always be "justified sinners," as Luther put it. But that is good news. Set free from the folly of our hubris and "concupiscence," as Augustine was fond of labeling it, we, too, can strive to be positive and useful as children of God in our time.

Far more could be said of the Wisdom Writers' conservative and pragmatic virtues, but suffice it to say that St. Paul offered the same in his letters to the Christian communities that, through his words, found hope and courage in the midst of Rome's grandeur and moral decay.

"O LORD, may we find such courage, too, as we pledge ourselves to be thy disciples in the mix of our own era, whatever befall!"

∼ ∼ ∼

> I am utterly bowed down and prostrate; all the day I go about mourning. . . . For I am ready to fall, and my pain is ever with me. . . . I am sorry for my sin.
>
> Psalm 38:6, 17–18

His son had warned me before visiting his father. "Poor Dad's old and crabby. The poor fellow's in his 90s, an invalid, bedfast and a misery unto himself and everyone else. His nurse will let you in. You'll find him upstairs, in the room on your left." He paused, while trying to smile. "Don't be offended by whatever he says. I should live to be so old myself. You know he's a veteran of the Spanish-American War—the only one left in town." So I drove to the house to make my visit. His nurse let me in and nodded up the stairwell. "He ain't in the best o' moods, sir! You gotta watch yerself," she frowned. "Ain't no tellin' what he'll say."

I knocked on his door. "Well, come on in!" he called, gruffly. "The damn thing's not locked." I eased the door open, peered inside, and entered the room. "Brad said you were coming," a hoarse voice greeted me. "Don't look much like a preacher to me." I glanced to my right, where the old Veteran lay in a wad of sheets and crumpled pink and green quilts. Lean and wiry, with a head full of brisling gray hair, he struggled to sit up, half flailing his withered arms, covered with the purple bruises of old age. "Well, I'm just what I am!" he blurted. "Don't shake my hand!"

he withdrew his fingers quickly. "Hurts too damn much," he rotated his sallow hands for me to see. "Preacher, if you're worth a crap, you'll do me a favor. See that drawer?" he pointed toward a dresser of peeling veneer against the wall. "Top drawer. Just pull it open. You'll see what I need." I turned toward the dresser and pulled open the drawer. There lay a pistol of some ancient vintage, with a chestnut handgrip, and a cylinder filled with lead bullets in tarnished brass shells. "Well! Hand me the thing! Helen's dead, and I want to join her. LORD, Preacher!" he suddenly sobbed. "I just want to die! I don't want to live another day. I want to die and be with her."

This is now the third psalm in the series of the Penitentials. "I am utterly bowed down and . . . all day I go about mourning. My pain is ever with me." In his commentary on its verses, Augustine devoted no less than eighteen long columns to its twenty-two Old Latin verses. Augustine, too, was ready to die and join his son and revered mother in the halls of heaven's paradise. I say "son," because he did have a son, who died at the age of 18. In the Latin version that Augustine used, the word for "fall" is actually "scourged." *Quia ego ad plagas paratus, et delor meus contra me est semper.* "For I am prepared for the scourges, and my sorrow is continually before me." He would go on to assert that no one can be a Christian who is not a mourner of his sin.

Augustine, however, saw far more than just his own misery in this confessional psalm. What does it mean to be sorry? He asks. And his answer cuts to the quick of our own confessional plights.

> Behold! Thou art from day to day mourning over thy sins; but perhaps thy tears indeed flow, but thy hands are unemployed. Do alms, . . . let the poor rejoice of thy bounty, that thou also mayest rejoice of the Grace of God. He is in want; so art thou in want also; he is in want at thy hands; so art thou also in want at God's hand. Dost thou despise one who needs thy aid; and shall God not despise thee when thou needest His.[6]

---

6. Schaff, *Augustine*, 110.

> "LORD, let me know my end, and what is the measure of my days; let me know how fleeting my life is! Behold, thou hast made my days a few handbreadths, and my lifetime is as nothing in thy sight. . . . Hear my prayer, O LORD, . . . hold not thy peace at my tears! For I am thy passing guest, a sojourner, like all my fathers. Look away from me, that I may know gladness, before I depart and be no more!"
>
> Psalm 39:4–5, 12–13

One hardly needs to reflect on these words before realizing how fleeting and brief life is. For any psalmist prior to the Exile, or before the period of the Maccabees, life was a gift, a precious gift, that ended when one's dust returned to dust and one's breath returned to God. Nonetheless, it was a gift to be enjoyed. Not wishing for God to hasten those coming hours, the Psalmist pleads for a few last days before he departs. The old Veteran's eyes emanated a similar wish, though he longed for the peace of death, as he lay there, confined in his room with the dresser nearby. In his *Notebooks of Malte Laurids Brigge*, Rilke describes how Malte's grandfather, Chamberlain Brigge, "still carried a death inside him. And what a death it was!" It took the old baron two months to die during which time his moans filled the manor with the roar of his death. Even the estate's Russian wolfhounds howled and paced the apartments as each increasing bone-chilling groan rose to terrifying crescendos. "I am afraid," Malte mutters. "One must take some action against fear, once one has come down with it."[7] The Psalmist was content to ask God to turn away, while he awaited his own death, departing "to be no more."

The glory of this psalm has to be in its stark honesty, however self-absorbed the writer was in his loneliest hour. To approach God with such sincerity, candor, and even disparagement is a blessing in disguise. We are not told if God turned away. Indeed, the Psalmist knew that God was on his side. "Hear my prayer, O LORD, and give ear to my cry." So too the

---

7. Rilke, *Notebooks*, 7 & 10.

old Veteran, whom I was blessed to visit and revisit many times before he died!

We belong to God in life and death. There can be no separation between the two. To know God *now* is to know God in his eternity, which can never fade or fail. The American philosopher Charles Hartshorne constructed his theory of the afterlife on the principle of God's eternity. There is no such thing as "to be no more" in his view. We shall forever belong to God. His memory is eternal. Our death may close the last chapter of our earthly book, but not our life as the content of that book. That unique and unrepeatable story can never cease to be or "unbecome," states Hartshorne.[8] God will forever cherish our individual stories. Like a beloved book, our lives are precious to God, beyond the brevity of time's horizon or the fleeting sands in the hourglass of our unique histories. Indeed, we are but sojourners, God's passing guests, as were our fathers. Still, God cared for them. Will he not also care for us? What is it that his own Son would one day say? "In my Father's house are many mansions. . . . I go to prepare a place for you, that where I am you may be also" (John 14:2–4).

⸻

> Be pleased, O LORD, to deliver me! O LORD, make haste to help me! Let them be put to shame and confusion altogether who seek to snatch away my life; let them be turned back and brought to dishonor who desire my hurt! . . . Who say to me, "Aha, Aha!"
>
> Psalm 40:13–15

Skeptics of religion have always sought to "snatch away" faith's hopes and dreams, or, at least, dim them as best they can. Their "Aha, Ahas!" ring out as loudly today as they rang out in David's time, or in the time of the returning Exiles, as they endured the bitter slurs of those who mocked them as they passed along. As brilliant as the works of Hawking, Wilson, and Dawkins are, their intended goal is to minimize the role of God in either the creation of the universe or the emergence and ascendance of

---

8. Hartshorne, *Omnipotence*, 32–37.

mankind. From their perspectives, God is simply unnecessary to account for the Big Bang or the arrival of human beings through Evolution.[9] Given the laws of the universe, both phenomena were able to occur without divine will, interest, or guidance. The foundation of their theories, however, is based on the supposition that matter alone matters, as matter alone can be verified. After all, how can you verify God, who transcends the world of objective material or subjective thought? "Aha, Aha!" they say. "You can't." But then how can they verify their own statements, which are constructs of reason and limited to their own values? The irony of their position, however, is that their descriptions of the Big Bang and the truth of mankind's long and convoluted Evolution need not be disputed. Far beyond disproving God's role in creation, the sheer expansion, wonder, and magnitude of the universe witnesses more to the likelihood of God's existence—as one who creates out of novelty and freedom—than to their view of God as an absentee landlord, who so transcends the universe as to cease to marvel at the arrival of his own self-consciousness in the consciousness of mankind.

The Psalmist's hope lay in his heart where God was inextricably present. Long before Augustine, Israel's wisest had already surmised that man's heart is restless until it rests in God. Indeed, what does matter "matter" without purpose, hope, or love? Israel's insight of "what is man that Thou are mindful of him?" lifts the soul to the heights of self-fulfillment as few other worldviews have or can. World Communism could not do it, while Humanism and Atheism, for all their bravery, suffer from an absence of a universal norm. As for "shame and confusion," that is not for us to say. God's love exists, not to condemn the world, but to save it and us through his grace.

The Psalmist's prayer is a welcome reminder of what endures, of what alone enjoys highest value, and of what regenerates the human soul. In its verses, God assures us that to dwell with him is to dwell poetically upon the earth in the fullest sense of that metaphor.

---

9. See Stephen Hawking's *The Grand Design*; Edward O. Wilson,'s *The Social Conquest of Earth*, and Richard Dawkins' *The God Delusion*. All are worth reading.

remorse and redemption

> Blessed is he who considers the poor. The LORD delivers him in the day of trouble; the LORD protects him and keeps him alive; . . . As for me, I said, O LORD, be gracious to me; heal me, for I have sinned against thee! . . . Blessed be the LORD, the God of Israel, from everlasting to everlasting!
>
> Psalm 41:1–2, 4, 13

So ends Book I of the Psalter—all 41 of its opening Psalms. Considered to be the psalms of David, or, at least, composed by others in his honor, Psalm 41 brings to a conclusion this particular portion of the Psalmist's collection. Throughout Book I, the Psalmist has provided readers with a variety of majestic hymns and songs of praise, lament, confession, and thanksgiving. Often accompanied to the now-lost melodies of lyre and flute, they made glad the heart of those who sang and prayed them. We may never know how many David composed, sang to his Court or priests, or whispered to himself when withdrawn and alone before God; nonetheless, through their power and grace, they continue to speak to hearts today. Especially do they comfort the poor, the troubled, the sinful soul, and all in need of God's healing touch.

The Hebrew word for "poor" [*dal*] includes the earth's wretched, its down-and-out, its *les miserables*, but it also incorporates the "weak," the "meek," the "forgotten," and "spiritually humble." In that regard, the Psalms truthfully become a mirror of the soul. They represent *our* cry to God as much as ancient Israel's. They mend our hearts as therapeutically as they mended Judah's. They bring God down to us as God lifts us up to himself. For all their devotion to the upright servant, which they longed to become, they witness equally to the God of grace, whose righteousness alone atones. Written by men, full of merit, they became and remain a beam of light and hope for all who dwell as passing guests upon God's earth. How could we ask for more? Why would we seek less?

"Lift up our hearts, indeed, O LORD, and bless our lives and dreams and hopes as Thou didst bless and guide and love your servant Israel long ago."

Book Two
Psalms 42–72

5
Songs of the Temple Singers

> As a hart longs for flowing streams, so longs my soul for thee.... Deep calls to deep at the thunder of thy cataracts; all thy waves and billows have gone over me.
>
> Psalm 42:1, 7

OF ALL THE CHANTS we intoned at Villemétrie, my favorite was the Center's Gregorian version of Psalm 42. Harmonizing in *a cappella*, our voices joined in melodic chord to chant the melodies of Korah's Sons—that ancient guild of Temple singers: "As a hart longs for flowing streams, so longs my soul for thee." Its closest adaptation in English remains that of Nicholas Brady's 1696 metrical quatrain:

> As pants the heart for cooling streams
> When heated in the chase,
> So longs my soul, O God, for Thee,
> And Thy refreshing grace.

Following dawn's cold *matins* (for it was bitterly cold in our small chapel), the chants' soulful tones would warm our hearts throughout the day and long into dusk's vesper hour. It was an idyllic time for a lonely soul in search of God. For every quest there is a season, and such was Villemétrie's passing hours. We were all God's guests, God's quiet sojourners, along life's path of early morns and vigil nights.

Mankind will always seek God, in spite of life's waves and billows. Yes, some will turn back midway, or trim their sails for a different tack. But most of us ply on in trust and love, sustained by God's hope and grace, whispered in the wash of our journey's wake, in the murmur of wind and waves. "Deep calls to deep at the thunder of thy cataracts," sang the sons of Korah.

In his earlier essays on religion, Sir Bertrand Russell—calculating the cost of the voyage—elected to cease believing in God. He was young, if not a bit sophomoric. "If everything needs a cause, then God requires a cause,"[1] he concluded, as he steered his life in a different direction. Again, his life is not ours to judge. He made his decision, and his keenness of mind is still valued among logicians and philosophers worldwide. In truth, every religion needs a caustic critic. In the time of Hezekiah and Ahab they were known as *nabiim*, "prophets."

Many years ago, an old man would stop by the house to converse with my grandmother. While she poured him a cup of coffee from the cook stove, and lathered up a biscuit with churned butter and blackberry jelly, he'd sit with his back to the window and stare at the stove. "Kate, I know God made you and me," he'd begin, "but you know what troubles me the most?" he'd stare up at her and pause. I would ease my chair forward to listen, positioning myself ever closer to the stove, for it was always cold in the farmhouse in winter. How his neck and hands bulged with ropes of wrinkles and grooves of sallow skin! He'd stir his coffee. "Kate, I know God made us and all these fields and farms about," he'd nod toward the granary and frost-white hills. "But, Kate, the question that troubles me is, who made God?" Unlike Russell, the conundrum only deepened his faith in the "Deep," rather than unravel his days with doubt and depression. The old man was my great uncle. One of his sons went on to become a chaplain.

As for the cataracts and their thunder, where might such have topographically existed for Korah's Sons to have heard and seen? What secret enclave did they know? Where to go to hear the same today, the roar of God's tumbling falls, with all their sparkling wonder? On the far corner of Israel's northeastern border with Syria, such a falls exists, its gushing springs swollen by Mount Hermon's melting snows. It is the headwaters of the Jordan River. I stood and listened with the others, as our kibbutz guide led us up the rocky path. Now it rushes through my soul in grateful memory. It can rush through yours, too, in all its thundering glory—the God who needs no cause other than himself! The God who is the "Deep"

---

1. Russell, *Why I Am Not a Christian*, 6–7.

within ourselves, calling to the "deep" within each of us, the true, one, and only God of every soul!

"Why are you cast down, O my soul, and why are you disquieted within me? Hope in God; for I shall again praise him, my help and my God" (Ps 42:11).

∼ ∼ ∼

> I say to God, my rock; "Why hast thou forgotten me?"
> . . . As with a deadly wound in my body, my adversaries taunt me, while they say continually, "Where is your God?" . . . Vindicate me, O God, and defend my cause. . . . Oh send out thy light and thy truth; let them lead me, let them bring me to thy holy hill and to thy dwelling!
>
> Psalm 42:9–10; Psalm 43:1, 3

The Psalmist knew what every saint wishes were not true: that faith will always have its adversaries. From the Stoics of old, who listened politely to Paul but declined further interest, to David Hume of John Locke's time, and later Schleiermacher who responded to the elite of the Enlightenment, down to the present despisers of religion—though they would not label themselves so—faith has always had its detractors. Sometimes, even mockers! Such as Richard Dawkins boasts of being:

> I decry supernaturalism in all its forms. . . . I am not attacking any particular version of God or gods. I am attacking God, all gods, anything and everything supernatural, wherever and whenever they have or will be invented.[2]

He makes his case, but it rests primarily on empiricism's supposition that the reality of matter is the only reality that matters. That we should ask the ultimate question, which only the soul can ask, does not diminish the soul's reality any more than an atom's quarks and particles, electrons and protons—posited but unseen—eliminate the molecules of visible matter. We cannot help but pose the question, "Does God exist?" And the only answer the heart will accept that makes a whit of sense is, "Yes."

2. Dawkins, *Delusion*, 57.

In the moment that risk is taken, our existential anxieties are taken up in God's embrace and rendered back as gifts of love, courage, and peace. That is the "light and truth" that leads the soul and guides the heart in its daily ascent up the holy hill where God resides. And where are those holy heights today, if not in your heart and mine? Schleiermacher's answer is still a lamp unto our feet. In the final analysis, our consciousness of God is an inevitable aspect of our feeling of absolute dependence of the finite upon the Infinite and Independent, which is God alone.

Remember, Psalms 42–49 are listed as "maskils," that is, hymns of understanding, laden with the sacred beliefs of Judah's Covenant with YHWH. *Thou shalt have no other gods before me.* That Credo says it all. As for the Sons of Korah, they were a guild of temple singers. They served as God's choir on Zion's hill, to the music of lyrical flutes, to summons us to faith and loyalty amid life's crowd of God-dissenters. Would Hölderlin have honored them, as much as he hallowed the Greek poets for dwelling poetically on our behalf? What are singers for if not to serve as echo-bearers of God's redeeming love? His maskil exists for us to sing, too, as happy guests of God's exquisite earth.

∼ ∼ ∼

> Thou hast made us like sheep for slaughter, and hast scattered us among the nations. . . . Nay, for thy sake we are slain all the day long, . . . Rouse thyself! . . . Rise up, come to our help! Deliver us for the sake of thy steadfast love!
>
> Psalm 44:11, 22–23, 26

Anyone who has ever read *Bury My Heart At Wounded Knee* can identify with the Psalmist's passage. It takes less than a paragraph to realize the extent to which the Psalmist's lines apply to America's Native People. From the thousands slaughtered during De Soto's march to the Mississippi, and from its confluence with other rivers as far upstream as the freezing plains of Wounded Knee, America treated its native tribes "like sheep for the slaughter." For all the glory of Manifest Destiny, they were "slain all the day long" from their longhouses along the Atlantic to the valleys of the Rockies and the once buffalo-teeming grasslands of the Great Plains.

The singers of Psalm 44 were no doubt descendents of Judah's Exiles and members of its vast Diaspora, dispersed across the Middle East following Samaria's fall in 722 and Jerusalem's in 587 BCE Scattered among the nations, and slain for YHWH's sake, they returned home never to rise to glory again, except briefly under the Maccabees and the heartless reign of Herod, the Idumean.

But the Psalm's focus reaches far beyond the fall of Israel, or Jewry's sad two millennia of persecution, pogroms, and Holocaust. Judah saw itself "slain all the day long" because of their loyalty to God's covenant. Where was God when they needed him? Had they not been loyal through thick and thin, one generation after the other?

There are times when we are tempted to feel the same way. "What have I ever done to deserve this?" we are wont to cry. "Why me, O LORD? Why me?" But there is a larger question that hangs over life, which all mankind answers in some form or other. Are we willing to believe in God when life's worse turns into the very worst? Job had to answer the question just as we must. "Though he slay me, yet will I trust him," replied Job. It is the creed of everyone, of every time and culture in the midst of disappointment or personal crisis, defeat or dying dream. Never could my father forget his Army comrades who suffered and died in the jungle heat, succumbing to the blows of Japanese rifle butts and bayonets on that infamous Death March of the Bataan Peninsula. Before the invasion, he had mulled signing on for one more tour of duty, but chose instead to return to the States with my sister, mother, and me.

Not every day is a good day, nor necessarily a bad day. But when our hearts are slain and cornered like sheep for the slaughter, do we still trust in God, as Job did? And what does "slay us" mean? Even the Stoics knew that some things are in our power and some are not. The former we can change; the latter we endure; the former are in our hands; not always so the latter. For faith and attitude remain within our power. As Epictetus reasoned long ago:

> Of all existing things some are in our power, and others are not . . . In our power are thought, impulse, will to get and will to avoid. . . . Things in our power are by nature free, unhindered, untrammeled; things not in our power are . . . subject to hindrance [and] dependent on others. . . . [Therefore] what disturbs men's minds is not events but their judgements on events.[3]

---

3. Oates, *Manual of Epictetus*, 468–469.

That might seem callous, but his ancient views are sound and valid.

"Rouse thyself! Help us, O LORD!" are, therefore, words of hope and value, for they are cries of faith and courage, cries of trust in God's salvation. In spite of fear and desperation—whether now or then—the Temple Singers' Songs possessed, and still retain, a power and wisdom that God has blessed across the ages, and which his singers summon us to claim.

∼ ∼ ∼

> Why dost thou hide thy face? Why dost thou forget our affliction and oppression? For our soul [*nephesh*] is bowed down to the dust [*yaphar*]; our body cleaves to the ground [*eretz*].
>
> Psalm 44:24-25

We must not suppose that the Singers' Song is meant to heighten our despair or pander to our resignation. Being finite and mortal, of *nephesh* and *yaphar*, our lives are replete with paranoia, since they are as fragile as the crumbly soil of the earth. It reminds us of what Jesus said. "Therefore do not be anxious about tomorrow, for tomorrow will be anxious for itself. Let the day's own trouble be sufficient for the day" (Matt 6:34).

Embracing each day as it comes has never been simple. The Greeks in particular understood the fickle vagaries of fate and fortune. Their myth of Prometheus, bound to his rock, flailing against the hunkering vultures eager to feed on his open wounds, or the hapless Sisyphus, condemned daily to roll his stone up life's steep hill, only to watch it roll back down come evening tide, galvanized the Greek heart to accept a tragic sense of life as an inseparable element of one's destiny. The truth behind the myths' archetypes cannot be denied, nor is there any need to. Who has not experienced the hiddenness of God, of his withdrawal from our private world of pain and sorrow? Indeed, we carry the seeds of these two giants—Prometheus and Sisyphus—as part of our subconscious code as human beings. That is why we need God, the God of Abraham, Isaac, and Jesus, who draws us to himself to heal our Promethean wounds and strengthen our minds and hearts for the daily ascent up life's hill.

songs of the temple singers

In his book *Being and Having*, Gabriel Marcel, one of France's eminent Catholic scholars, reminds us that our "hill of destiny" is hardly one we climb alone. When open to the grace of what he calls "transcendence," it makes all the difference in the world. Writes Marcel:

> I want to stretch out a helping hand to all who climb the dark hill of Destiny; our common fate. We never climb alone, though we often seem to do so; belief in loneliness is the first illusion to dispel, the first temptation to conquer. I address myself to those who despair of ever reaching the summit of the mountain, or who are persuaded that there is no summit and no ascent, and that the adventure of life is reduced to tramping miserably about in the mists.[4]

In another work, he explains what he means by "transcendence."

> A man cannot be free or remain free, except in the degree to which he remains linked with that which transcends him. . . . When I myself speak here of a recourse to the transcendent, I mean . . . a level of being, an order of the spirit, which is also the level and order of grace, of mercy, of charity; and to proclaim . . . that we do not belong entirely to the world of objects . . . [rather] we have to proclaim that this life of ours . . . may in reality be only the most significant aspect of a grand process unfolding itself far beyond the boundaries of the visible world.[5]

What makes all the Psalms of enduring value is their recognition that we are not alone. There is a summit toward which we climb, an ascent that leads us to the Father's hill, to the House of Zion, and the cross that binds us to God's Son, now and forever. It is a common journey, a common ascent, filled with grace and salvation, empowerment and courage. To be truthful, the journey will always encounter obstacles and its share of hardships, but as the Psalmist's generation knew, all that is part of God's grand unfolding process that gives meaning to life beyond the boundaries of our visible horizons.

---

4. Marcel, *Being and Having*, 23
5. Solomon, *Existentialism*, 131.

> Hear, O daughter, consider, and incline your ear; forget your people and your father's house; and the king will desire your beauty. Since he is your lord, bow to him; . . . The princess is decked in her chamber with gold-woven robes; in many-colored robes she is led to the king, with her virgin companions, her escort, in her train. With joy and gladness they are led along as they enter the palace of the king.
>
> Psalm 45:10–11, 12b–15

How the Poet's anthem appeals to our aesthetic and joyful hearts! In all her tender beauty and glittering gowns of golden slips, her attendants led the young Phoenician Princess to the waiting side of her stalwart groom—the King of Israel in his own refinement. Weddings have a way of charming us. Their symbolism of love and union, happiness and hope, appeals to the very essence of what is pure, innocent, and chaste, even when innocence is beyond our reach. It announces a new beginning, a risk of pledge and passion, a commitment to endure together the ills and joys of the coming days. And so we have something of both the historical and allegorical in this Psalm. One really needs to read it in full.

But there is a message within its message that the Poet makes unmistakably clear. "Forget your people and your father's house; and the king will desire your beauty. Since he is your lord" (Ps 45:11). How succinct and straight to the heart his larger meaning. Who is our King? Who is my King? Have we ever left our father's house, that former home and former life with all its former values to belong to Another—that Redeeming Other of the Patriarchs, Prophets, and Apostles? We are not speaking here of a mom and dad, or of wedding vows, recited with glowing eyes. No! The Temple Singers are pressing us to surrender something far more. Their nuptial song is calling us to surrender our deepest fears, suppressed thoughts, and gnawing archetypes, in order to allow God alone to be the healing consciousness of our todays and tomorrows. Such is God's desire, with his extended hand to lead us in pageantry into the chambers of his heart and into his house of many mansions.

songs of the temple singers

∽ ∽ ∽

> God is our refuge and strength, a very present help in trouble.... The nations rage, the earth melts. The LORD of hosts in with us; the God of Jacob is our refuge [*ma-ha-seh*].
>
> Psalm 46:1, 6

High above Eisenach's ancient German walls rises the Wartburg, constructed as early as the eleventh century. Here behind its medieval walls, Frederick the Wise consented for his favorite scholar-priest to hide while translating the Greek New Testament into German. Luther's tiny room and tiny table may still be visited. On these same heights the castle's owners later added the magnificent hall in which Wagner's famed *Tannhauser* opera enjoyed repeated performances during Germany's great musical festivals. On the way up to the Wartburg, one passes Johann Sebastian Bach's birthplace and Luther's childhood home. Even one of Wagner's summerhouses (now a museum) may be toured along the way. So much history, so much greatness, so much passion, so much flowering of genius! And all of it dedicated to the God of Jacob, as well as Wagner's thundering gods of primal genesis! All of it here in one place!

We know that it was this Psalm that inspired Luther's *Ein' Feste Burg ist Unser Gott*. Sung in countless churches worldwide, it celebrates the Living God's protective hand, mighty arm, and caring love for all mankind—"a bulwark never failing, our helper he amid the flood of mortal ills prevailing." Its sonorous verses still uplift fearful hearts, filling souls with inspiration. The Psalmist would have been thrilled to claim Luther's lines as his own. With what passion and soul the Temple Singers would have sung them on the heights of Zion's steps in front of their own Wartburg! "God is our refuge and our strength, a very present help in trouble!" Indeed, he was—for Jacob, Abraham, Sarah, and Rachel, Moses, David, Mary and her first-born Son.

Ours too is a time of trouble, of mortal ills prevailing. From our personal ills and broken hopes to our nation's woes and mankind's struggles, the power of God's love and restorative grace remain unchanged and available. Man can prevail, you can prevail, I can prevail, if we welcome God as our *Feste Burg*, our *ma-ha-seh*, our bulwark never failing.

> ∽ ∽ ∽
>
> There is a river whose streams make glad the city of God, the holy habitation of the Most High. God is in the midst of her, she shall not be moved; God will help her right early. . . . Come, behold the works of the LORD, how he has wrought desolation in the earth. He makes wars cease; . . . he breaks the bow, and shatters the spear, he burns the chariots with fire! "Be Still and Know that I am God."
>
> Psalm 46:4–5, 8–10

Few theologians seized upon the insight of this Psalm as brilliantly as Augustine of Hippo. It was the year 410. Rome had fallen, her armies scattered, her ancient senators and grandees humiliated, her walls breached; her temples robbed and set ablaze; her monuments toppled; her churches ravaged, and innocents violated. The old elite wagged their heads. They wrung their hands and blamed the City's fall on the Christian State that had dethroned the pagan gods. Letters poured in to Hippo, reports of ruin, rape and atrocity, as fleeing citizens made their way to Gaul or North Africa. Thus began the bishop-monk to write his thoughts on *De Civitate Dei* and the rise and fall of the City of Man.

Augustine knew that the City of God represented the highest ideal to which a soul can aspire, though while on earth we live within, and are buffeted by, the rules and fears of the City of Man. The two exist side by side. The earthly city will one day end; the heavenly will forever abide. The earthly is governed by insatiable pride and the quest for glory. It is motivated by power and lust, but subject to the limits of reason, compounded by avarice and indifference toward the poor and lowly. In contrast, the heavenly city is governed by grace and inspired by faith, hope and love. Within its halls, the meek are praised, the poor embraced, the lonely welcomed, the hungry fed, and mourner comforted. Peace prevails instead of war; joy instead of fear, forgiveness and order instead of sin and caprice, life instead of death. The two cities interact and overlap until the end of time, when God shall bring the City of Man to full account and earthly rest. Until that time, we dwell in both, inspired by faith and hope, courage and grace. Though the City of Man extends out on every side, our faith can make a difference if our hearts are fixed on the City of God.

It is God's love that ennobles us and deepens our vision of who we are and of what we can do and become. "O God, may we ever be haunted, as was Augustine, by thy shining City of kindness and love, justice and mercy, joy and peace! Amen!"

~~~

"Be still [*ha-rapho*] and know that I am God."
Psalm 46:10

It is purported that the most effective "sermon" the Buddha ever "preached" was done in complete silence. Neither he nor his disciples exchanged a single word. Holding a pure white lotus blossom in his lap, he sat in front of his monks in quiet stillness with a serenity none could ever forget. Words would have only produced a substitute for the reality of the inimitable blossom in the Master's hands. Silence is a huge facet of Buddhism, just as it is for any religion that values self-emptying, humility, and quietness before the eternal. How can your soul be receptive of anything if it is already satiated with everything else?

"Be still and know that I am God," represents the Psalmist's realization of the Hebrew notion of emptiness and respect. What can we offer God but our silence? In the presence of his eternity, love, and might, what words of praise or awe add anything to God that he does not already possess in himself? Is he not already *that than which none greater can be conceived*? as Anselm of Canterbury struggled to comprehend God.

"The highest form of worship is silence and hope," quotes Rabbi Heschel, citing Rabbi ibn Gabirol.[6] From Ibn Ezra he quotes: "For there is a form of knowledge that precedes the process of expression . . . and it is God who understands it."[7] It is mirrored in Habakkuk 2:20: "The LORD is in his holy temple; let all the earth keep silence before him." Adds Heschel: "One must never forget the ancient maxim: 'The best medication is silence.'"[8] The grandeur of God carries within itself that which surpasses

6. Heschel, *Quest for God*, 41.
7. Ibid.
8. Ibid., 43.

all knowledge and expression. This is especially true of the Sabbath. As Heschel notes: "It is one thing to . . . be driven by the vicissitudes that menace life, and another thing to stand still and to embrace the presence of an eternal moment."[9]

There was a professor of philosophy and religion who used to taunt his students concerning unanswerable questions: "Over the years," he'd say, "I've amassed quite a few indomitable questions, I mean impossible ones to answer, and have stuffed them into two ragged valises," he'd smile. "I plan to carry them into heaven, walk right past Saint Peter, and demand an immediate audience with God. That's right! With God! But I have the sneaky feeling that once I behold his glorious countenance, as I stride down his hall of a trillion lights, it'll be unnecessary to open either valise."

In the Hebrew, *ha-rah-pho* carries a treasure of meanings within its root. Not only does it mean, "to be silent" or "still" but it enjoins us to surrender our preconceived notions about God, as well as about ourselves. "Let them go!" whispers the word *ha-rah-pho*. "Empty your cup," as a Buddhist might say. Be still, and know that God is God. He and he alone is "exalted among the nations . . . exalted in the earth" (Ps 46:11). For that reason we can surmount all ills, whether in good or bad times, joyful or sad! "Let it all go!" the Psalmist advises. "Give it up. Your anxieties and fears! At least on the Sabbath, or when you enter God's temple. Let it all go. And let God be God in your life, both now and as far out on the horizon as your dreams flow."

∽ ∽ ∽

> Clap your hands, all peoples! Shout to God with loud songs of joy! For the LORD, the Most High, is terrible [*yah-ray*], a great king over all the earth. He subdued peoples under us, and nations under our feet. He chose our heritage for us, the pride of Jacob whom he loves.
>
> Psalm 47:1–4

---

9. Heschel, *Sabbath*, 29.

Martin Buber warns that we do ourselves an injustice if we cling to God only on the basis of his *hesed* love. Equally important is that ancient and fearful side of God that nurtured and upheld his people across the troubled times of their history. Yes, he is the God of loyalty and compassion, but *yah-ray* summons us to embrace that fathomless side of God that reawakens our sensibilities, resulting in authentic renewal and peace. As Buber explains:

> All religious reality begins with what Biblical religion calls the "fear of God." It comes when our existence between birth and death becomes incomprehensible and uncanny, when all security is shattered through the mystery. This is not the relative mystery of that which is inaccessible . . . It is the essential mystery, the inscrutableness of which belongs to its very nature; it is the unknowable. Through this dark gate . . . the believing man steps forth into the everyday which is . . . hallowed as the place in which he has to live with the mystery. . . . He who begins with the love of God without having previously experienced the fear of God, loves an idol which he himself has made, a god whom it is easy enough to love. He does not love the real God who is . . . dreadful and incomprehensible. . . That the believing man who goes through the gate of dread is directed to the concrete contextual situations of his existence means just this: that he endures in the face of God the reality of lived life, dreadful and incomprehensible though it be. He loves it in the love of God, whom he has learned to love.[10]

This is the heritage of Jacob, Moses, Jesus, and Augustine; of Ezra, Hillel, Maimonides, and Heschel. It is this lineage that keeps us human and which the Temple Singers urge us to join. "Dreadful and loving, O God, be our guide, now and forever! This do we pray in thy hallowed Name!"

---

10. Buber, *Eclipse*, 36–37.

~ ~ ~

> Great is the LORD and greatly to be praised in the city of our God! . . . By the east wind thou didst shatter the ships of Tarshish. . . . Walk about Zion, go round about her walls, number her towers, consider well her ramparts, go through her citadels; that you may tell the next generation that this is God, our God for ever and ever. He will be our guide for ever.
>
> Psalm 48:1, 7, 12–14

No date is assigned to this Psalm, but it reflects an era quite past David's, if not in the reign of Jehoshaphat, Amaziah, Uzziah, or Hezekiah. Each of the latter's years knew periods of prosperity and power. Even as late as Jehoiakim's era, Judah could boast of its walls and gleaming towers. So impregnable Zion seemed! Even the Temple Singers clapped their hands! What ships of Tarshish, from far off Spain, would dare brave the winds that shattered fleets? But, alas, alas! Jerusalem fell; its walls were razed; it towers and citadels leveled to the ground. What was the Psalter's editor thinking? Why preserve this boastful piece of Judah's past well into the era of the Second Temple's baleful liturgy? We could write it off as a remorseful or nostalgic memory of what once was, but our souls long to be assuaged otherwise.

In his letter to the Romans, Paul reminds his readers to, "Rejoice with those who rejoice and weep with those who weep" (Rom 12:15). He understood the vagaries of history, of his own Jewish past and the pining of her people for a peace and wholeness that always seemed just a generation away. Augustine read the Psalmist's words without blinking an eye, seeing in the shattered ships of Tarshish the demise of every vain power opposed to God. At the same time, he hailed Zion's walls and towers, ramparts and citadels as anagogical signs of God's triumphant love. "Walk about Zion, and embrace her," he quotes from his Latin Bible. "Walk about Zion." "But how?" he asks. By "embracing her," he replies. "What is the might of this city?" he taunts. His answer: "Whoso would understand the might of this city, let him understand the force of love. That is a virtue which none conquereth . . . No waves of the world, no streams of temptation," can "extinguish . . . love's flame."[11] So it is with the City of God, whose towers and walls surround us, and emboldens our faith. Though we fall, yet God loves us; though we weep, yet we rejoice. So did the Psalter's editor remember and preserve this happy verse.

∼ ∼ ∼

Why should I fear in times of trouble, when the iniquity of my persecutors surrounds me, men who trust in their wealth and boast of the abundance of their riches? Truly, no man can ransom himself, or give to God the price of his life, for the ransom of his life is costly, and can never suffice, that he should continue to live on for ever, and never see the Pit.

Psalm 49:5–9

This Psalm clearly hosts a double entendre, a two-fold theme that the Psalmist has woven into one. Both speak to the heart, while nudging our consciences and fearful souls. Sadly, the first exposes a lingering envy we bear toward the rich and affluent. Even the Wisdom Writers fell victim to its persuasive logic. The wealthy die too, just as the poor, and all go down together to the Pit, from whence none returns. Thus, what lasting advantage, infer the Writers, do the shameless rich have over the poor? Nietzsche called such reasoning "resentment," a vice he associated with the meek, the weak, and cowardly. He dubbed it a form of spite, as venal as envy. His *Ubermensch,* or man of virtue, should be above such backhanded covetousness.[12] In truth, his criticism is not without integrity, though his dismissal of the meek borders on venality itself. Nevertheless, he compels our consciences to review our souls' values, to ferret out those pockets of envy, spite, and resentment that still lurk there. That we can never rid ourselves of all of them humbles our hearts to realize how much and why we need God's forgiveness and love.

---

11. Schaff, *Augustine,* 167.

12. Nietzsche, *Genealogy of Morals*; see in particular his references to "*ressentiment*" which abound throughout the work.

The second nuance reminds us of how transitory human life is. Who can give God the price of his or her life, ransom one's own soul, or buy one's future beyond the mortal span of time's inverted hourglass? The one theme that Heidegger refused to renege on was mankind's mortality. For him, death is a not-to-be-outstripped reality. Once aware of death's finality, our remaining time assumes the category of a gracious gift, not-to-be-outstripped, forfeited, or denied. It becomes our unique span of time, never to be experienced on earth again, nor enjoyed anew if we cast it away as a meaningless impediment.[13] Far from being negative, his analysis opens us to the richness and redemptive power of grace.

So too, Moses Maimonides mulled the mystery of this Psalm's insight in his unforgettable *The Guide For the Perplexed*. In Chapter XVII, in which he explores no fewer than five theories of providence, he concludes that it is only the extent to which we allow the gift of Intelligence to illuminate our lives that we enjoy the fruits of Providence; otherwise we become "like the beasts that perish" (Ps 49:20).[14]

> Now consider . . . the truth taught by the Prophets, that every person has his individual share of Divine Providence in proportion to his perfection. For . . . research leads to this conclusion, . . . that Divine Providence is in each case proportional to the person's intellectual development.[15]

However Platonic Maimonides' view, the Psalmist would have concurred, at least in part, though he might have added "spiritual" along with Maimonides' "intellectual development." Both leave us with a question. To what extent is God in our lives, free of envy, spite, and resentment? In that respect it is a reflective Psalm, for it reminds us that God alone redeems us from the Pit. In concomitance, it calls us to embrace a life of reason, self-control, and courage. With the Gospel, it enjoins us to worship God, not only with all our heart and soul, but also with all our "mind" (Matt 22:37).

---

13. Heidegger, *Being and Time*, sects. 50–53.
14. Maimonides, *Guide*, 475–483.
15. Ibid., 485–86.

> The Mighty One, God the LORD, speaks and summons the earth from the rising of the sun to its setting. . . . The heavens declare his righteousness, for God himself is judge! . . . "I . . . accept no bull . . . nor he-goat from your folds. For every beast of the forest is mine, the cattle on a thousand hills . . . Offer to God a sacrifice of thanksgiving, and pay your vows to the Most High; and call upon me in the day of trouble; I will deliver you, and you shall glorify me."
>
> Psalm 50:1, 7, 9–10, & 14–15

In his poem "*Reisezehrung*," Goethe expresses poetically what the Psalmist and the Prophets knew from Israel's earliest days: that the one indispensable thing that life's journey requires is love. In their case it was love of God, combined with obedience to the Mosaic covenant. In Goethe's case, a passion for life and love of another.

> Thus I now travel through the world with joy
> For what I need can be found anywhere.
> And I take it with me wherever I go
> That *indispensable* essence—"Love."[16]

From the time of Samuel forward, the prophets taught that obedience surpasses sacrifice (1 Sam 15:22). "For I desire steadfast love [*hesed*] and not sacrifice, the knowledge of God, rather than burnt offerings" (Hos 6:6). Amos was even harsher: "Even though you offer me your burnt offerings . . . I will not accept them" (Amos 5:22). Micah softened the blow, while delivering the same injunction: "With what shall I come before the LORD, and bow myself before God on high? . . . He has showed you, O man, what is good; . . . to do justice, and to love kindness, and to walk humbly with your God" (Mic 6:6, 8). Of additional interest is Maimonides's own distinction between what he calls "chief and secondary lessons." He assigns the Ten Commandments, with its respect for the sacredness of the Sabbath, to the first order and Judah's love of festivals

---

16. *Goethe: Selected Verse*, 201

and celebrations to the second category. To enjoy the latter while spurning the first is to sabotage the very greatness of God and undermine the joy and strength that faith makes possible. [17]

As in all cases with the Psalms, the Sons of Asaph [writers of this hymn] put our faith once again to the question. It is so easy to subvert the "chief" element of worship. We seem to fall into it naturally, compromising genuine spirituality in favor of something less like rote attendance, vestments, and aesthetics, instead of practicing the higher lessons of faith, hope, and love. It is both a personal and congregational matter of "chief" concern, as the Psalmist implores us to seek the primary over the secondary.

---

17. Maimonides, *Guide*, 544.

6
A Broken and a Contrite Heart

> Have mercy on me, O God, according to thy steadfast love; . . . wash me thoroughly from my iniquity, and cleanse me from my sin! . . . For thou hast no delight in sacrifice; were I to give a burnt offering, . . . The sacrifice acceptable to God is a broken spirit; a broken and contrite heart, O God, thou wilt not despise."
>
> Psalm 51:1–2, 16–17

This was David's mirror of mirrors, though it has as much to do with us as it did with David and his affair with Bathsheba. Nathan's sharp rebuke cut to his heart. After all, the trauma of the couple's amorous affair resulted in the death of their first-born child, as well as in the loss of Bathsheba's husband, Uriah, at David's instigation (2 Sam 11–12). One might argue that Bathsheba was innocent, for what choice did she have? Still, sin has a way of polluting our hearts and, however silently sequestered, slips past our guarded consciences to appear in the public arena of our souls.

True, we might not be guilty of adultery, or murder, but our battered lives know of instances we wish we could forget, or wish had never happened. We might not have even instigated them, yet they occurred and stick in our throats when we pray. The glory of this passage is its unassailable realism that demands our honesty of soul. However "full of merit," in Hölderlin's finest sense of the word, we are still only human. Justified and sinful, indeed! How true and right, grateful and humble.

There was a youth once who experienced an event he could never forget and which in his later years he felt compelled to share with a nephew. In his younger travels he had loved a girl who bore tattoos on her hips. On her left hip an indelible rose caught his eye, and on her right an angel with outstretched welcoming wings. Years later, when she was only a memory, he often pondered the symbolism of the tattoos. What did they mean? Why did she choose them? And, for heaven's sake, place them where she had? No one who loved her would ever be able to forget the tattoos. Then one day, while singing in church:

> Jesus sought me when a stranger,
> Wandering from the fold of God;
> He, to rescue me from danger,
> Interposed His precious blood

he suddenly realized their meaning. The nephew listened. What was the clue? Replied his uncle, "Any life is salvageable that wants to be."

Jesus did not condemn the woman caught in adultery, for he had not come into the world to condemn the world, but to save it. "Go and sin no more," he told her (John 8:11). I find it interesting that modern editions of Scripture drop this story as a late addition and not truly of Jesus' ministry. How do they know? She was humble, if not of a broken and contrite spirit. Jesus forgave her, as no doubt he would have forgiven the ache and loneliness of the tattooed girl, as well as her young lover.

"A broken and a contrite heart God will not despise" are God's words of love for each of us, too. Perhaps we might rephrase Jesus' therapeutic blessing: "Go and judge no more. Be kind, forgiving, patient, long-suffering, and merciful as the LORD, our Heavenly Father, is merciful to you."

Suffice it to add that Psalm 51 is the fourth of the seven Penitential Psalms. To it we now turn in honor of Augustine, out of respect for David and God's abounding love.

~ ~ ~

For I know my transgressions, and sin is ever before me.

Psalm 51:3

Augustine devoted no less than 16 columns to this peerless psalm. In his last days, it became his prayer of confession, along with the other Penitentials. Like David, he too had had his Bathsheba, though at a much earlier age. Her name remains a secret, as nowhere in all his writings does he reveal it. His mother implored him to put her aside, though he had lived with her seventeen years. She mothered his son, Adeodatus, who died shortly after Augustine left her for a life of seclusion in a North African community. He had taken Adeodatus with him and grieved for months following the boy's death. Anyone who has lost a spouse or son or daughter can readily imagine the cavernous hole the youth's death left in Augustine's heart. But after arriving in North Africa, he accepted the double loss with grace. He loved God too much and trusted God too much to hunger for anything other than knowing God and exploring the depths of his soul.

Augustine knew he had been a transgressor and slave of years of willful concupiscence. With humility, though often masked under the sheer brilliance of his classical education, he nonetheless earned the title of "Saint" that the Church bestowed upon him. Combining eloquence with a love for Platonic philosophy and the joy of Holy Scripture, his insight and spirit still nurture the hearts of readers today. It is present in this Psalm, in which he saw a mirror of the self and the gateway to grace. Here are only a few of his thoughts:

> For many men will fall with David, and will not rise with David. Not then for falling is the example set forth, but if thou shalt have fallen for rising again.... [So] let them hear that have not fallen, lest they fall; let them hear that have fallen, that they may rise. [Thus] Hear him crying, and with him cry; hear him groaning, and with him groan; hear him weeping, and mingle tears; hear him amended and with him rejoice.... For sin with despair is certain death.... So shall we come to God? And whence shall we propitiate Him? Offer; certainly in thyself thou hast what thou mayest offer, "In me are, O God, Thy vows, which I will render of praise to Thee." Do not from without seek cattle to slay, thou hast in thyself what thou mayest kill. The sacrifice of a broken and contrite heart.[1]

---

1. Schaff, *Augustine*, 190–191, 196. Slightly revised.

> Why do you boast, O mighty man, of mischief done
> ...Your tongue is like a sharp razor, ... You love evil
> more than good, ... But God will break you down ... He
> will uproot you from the land. ... But I am like a green
> olive tree in the house of God. I trust in the
> steadfast love of God.
>
> Psalm 52:1–3, 5, 8

Historically, Psalm 52 represents David's response to Doeg. The latter, an Edomite, had betrayed David to Saul at a time when David was seeking refuge in the house of Ahimelech, the chief priest of the shrine at Nob. Saul's jealousy and decline into dementia had soured the soul of the old king, who now feared the rising star of Jesse's son. Though Saul had to see the handwriting on the wall, he could not bring himself to endorse the young adversary. He wanted him eliminated. It's an old story, as universal as Cain's jealously of Abel.

To love evil more than good unhinges a human heart. If not evil, jealously is equal to the task, along with revenge, betrayal, and spite. David had to endure a lifetime of such. Still, the Psalm is written as much for us as it was against Doeg. Vengeance, reprisal, and violence destroy the soul. "If only God would strike down my tormentors!" is an ancient cry. Certainly, David had to steel his heart against the pernicious treachery of Doeg. For it was Doeg, upon Saul's command, who slew Ahimelech and his 85 priests at Israel's sacred shrine. Though the Bible is silent on the fate of Doeg, the story of Saul's death on Mt. Gilboa brings to an end Israel's first attempt to establish a kingship. Nonetheless, what Doeg meant for evil, David transferred into good. Surviving Doeg's slaughter of the officiates of Nob, was a young priest named Abiathar. Moved by the horror of the atrocity, and equally by the spirit of God, David named him his High Priest. Through the thick and thin of the young warrior's rise to power, as well as through the sordid and heartbreaking events of David's later years, Abiathar never failed him. With gratitude and grace he stood by David to the very end. Whether David ever took action against Doeg is nowhere recorded. He grieved over the death of Saul and especially over the death of Jonathan. David did not seek revenge, though well he might have.

Who among us has not felt betrayed at one time or other, wounded to the heart by someone's tongue, or made the brunt of an evil will? O how powerful the urge to seek reprisal! Justice in a civil court is one thing, but evil in a vengeful heart is another. O to be an olive tree in the house of the LORD, and a green and watered one at that! It is we who need the steadfast love of God, if evil is ever to be conquered. Otherwise, the value of a broken and contrite heart is negated, to everyone's sorrow.

It does not have to be that way. "O heavenly Father, guide and protect us from a bitter spirit and twisted heart. Help us to remember the kindness of David throughout his own troubles and temptation to fault others. Plant thy green tree of goodness in the soil of our own hearts, that we may grow in wisdom, love, and courage all the days of our life."

~ ~ ~

> The fool says in his heart, "There is no God.". . . God looks down from heaven upon the sons of men [*ha-beni-atham*] to see if there are any that are wise, that seek after God. They have all fallen away; they are all alike depraved; . . .
>
> Psalm 53:1–3

Note that this is the second time the Psalter's editor includes this "*maskil*," which is, remember, a psalm laden with Israel's understanding of YHWH's Covenant. True, it is basically identical with Psalm 14. But questions remain. For example, exactly who is this "fool" who says in his heart, "There is no God?" Granted, from time to time we may all qualify, there exists a second level of interpreting this psalm that suggests an even deeper stage of spirituality than described in Psalm14. It resides in the distinction between "the sons of men" in general, and Israel's self-identity, symbolized in the words "Zion," "Jacob," and "Israel."

Who are these "sons of Adam," also translated as "children of God" or "humankind"? They represent universal man, mankind, or humankind in general—all of us as a species. Yes, because, from time to time, all of us as *ha-beni-atham* have drifted from God and lost our way. But

"Zion," "Jacob," and "Israel" refer specifically to that unique class of "people" whom God elected, beginning with Abraham and afterwards his offspring. The Hebrew Bible confines this invitation to the arrival of Abraham on the scene, but it began long before. Cro-Magnon Man's haunting handprints, smudged in smoke and poked on cave ceilings, witness to God's call millennia earlier. That Abraham heard it and followed God began a spiritual journey that now includes you and me, along with the sons of Abraham. Hence, that any should say in his heart: "There is no God," or act as if God were a matter of mere indifference, is what underscores the Psalmist's grief. How can mankind say: "There is no God!" when our entire existence and identity is, and remains, founded on God's initiating grace and love? What were "the sons of Adam" thinking? What are we?

While attending a recent conference, a Jewish gentleman seated near me acknowledged his longing to claim his heritage again. "I have enrolled in Torah Studies and hope to visit Israel soon," he began. "For years I postponed returning to the synagogue, but find it renewing and enriching after all these years. I'm even studying the Talmud, and, O, how fascinating and esoteric it is. I love it!"

Heschel captures this dichotomy in a series of remarkable insights. Reflecting on the absence of God for many contemporary *ha-beni-atham*, he observes:

> Now this seems to be a fact: God is of no concern to us . . . [But] His being of no concern to us has become a profound concern. . . . God may be of no concern to man, but man is of much concern to God . . . God is of no importance unless He is of supreme importance. . . The man who betrays Him day after day, drunk with vanity, resentment, or reckless ambition, lives in a ghostly mist of misgivings. . . . God is not alone when discarded by man. But man is alone.[2]

"O LORD God, fill our days with thy presence, our loneliness with thine eternal attendance; our fear with thy reassurance; our conceit and antipathy with thy call to humility and greatness; our selfishness with thy summons to care for neighbor and others; and our lassitude with thy righteous admonitions to become servants of joy, courage, and peace."

---

2. Hesschel, *Man's Quest For God*, xii–xiii, 11.

∽ ∽ ∽

> Save me, O God, by thy name, and vindicate me by thy might. Hear my prayer, O God; . . .
>
> Psalm 54:1–2a

The skeptic within us smiles at the word "salvation." After all, just how many "Jesus-Saves-signs" must a person endure? Why can't the world's religious enthusiasts leave us alone? What is the guilt they want us to bear? O well, we may dismiss them, but the signs arouse something endemic in our souls. Why won't the emptiness go away? Why does the Void keep coming back? When do we finally master its presence?

Camus called it the "absurd," something we can't evade and with which we simply live. Freud labeled it a neurosis; Dawkins a delusion; less kindly souls, a waste of time. But it is there. Pretending it isn't only prolongs the human conundrum and the quiet anxiety of one's lonely existence. No amount of scientific investigation that reduces us to a biological form of conscious vitality quiets the quest for wholeness, either. We simply cannot be reduced to matter in motion, or even Aristotle's "rational animal," and derive satisfaction. We still want more, "crave more," as the Buddha put it, until we experience release from the weary cycles of our aimless sojourns. But it isn't just sojourns, dwelling, or order, direction, enlightenment over chaos that's the issue. No. It is still more. Something still higher, magnanimous, inescapable, and intensely worthwhile! Why? Because we are souls, not just protons, neurons, and electrons, swirling in elliptical fields. We are persons, unique individuals, with feelings and dreams, questions and sorrows, always conscious of "that than which none greater can be conceived," ever driven by the mystical and wonder within ourselves. And that is God, the Creator of the soul, which he fashioned in his image and set with joy on the earth.

In retrospect, many and varied individuals came to Villemétrie for renewal and reflection. Some came to meditate alone in the chapel's serene quiet and cold; others to wander the Center's paths and park; still more to enjoy camaraderie about the table, set with white linen, baskets of bread, fruit, cheese, and bottles of wine; however, what drew them, one and all, was a single human being, André de Robert, in whom the patience and spirit of Christ reached out to all. His countenance, speech, and oftentimes silence pointed to that alone which confirms the heart's search and calms the soul—God. Yes, God, and GOD alone.

∽ ∽ ∽

> My heart is in anguish within me, the terrors of death have fallen upon me. Fear and trembling overwhelms me. And I say, "O that I had wings like a dove! I would fly away and be at rest; yea, I would wander afar, I would lodge in the wilderness, . . ." Cast your burden on the LORD, and he will sustain you; he will never permit the righteous to be moved.
>
> Psalm 55:4-7, 22

The above pattern of lament and deliverance is as ancient as Ice-Age Man. A bead here, a weapon there, caressed together in a leather pouch, placed in tenderness within a grave, all of it is there for the heart to see. What would we do without the heart's freedom to grieve in anguish and silent prayer? O to fly away like a bird, like the innocent dove! To hide oneself in a cleft in a mountain to mourn and cry, be silent and still! We are not the first to long so. The Psalmist offers such freedom to grieve and the need to pray in the confident knowledge that God will find us in both. He will never forget his servants or believers among the sons of men.

Even ministers experience fear and trembling. He sat on the couch in front of a colleague and crossed his legs. "Will you let me read this eulogy before I head to the funeral? It's for my favorite friend's father," he added. "Sure," the colleague nodded. "Go ahead." And so he began. With an eloquent voice, graced by dignity, he traced the happy times the three had known. He quoted from Shakespeare and Seamus Heaney, spoke of laughter, politics, and golf; times of pleasure and times of teasing. His voice grew tight, his hands cold, knuckles pale and clammy. He all but whispered the last few lines, stared at his host, paused, and burst into tears. In truth he sobbed. He cleared his voice, then added: "I know the passages we're supposed to read in order to comfort the bereaved, but how I feel and what I miss words can never salve." He laid his eulogy aside and once more shook with sobs. His friend rose to go to him; he rose to meet his friend, and, the latter wrapping his arms around his fellow-cleric's shoulders, held him while he wept and sobbed even more.

"Come cast your burden upon the LORD and he will sustain you." It may not be through words, nor while stolen away in a silent enclosure far from the rumble of man, but a friend's arms in time of sorrow. Has he not ministered to you and me in a similar manner? When our time comes to listen to another's troubles, may we open our hearts to bear our neighbors' burdens! Why? Because we are each an earthen tabernacle of God through whom his sacred love embraces humankind.

∽ ∽ ∽

> Be gracious to me, O God, for men trample upon me;
> ... When I am afraid, I put my trust in thee. ... In God,
> whose word I praise, ... What can flesh do to me?
>
> Psalm 56:1, 3–4

Of course, flesh can require flesh, as the world knows. What civilization hasn't used torture to terrify the brave or cower the craven, or whip the servant or prisoner of war into submission and despair? The horror of the rack, the bone-breaking blows of the gauntlet, the flogging of the bowed and shackled, as well as the singeing odor of the stake—all sadly, yes all swell the legacy of our species.

But other torments exist as well, embedded in a list of fears and trampling, bitter enough to test the bravest soul. O to assuage those spells of sorrow with the swift justice of Michael's sword! Nowhere does God countenance evil, or grant impunity to the wheelers of wrong. Yet, the LORD is ever present, the Psalmist reminds us, even in the halls of Holocaust's chambers and the soul's cry for justice and right. "This I know, that God is for me. ... What can men do to me?" (Ps 56:9, 11)

Though hardly a call to pursue martyrdom, David's Psalm cauterizes our wounds and soothes our pains. Men can be ruthless, depraved, and mean, and in fact are, driven by *hubris* and vanity. We find such in all walks of life, careers and economic classes, social strata, hiding behind religion and wealth, or stymied in resentment and ignorance. "What can man do to me?" He can bring you down to the level of his or her odious state, but only if you let them. "Trust in God," the Psalmist pleads, and you will never sink into that pit. God will sustain you and mend your wounds. God will embrace you in bad and good. He will fill your heart with strength and love. He will provide you the courage to stand for right; to fight with a noble conscience and will; to care for the anxious, fearful, and weak; to return good for evil, a blessing for a curse; and love and encouragement for the timid and poor.

"O for such faith and strength, dear God! For a character honed by your perfect love! May it come to us as we come to you, in fear and trembling, and in trust and hope! Be with us, God, and bear us up, for we are weak and selfish at best. We need your presence and guiding hand, your eternal arms about our mortal frame, the calm of your Son in our troubled hearts. Yea, have you not made us like yourself, capable of courage, mercy, and right! Why do we waver, dear God? Inspire us anew with David's verse. Help us to claim what in faith is ours—the gifts and the power to praise you for life, and the wisdom and fortitude to help transform lives."

~ ~ ~

Be merciful to me, O God, . . . in the shadow of thy wings I . . . take refuge, . . . I lie in the midst of lions that greedily devour the sons of men; . . . I will sing and make melody! . . . Awake, O harp and lyre! I will awake the dawn!

Psalm 57:1, 4, 7–8

It was the winter of 1961. At the age of 25 I had arrived on youthful wings to the hills of Galilee. From Italy I had sailed to Pella's shores, and then, via air, from Athens to Israel. Our group was assigned to a thriving kibbutz, just north of Haifa and southeast of Acre. My assignment: to labor with Palestinians in the farm's sprawling banana groves. With joy I shouldered my share of burlap-covered stalks to be carried to the tractor's cart. Their market: Greece, Cyprus, and Turkey. In time, I was made the "foreman" of the gang. An awkward task to be sure, but they accepted me as if I were one of their own. Soon we enjoyed each other's respect; nonetheless, they would drop into quiet chatter when the boss returned. That was long ago, before the war of '67 and the flight of so many to refugee camps. It was not mine to say who was right or wrong, which group was the lion amid this fold of the sons of men! Was it the children of Ammon, or the children of Ephraim? Both laid claim to the sacred land, to its sandy soil and yellow marl. It hurt to walk between the rows of sweating men and trampled fronds, or stare into the men's faces. They were citizens of Israel, too.

Life is a twist of fair and ill, a web of joy and trials. But of fair and joy it was for the kibbutz when the Festival of Purim came around. The refectory chairs were pulled aside. Young and old danced till dawn to harp and lyre, horn and drum, fiddle and feet and swirling arms. I stood on a table in the corner of the hall and handed out bottles of cold beverage. It sounds poetic, if not carefree, or a bit bizarre. But it was Purim! Judah's festival of deliverance from tyranny's hand! Say what you will, but there is a time to dance, and a time for woe, a time to reflect and recall the past, along with the pain and dreams of tomorrow.

Will Muslim and Jew, or Westerner and Arab, ever join in joyful dance, and, putting aside guns and bombs, embrace the Highest that ennobles humankind? Let us pray, dear God, that it may be so! "Be exalted, O God, above the heavens! Let thy glory be over all the earth!" (Ps 57:11) May all hearts awake to dance each dawn!

~~~

> Do you indeed decree what is right, you gods [*beni-atham*]? . . . Nay, in your hearts you devise wrongs. . . . O God, break the teeth in their mouths; tear out their fangs. . . . [Then] the righteous will rejoice when he sees . . . vengeance; he will bathe his feet in the blood of the wicked.
>
> Psalm 58:1–2, 6, 10

Hardly the voice of a saint, you say. Remember, this is the Old Testament. The Sermon on the Mount is centuries away. The culture was different; old runes applied—curse for a curse, the second minimizing the venom of the first. It was an ancient law, an established rite. If your enemy rails against you, you have the right to denounce him, too. Jesus of Nazareth turned it into a lament: "Jerusalem, Jerusalem! How often would I have gathered your children together as a hen gathers her brood under her wings, and you would not!" (Luke 13:34)

On the farm where I was reared, my uncles would come to visit their mother, my grandmother Kate. They would sit in the kitchen and bemoan the war, along with their mounting debts. Foreclosures were a steady threat. They would curse their debtors, especially the banks. "A curse on them all!" they would pace, then return to the table for another cup of their mother's black coffee. Sometimes she'd lace it with a tablespoon of brandy. "Ah, Mom! Somehow we'll get through this," they would finally announce. After all, they were each (all three of them) Presbyterian elders, though their language was rich with farmhand words. Later alone on the farmhouse's porch my mother, Aunt Evelyn, and grandmother would rock. When totally alone, they'd talk to themselves, stopping in mid-rock to lean forward, then gesturing and mumbling, push a foot back and rock some more.

We could call it venting, which of course it is. It brings solace and closure to some of our turmoil. But its deeper meaning is far, far more. It's a form of a prayer, however fractured. "Here, LORD, am I. Warts and all! Please hear me and come to my rescue. Forgive my bitterness and inappropriate words. Help me to become more like your Son, or Mary, or Martha."

That is the beauty of any rite, blessing, or curse, whispered to God. "I need you. O God! I need you!" That is its meaning beyond the hurt.

∽ ∽ ∽

> Rouse thyself, come to my help, and see! . . . Each evening they come back, howling like dogs and prowling about the city. . . . My God in his steadfast love . . . will let me look in triumph on my enemies. . . . Consume them till they are no more . . .
>
> Psalm 59:4b, 6, 10, 13

So much for a broken and contrite heart! But Saul was after David once again, his henchmen "prowling like dogs" outside his secluded and camouflaged shelter. Wherever he looked, they were there.

Life's enemies rarely give up. We carry their curses and irate glances deep in our hearts, sometimes for years, until we finally let God take them in his love. Sometimes we go out of our way to avoid our enemies, or take a different path. Their words sink like poison-tipped arrows into our souls. It is difficult to escape them. Sartre devoted an entire chapter to "The Other" and their "glance" in his *Being and Nothingness*. His point: to encourage Existentialists to remain true to their sense of self and not be defined by others. The point is instructive for seekers of God as well. "Know thyself!" is as ancient as Socrates' injunction, which he found inscribed in the Temple of Apollo at Delphi. The Psalmist understood it as well, though he likely never laid eyes on the famous temple. His heart belonged to another temple. His soul was enjoined with the soul of God, the God of Abraham, Isaac, and Jacob, not Apollo. His was that larger self of whom Jesus spoke to his Disciples: "Whoever loses his life for my sake and the gospel's will save it" (Mark 8:35). David encourages us not to retreat from the "prowling dogs" that would steal the food that nourishes our soul. "No! You may not have it! Snarl all you wish! It belongs to God and God alone, to myself and God, to whom I owe it."

The dogs at the gate, however, are not the primary beasts we have to fear. It's the ones within, the hounds of our deep unconscious, with their eerie howls of maniacal strife that Jesus tamed time and again. "Come out!" he called in his therapeutic voice. "Never enter again." And whining and sniffling and cowering and crawling the demons crept out from the souls they had stolen. They still lurk about the City of Man and its unguarded walls. "Do not render unto dogs what is holy," said Jesus (Matt 7:6). Your soul belongs solely to God.

How wise of the Church Fathers to endorse tropological and anagogical metaphors to probe our repressions and fears! Augustine saw in Saul's henchmen-hounds the sleeping soldiers at Jesus' tomb. At best their efforts were of no avail. Now, it is we who must be on guard, ever vigilant lest we succumb to the worst within us. To be good, to be wise, to be just, to be strong; to be faithful, to be kind, to be merciful, even shrewd, that is the pulse of this Psalm, while never forgetting that at best we are justified sinners, lest we boast in our courage and pride. "Come to my help, and see! . . . [For] God in his steadfast love will provide the triumph!"

7
Solace for Times of *Storm and Stress*

O God, thou hast rejected us, broken our defenses; thou
hast been angry; oh, restore us.... O grant us help
against the foe, for vain is the help of man!

Psalm 60:1, 11

For all David's joyful moments and the adulations he received across the years, a thoughtful reading of his life reveals the Storm and Stress that marked his days. According to the Psalm's title, a war with Aram initially went bad. It was only through the prowess of David's commander, Jo'ab, that victory was salvaged from defeat. The carnage, however, resulted in the deaths of twelve thousand Edomites scattered across the Valley of Salt. It was such a great victory that the Psalmist attributed it singularly to the presence and power of God. "For vain is the help of man!" he announced somberly.

Not all our days enjoy triumph, nor end in blissful peace. With an adventurer's memory I still recall the Valley of Salt, which hugs the southern Israeli-Jordanian border. I had joined a guided tour to view the ruins of fabled Nabataea. As we mounted horses in the shadows of its tall red cliffs, our guide commented dryly: "Only last week two Israeli youths were shot trying to cross the border." With that introduction, we turned the horses toward the pass. With quiet awe, we trotted single-file down the rocky road between the dark-red, Behemoth-cliffs. Near the egress, we slowed our pace to admire the remaining cobblestones the Romans had laid centuries earlier, then, picking up gait, trotted past the oleanders and into the valley of Petra's rock-hewn facades. While there, a Jordanian soldier pointed to the mesa where thousands of Judah's enemies had been slaughtered and cast off the mountain's face. How horrendous the battle must have been, whether the victory accredited was to David's forces, or the mesa-triumph of Omri's army! (1 Kings 16:21–28, fn in RSV; 2 Sam. 8:13–14) In the latter's case, the victims were Moabites.

So much simmers in this Psalm, couched in plaintive verse! How vain the help of man! Equally, how vain human glory! When we stare into the pools of our own souls, what flaunted triumphs and cheerless defeats still bubble to the surface? Are there times we might have called on God, yet failed to do so? Or times we claimed credit for achievements not our own? Or, even worse, accused others of culpabilities entirely of our doing? Even Goethe in his early youth had to decide between a life devoted purely to Eros, or the *Sturm und Drang* of a passionate aesthete, committed to his art. He chose the latter, though often feeling alone in the company of others. Shortly after devoting himself to his craft, he sat down one evening and began writing *Werthers Leiden, The Sufferings of Werther*, his first enduring masterpiece.[1]

At some point, we too have to choose between a life based on vanity and pride, or a life committed to something higher, to the unconditional and ineffable summons of God. And that we do in the midst of life's Storm and Stress, which truly never goes away.

"O God, help us to choose wisely, for vain we are—alone or in the company of others! Do not cast us off, but be our guide as we journey down life's rocky path and past the ruins of choices that might have been, save for thy grace and salvation, thy providence and faithful care!"

∽ ∽ ∽

> Hear my cry, O God, listen to my prayer; from the end of the earth I call to thee, when my heart is faint [*ay-theph, ayeph*]. . . . Let me dwell in thy tent for ever! Oh to be safe under the shelter [*mak-shesh*] of thy wings! For thou, O God, hast heard my vows, thou hast given me the heritage of those who fear thy name.
>
> Psalm 61:1, 4

---

1. Ludwig, *Goethe*, 81 and 108.

However far away the "end of the earth" may have seemed to the Psalmist, we grasp the phrase's meaning immediately. God is present everywhere, whether on the glowing edge of the farthest reaches of galactic stars, or as close as the wondrous universe within ourselves. God is present, always there. Indeed, how could space, time, or distance ever limit God? Theologically, it is dubbed "the ubiquity of God," a principle to which Luther appealed to explain Jesus' presence at the LORD'S Supper. "*Hoc est corpus meum*! This is my body."

Even more, the Psalmist's metaphors invite us to experience anew the ubiquity of God. *Faint, tent, shelter, wings*, each carries a message of its own, or a story within a story as all metaphors do. Rilke reminds us that a poem is far more than a set of "emotions," but represents "experiences" that affect the soul. His insight applies especially to the power of the Psalms. Who among us has not succumbed to moments of longing, or suffered from a languid weariness that won't go away? That it may linger as the result of depression cannot be ignored. Often languor is the tip of a chronic disorder that may require hours of counseling to resolve. In the Psalm above, the plaint seems to float on the surface of a deep ill-ease—the fear that he, the suppliant, may lose his spiritual foundation. Whether in Beijing or Rome, Atlanta or Paris, the feeling is virtually the same.

I have never forgotten how lonely I felt "Thanksgiving Day" the year I spent at Villemétrie. Even André's attempt to console my dejection proved of little avail. But his concern and warmth did act as a medicament. Finally, by evening time and the hour of the *capitule*,[2] the brotherhood joined in laughing about America's taste for "turkey" and the fact that Franklin preferred the ruffled gobbler to the stately bald eagle.

When life is down, however, the reality of the ubiquity of God can bear us through the weariest of times. One might call it "separation anxiety," but it applies to the spirit as well. Abandonment, dejection, separation, and despair are as spiritual in constitution as they are psychological.

What the Psalmist provides is an exquisite occasion to experience the providential oversight of God; an opportunity to be enfolded in God's ineffable holiness, sheltered by his everlasting arms, protected by the shield of his wings. Yes, these are metaphors, but they sound the depth of our fearful hearts and assure us of the nearness of God. In doing so, they address Tillich's list of urgent concerns that require resolving if we are

---

2. The *capitule* refers to the brotherhood's practice of choosing a memory verse each evening to be held in prayerful thought by all throughout the next day.

ever to be whole: the threat of non-being, the anxiety of existential doubt, and the sinking feeling of a life without meaning. They have to be answered. "Arise, dear soul," the Psalmist summons us. "For God hast heard your vows and hast given you the heritage of those who revere his name."

~ ~ ~

> For God alone my soul waits in silence; from him comes my salvation.... Trust in him at all times, O people; God is a refuge for us.... Put no confidence in extortion, set no vain hopes on robbery; if riches increase, set not your heart on them.... [For] power belongs to God; and ... to thee, O LORD, belongs steadfast love. For thou dost requite a man according to his work.
>
> Psalm 62:1, 8, 10, 12

"You cannot serve God and mammon," taught Jesus (Luke 16:13). "No servant can serve two masters; for either he will hate the one and love the other, or he will be devoted to the one and despise the other." Jesus left very little room for waffling. So, too, did the Wisdom Writers. Either we trust in God, or trust in mammon. And mammon of course can represent anything other than love for God, alone. Jesus and the Psalmist put us to the question. Which is it? Jesus' reference in Luke's Gospel, however, is to "unrighteous mammon," not wages earned through honest labor. Thank heavens, we might breathe with a sigh of relief; nevertheless, the Psalmist's intention remains unmistakable. To whom is your heart given? To whose is mine? To what or to whom are we devoted? And at what point do we chain mammon to its post? In other words, what lifts our heart to its highest satisfaction? Is it God or something else?

In Rilke's *Notebooks of Malte Brigge*, he mocks traditional faith with a piercing thrust of his poetic pen: "Is it possible to believe we could have a God without using him?"[3] His insight is threefold: Are we merely using God to boost our restless egos, or is God simply an empty metaphor for that which we snub as inconsequential, something we seldom use or have need of anymore? The latter is more likely the meaning of his comment.

3. Rilke, *Notebooks*, 24

Yet a third meaning also comes to mind—shouldn't God be above all temptation to use him? Anticipating the same, the Psalmist urges us to embrace God as our "ultimate concern," as Tillich rephrased the question in his *The Dynamics of Faith*. For Tillich, faith is a state of ultimate concern; there can be no middle ground. Either God is our ultimate concern, or just a concern among many.

This brings us once more to the Psalmist's opening verse: "For God alone my soul waits in silence, from him comes my salvation." We cannot rush God's agenda or storm it to suit our will. To "wait" upon the LORD for one's "salvation" is the only path to redemption. Historically speaking, it was long in coming for Exiled Judah. Fifty years separated the Exiles from the fall of Jerusalem to the time of Cyrus' "Edict of Liberation." It was the latter that permitted Judah to return home and why Isaiah hailed Cyrus as God's Anointed (Isa 44–45). Another fifty years would elapse before Ezra was authorized to restore Torah Studies. Upon accomplishing his commission, the Second Temple's rituals soon became stylized, as we know them in the Psalms.

We are tempted to surround ourselves with numerous urgent concerns, so many that we often lose sight of the ULTIMATE. When that occurs, then our hearts are guided by the City of Man and its alluring values. But true salvation, the Psalmist proclaims, comes only from God and his steadfast grace and redemption. No wonder the Psalmist's cry goes out to God from the "ends of the earth."

～～～

> O God, thou art my God, I seek thee, my soul thirsts for thee; my flesh pants for thee; as in a dry and weary land where no water is. . . . But those who seek to destroy my life . . . shall be given over to the power of the sword, they shall be prey for jackals.
>
> Psalm 63:1, 9–10

Revenge is a common desire of all who have suffered spiteful actions or words. Truly, it is universal and rises from a soul's entreaty for justice. The idea of an eye for an eye and a tooth for a tooth at least addressed man's legitimate demand for compensation. As noted earlier (in Psalm

34), the *lex talionis* rightfully sought to render a fair and judicious settlement. That Israel's prophets and psalmists voice a similar cry should not surprise us. Actually, their uncensored and anguished aspirations for God to destroy their adversaries redound to our benefit, for they serve as an emotional valve for our beseeching God to address our wounds and sorrows. That Jesus would take a different view (Matt 5:38–42) hardly changes the equation. When you hurt you hurt, and if another party is responsible, you have a right to demand reparation. In Jesus' case, his preferred response was to return evil with good, anger with calm, if not forbearance. With that, we cannot argue either, no more than tamp down the Psalmist's exquisite opener: "O God, thou art my God, . . . my soul thirsts for thee" (vs. 1). The power of the latter becomes especially apparent in the metaphorical verse: "they shall be prey for jackals."

I had never heard, nor let alone seen, a jackal until the first night I spent in Israel. Our flight had been delayed between Athens and Tel Aviv, and several of us had not arrived with the larger group. In fact, two of us arrived only after sunset. Soon enough, however, we were driven to a rustic kibbutz on the then-Jordanian/Israeli border, to join the others and bed down for the night. The group was known as: "The Christian Movement for Peace." It consisted largely of German young people, who wished to demonstrate their nation's regret for the horrendous crimes of the Holocaust. Now it was night, and from my bedroom widow I watched as a small squad of Israeli soldiers made their way to a wooden pillbox, protected by sandbags. Each soldier shouldered a machine gun and a bag of grenades. I fell asleep, only to be awakened by the rap-tap-tap of weapons fire. As it grew louder and louder, I lunged out of bed to peer out the window. There in the moonlight scampered a pack of feisty jackals, yapping and fighting over scraps in the kibbutz' garbage pile. They were boisterous little devils, hopping and stealing food from each other's narrow snouts. "So this is Israel!" I thought. "The land of Abraham and Sarah! Of Samuel and David! And of all the prophets, as well as the stony soil of the olive groves that the Palestinians equally cherished!" Even more so for me, it was the ground over which Jesus had traveled, and in whose villages and synagogues he had taught and healed. As Jesus said, "Foxes have holes, and birds of the air have nests, but the Son of man has nowhere to lay his head" (Matt 8:20). Or again, "Go and tell that fox, 'Behold, I cast out demons and perform cures today and tomorrow, and the third day I finish my course'" (Luke 13:32).

How Israel longed for its enemies' towns to be razed to rubble and turned into mounds for jackals and foxes! And how profound was Jesus' statement concerning Herod, "that fox," whom he assigned to his deserved place in history! In irony, however, the Prophets warned both Israel and Judah that unless they repented, they too would become as lairs for jackals and their cities mounds of toppled ruins.

How fitting a symbol of our own hearts! Anger, hate, and strife; jealousy, cunning, and avarice—all create ruins in a divided soul. Like Jung's buried archetypes, they swell in our hearts until our inner spirit collapses in rubble. It takes time to expose the unexamined repressions that control our lives. We have to acknowledge them and bring them to consciousness, if we hope to find salvation. Otherwise, we never experience the full measure of a life that God's love can make possible.

"Ah holy Jesus, thou sacred Son of Man, come lay your head in our hearts, for we too hunger and thirst for that which only thy passion and cross can provide. And in thy holiness, cast out that clever fox that leaps from lair to lair, seeking a permanent home in the chambers of our souls."

~ ~ ~

> Hear my voice, O God, . . . preserve my life from dread of the enemy, . . . [who] hold fast to their evil purposes; they talk of laying snares secretly, thinking, "Who can see us?" . . . For the inward mind and heart of a man are deep!
>
> Psalm 64:1, 5–6

Few modern writers grasped the significance of human perversity as powerfully as Fyodor Dostoevsky. Sweeping aside all clichés about the goodness of man, Dostoevsky determined to paint man's stubborn and uncontrollable side as it was and is. His purpose was to counter the rising tide of Western rationalism, idealism, and socialism, which he perceived could have no worthy end. Having witnessed degradation and suffering from the time of his childhood to his years of incarceration in Czarist prison camps, he dared to challenge the late 1880s' optimism that threatened to undermine personal freedom. In the process, he unmasked the depths of mankind's willingness to choose evil to rebuff the grandiose idealism that blinds society. Contending against the Socratic theory that "man only does nasty things because he does not know his own real interests," he maintained instead that man deliberately chooses the "nasty" in order to establish his personal independence. Thus he concludes that "man is stupid, phenomenally stupid," and will choose to suffer destruction and chaos to cling to his own sense of selfhood. Indeed, he protests: "that the best definition of man is—a creature that walks on two legs and is ungrateful."[4] Obviously, Dostoevsky's definition of man preserves an element of man's nobility, but of his perversity, Dostoevsky harbored no doubts.

Closer to the Psalmist's view is the Apostle Paul's assessment of the depth and hopelessness of the human situation. As Paul states: "I can will what is right, but I cannot do it. For I do not do the good I want, but the evil I do not want is what I do" (Rom 7:18b–19). The Psalmist's critique that "the inward mind and heart of man are deep" poses two questions. Is our inability to choose good due to a *captive will*, resulting in chaos and self-immolation (Paul's dilemma), or is it the result of a *rebellious will*, determined to establish its own identity and self-fulfillment, knowing quite well that what it wills is perverse and self-destructive (Dostoevsky)? There is a difference. In Paul's case the will is captive to an already damaged state. It wills what is right but cannot fulfill what it wills. In Dostoevsky's case, one deliberately wills what is wrong and succeeds in doing it. Perhaps the true status of our "inward mind and heart" is a combination of the two. Thus the good news of the Psalmist's lament lies in its opening our eyes to the "deep" truth about ourselves, not just about our enemies. Thereby it paves the way for our confession, contrition, and thanksgiving for God's grace that can transform and save our mortal existence.

"O God of highest desires, in our *inability* to rise to thy will, forgive, guide, and grant us thy peace. O God of purity and mercy, in our moments of *rebellion* and acerbic spitefulness, again forgive, guide, and grant us thy peace, for we are weak and delirious, and need thy holiness and love to mend our fractured being."

---

4. Dostoevsky, *Notes*, 221–223

> Praise is due to thee, of God, in Zion; . . . When our transgressions prevail over us, thou dost forgive them. . . . O God of our salvation, who art the hope of all the ends of the earth, and of the farthest seas. . . . Thou makest the outgoing of the morning and the evening to shout for joy.
>
> Psalm 65:1, 3, 5, 8

This expansive hymn of thanksgiving reaches out to every corner of human life. From our personal salvation to the beauty of Nature, and from its slopes and valleys, vineyards and fields, the Psalmist praises God as life's sole creator and sole sustainer. It reminds one of the *Rig Veda* and the myriad gods whom ancient India praised, lauding each god or goddess for fulfilling his or her task that makes life palatable. There was Indra, god of rain and storm; Rudra, the dreadful lord of pending destruction; Vishnu, god of life and love; Varuna, god of the lofty sky and giver of moral law; and above all, the goddess Dawn, who chased away her sister Night each morn to fill her devotees with hope and joy. O how her golden crown sent shimmering rays across the sky to inspire all each day! Considering the era that produced the *Rig Veda*, surely YHWH would have bent his ear and shown his mercy to one and all.

In Israel's case, we know that at least by the time of Moses, the Israelites had centralized the hosts of heaven under one deity, Elohim. In Hebrew, "im" refers to the masculine plural. No longer was Israel's heart to be torn by competing elemental powers, but all belonged supremely to one God alone—Elohim! Later, God revealed himself to Moses as YHWH. "I am who I am," a name in which God concealed as much about himself as God revealed. Later he would share with Moses: "There can be none beside me, nor can any image ever capture the I Am that makes me God." No wonder we are asked to be still and know that God is God.

Sunrise and sunset, rain and storm, summer, winter, spring or drought, God remains one and the same—the sole God of the universe in whom all justice and mercy abound. There is strength in knowing that God alone is God. There is peace in opening our hearts to God and seizing every opportunity that God provides for goodness and joy: "for he makes his sun rise on the evil and on the good, and sends rain on the just and on the unjust," said Jesus (Matt 5:45). "O thou who hearest prayer!" praises the Psalmist. "Blessed is he whom thou dost choose and bring near, to dwell in thy courts" (Ps 65:1, 4).

∾ ∾ ∾

To you silence is praise.
Psalm 65:1

It may come as a surprise to realize that Psalm 65:1 can be translated as above. Actually, in Hebrew the text reads *lak demoath thhalah*, "to *You* silence is praise." The "Thou" whom we meet in our hearts requires no other name. The Vulgate's translation of the old Hebrew renders the text: "*Tibi silens laus, Deus*," i.e., "to you, *God*, silence is praise." To understand the text's deepest meaning, Maimonides resorted to a story preserved in the Talmud. It is wonderfully simple and demonstrates the highest way to praise God. Quotes Maimonides:

> A certain person, reading prayers in the presence of Rabbi Haninah, said: "God, the great, the valiant and the tremendous, the powerful, the strong, and the mighty." The rabbi said to him, "Have you finished all the praises of your Master? The three epithets, 'God, the great, the valiant and the tremendous,' we should not have applied to God, had Moses not mentioned them in the Law, and had not the men of the Great Synagogue come forward subsequently and established their use in the prayer; and you say all this! Let this be illustrated by a parable. There was once an earthly king, possessing millions of gold coin; he was praised for owning millions of silver coin, was this not really dispraise to him?"[5]

Maimonides warns that when flowery phrases are used to praise God, their general intent is to manipulate or influence God, which truly amounts to a form of blasphemy. That is why "silence" before God is the truest form of "praise" we can render the Eternal. May it be so with us!

5. Maimonides, *Guide*, 156.

∾ ∾ ∾

> For thou, O God, hast tested us; thou hast tried [*zed-raph*] us as silver is tried; . . . yet thou hast brought us forth to a spacious place.
>
> Psalm 66:11

The word for test in Hebrew is *zed-raph*. It means to be *refined,* if not purified, although the idea of being tested possesses a validity all its own. The process of smelting silver in the Psalmist's era required an intense flame, hot enough to burn off all dross. Are we willing to be that refined? The Psalmist wants to know. Are we willing to allow God to burn off all that cheapens our hearts and prevents us from serving him? It took the Exile to do that for Israel and to launch the nation of Judah of Jesus' day.

What career does not require intense study, testing, and mastery in order for a candidate to be certified to practice in his or her chosen field? It's just that we hate to give up aspects of our selfhood that we have come to enjoy, even, when like Dostoevsky's underground man, we know they are detrimental to ourselves and those whom we love.

"O God, it is we who need to be 'brought forth to [that] spacious place,' which only thou canst provide, free of dross and imperfection, though only in thy eyes."

∾ ∾ ∾

> May God be gracious to us and bless us and make his face to shine upon us, . . . The earth has yielded its increase, God our God, has blessed us.
>
> Psalm 67:1, 6

While on our way to Petra that spring, we frequently traveled over sections of the King's Highway that both the Romans and the Ottoman Turks had paved, each empire in its time. To our east stretched miles of wafting wheat as far as the eye could see. Vast fields of tawny grain dominated the horizon, hugging the blinding hills in endless waves of lambent gold—ripe for the harvest. "Bedouin!" commented our guide. "They are reserved for the Bedouin."

While on a jaunt to Shechem, I watched a lone Palestinian, with his headscarf whipping in the wind, harvest a small field of wheat. As I gazed out the bus's open window, I took photos of the man and his two companions: a donkey and an ox, slowing turning a heavy weight over the farmer's threshing floor. As the farmer cast pitchforks full of shiny sheaves under the rig, a breeze lifted the chaff slowly and blew it in glittering sheets across the field.

That same month, the kibbutz set aside an evening to pay homage to the venerable rites of spring, celebrated by their Hebrew ancestors of old. It was the festival of first sheaves, or the Feast of Weeks, as commanded in Exodus 14:22. As we sat on the edge of a wheat field, young and shapely *Sabra* [*tsabrah—Isareli-born girls*] danced to the music of flute and tambourine. With upraised arms they slapped their tambourines, dancing with nimble feet while others waved sheaves of wheat. "You should stay and marry one," our kibbutz president teased me. "*Sabra*? Do you know what it means? Prickly on the outside, but sweet and tender within!" he smiled. I smiled in turn. Yes, they were svelte and lovely, but I had "miles to go before" returning home; plus, I wanted to spend at least another two months with André's équipe, before my journey back to the States.

As a child on my grandmother's farm, I savored the end of June, when farmers came from miles about to assist each other complete their wheat harvest. Scores of men would descend on the land and funnel wagon loads of sheaves into a giant threshing machine. A tractor's motor, attached to the lumbering giant by way of a flapping belt, provided the sole muscle to power these communal Behemoths. Sacs of flaxen grain would be collected from the machine's chute, tied, and carted by hand to wagons to be piled in dusty rows in a barn or granary. Then, the men would break for lunch, crowding about tables set up in the farmer's yard for their well-deserved repast. Piles of fried chicken, mounds of potatoes, slices of ripe tomatoes, and plates of pickles and condiments, along with stacks of biscuits and bowls of chicken gravy would disappear down the hungry harvesters' gullets. Then the women in their flour sac dresses would bring out trays of cakes and apple pies for the grand finale.

"O Father in Heaven, how you make your face to shine upon us and still do! How you have blessed us over the years! May we, and all the ends of the earth, praise you all the days of our life!"

> Father of the fatherless and protector of widows is
> God in his holy habitation.
>
> Psalm 68:5

One of the more poignant stories preserved by the Court Historian revolves about Jonathan's last son, Mephibosheth (2 Sam 9:6–13; 19:24–30; 21:7). Jonathan, you may recall, was Saul's proudest son and the closest friend David ever had. Both Jonathan and Saul perished together on Mt. Gilboa, defending the last remnants of Israel's first monarchy. The Philistines had encircled them and one by one cut down each valiant warrior. When word reached Jonathan's home, Mephibosheth's nurse grabbed him up to flee, but in her haste she dropped the child, causing him to be lame the rest of his life. Upon the news of Saul's death, David was deeply troubled and set about eliminating all remaining Philistine footholds. Finally, out of respect for Jonathan, he asked if there were any members of his friend's household left. Being apprised of Mephibosheth, he invited him to eat at the king's table for the rest of his life (2 Sam 9:7).

As a young minister in rural Virginia, it was my duty to call upon our church's widows, wherever they lived and as often as possible. Most lived alone along dusty roads or up steep mountain grades, though a few resided in nearby retirement centers. They were always glad to see me, although the first time I visited each, I was reprimanded for interrupting their favorite TV–daytime serials. Between 2 and 4 p.m., I needed to be elsewhere. The one exception was a nursing home. It lay nestled in a vine-covered valley beside a pleasant stream, guarded by giant sycamores, with a plot of rich creek bottom beside it, perfect for flowers and vegetables. Clusters of grape hung from its grapevines, and delicious apples grew on an orchard just across the stream. Here I was wanted anytime, every time, night or day, throughout the year. The residents were widows, each housed in a separate room. My church affiliation was their least concern, although the owner was an elder in the rural-most church I served. Even when the residents were sad they greeted me with smiles. "Preacher, please come in and sit down." Today, a home health inspection agency would have condemned the owner's residence. But she provided the only long-term care facility for miles around. Besides, her house

solace for times of storm and stress 111

was far from unkempt and was always free of odors and sour fumes. As owner and manager, she was a delightful, energetic soul, about four-feet six-inches tall, gray-headed, favoring colorful blossomy blouses and long dark skirts. I guessed her to be in her late sixties. Like Mephibosheth, she too was lame in one leg. In spite of that, she cooked, cared for, fed, and administered her residents' medications as prescribed by their family doctors. She cleaned every room, raised and maintained the garden alone, and picked and canned every salvageable apple possible. She never fussed or complained, and, being a widow herself, knew and understood the cares of her clients. "Preacher, it is so good to see you!" she'd smile. "So and So's hurting the most today," or "Mattie has just lost a son, and Ms. B down the hall can't remember her name anymore, but she'll sit up for you when you come in." And so I'd make my rounds, visit everyone, and have a prayer with each widow before I left. My reward was always a slice of pie, or biscuit with jelly, along with a grateful smile from the owner. Then she would reach for my hand, with her withered fingers and knobby knuckles, and I would have a prayer with her.

We must never think that God neglects his own, or ceases to care for us when we are poor and needy, lonely or decrepit. The question he puts to us, along with the Psalmist, however, is when did we last help a fatherless child, or visit and aid some lonely widow? Even a card can lift the human spirit, or a tussle of a child's head of uncombed hair when his or her daddy is far from home.

~ ~ ~

> They gave me poison for food, and for my thirst they game me vinegar to drink.
>
> Psalm 69:21

The text above is quoted in all four of the gospels—Matt 27:34, 48; Mark 15:23, 36; Luke 23:36: and John 19:29. Each writer considered it an anagogical reference to the Passion story. David would not have suspected this, or the Psalmist, as neither was prophesying about the future. Sufficient enemies and critics abounded in both David and the Psalmist's time. Some scholars date this psalm after the Exile, during which time the Second Temple was being built. "For zeal for thy house has consumed me, and the insults of those who insult thee have fallen on me" (Ps 69:9). So also verses 35–36 suggest a post-Exilic time. It is difficult to know; still many of its verses recall David's days of *Sturm und Drang*, both before and during his kingship.

It is a powerful hymn, because it enables us to approach God with our own anxieties and troubles and to do so without mincing a single word. "I sink in deep mire, . . . I have come into deep waters, . . . I am weary with my crying; . . . My eyes grow dim with waiting for . . . God" (Ps 69:2–3). It is a prayer we have each made, a desperate appeal to God for help—here, now, in this instance—when everything is going wrong at the same time. "For heaven's sake, God, help me. Please!" our hearts cry. It all comes out in a torrent of rapid thought, uncensored, raw and bitter. Yes, even bitter, though we snatch those thoughts back as quickly as possible. And sometimes with tears! With glistening eyes and sobs that shake the whole body. Like the woman on the park bench in Paris, whom Rilke passed. As she looked up suddenly, her face calmin in her hands, still wet with tears. A "mirror" of the soul, says Calvin! The Psalmist allows us to let it all out when we can bear it no longer, or when God seems as indifferent as a wall. Yes, sob! Sob if you must! Didn't the woman at Jesus' feet do the same?

Tears clear the eyes of harmful irritants just as tears clear the heart of multiple trials when poured out to God. "Let the oppressed see and be glad," says the Psalmist. "You who seek God, let your hearts revive. For the LORD hears . . . and does not despise his own" (Ps 69:32–33). "Rise up, dear friend. Dry your eyes; and let God mend your soul. For God's Spirit has never rejected a broken and contrite heart."

∽∽∽

> May all who seek [*ke-kosh*] thee rejoice
> and be glad in thee!
>
> Psalm 70:4a

The human heart has always sought the source of its existence. At some point in life's journey we are impelled to ask, "What is man that thou art mindful of him?" (Psalm 8:4) The question may not be asked quite in those words, but asked it is. As Socrates put it: "The unexamined life is unworthy of a person." We are more than a swirling band of orbiting atoms with a molecular structure. We want to know what and why. We are *Homo sapiens*, thinking beings, curious and desirous to know and explore life's twin domains: the world outside and the self within. Even Protagoras, one of Athens' keenest sophists, sought a solution befitting humankind. He summed it up in his famous statement: "Man is the measure of all things, of things that are that they are and of things that are not that they are not." He doubted if more than that could be proven, thus curtailing any objective criterion outside what the mind can know. His was a conservative approach, casting a dim light, if not a veil of darkness, on any absolute value outside a thinking soul. It took Plato and his mentor Socrates to offer an alternative view. They wanted to lift hope beyond the sophists' decline into solipsism—the view that I can only know my own thoughts and emotions and can never get outside myself to know anything else. "O, but we can!" the Psalmist insists. "We can at least know and experience a restlessness in our hearts that only Transcendence can quell." That is why all who seek God may rejoice, for truly God is the Measurer of all things, even sharing with mankind the right to name everything in the universe that he created (Gen 2:19–20).

Jesus faced a world of skeptics who expressed anxieties about life. "Do not be anxious about your life," said Jesus, "what you shall eat or what you shall drink, nor about what you shall put on. Is not life more than food, and the body more than clothing?" (Matt 6:25) He would have made an invincible match against Bertrand Russell, Stephen Hawking, and Richard Dawkins. But he would have answered them in parables or with silence, the way he did Pilate. One wonders what Pilate thought as he studied Jesus' face. "I find him innocent," he whispered to his Roman cohort. Then quickly, with an anxious glance, he nodded for a basin of water, with which to wash his hands. Think about that! The need to wash his hands! We can't eliminate the question so easily by simply washing our hands. There is something we seek more urgent than anything else. It is God, the Ultimate, and his kingdom—that reality of justice and peace, of salvation and joy—that can never be washed away, but on the contrary cleanses us.

By the Waters of Babylon

∽ ∽ ∽

> O God, from my youth thou hast taught me, and I still proclaim thy wondrous deeds. So even to old age and gray hairs, O God, do not forsake me.
>
> Psalm 71:17–18a

Toward the end of his life, friends of Boris Pasternak published his novel, *Dr. Zhivago*, the likes of which captured literary imaginations worldwide. *Zhivago* contained the story of a Russian poet-physician, whose life and times are traced from the rise of Bolshevism to the overthrow of the Romanov dynasty and well into the emergence of the Soviet State. Artistic, yet sad, Yuri's love for his wife, as well as for Lara, sweep the reader along through his intense passionate life. We witness his personal trials, along with the suffocating changes that befell the people of the Soviet Union. In an addendum, the editor included a number of Pasternak's poems in order to introduce him to the Western world. In the lead poem, Pasternak concluded that living life to the end is hardly a childish task. Anyone 60 and older can identify with Pasternak's story and the ending of his poem, "Hamlet."

Life is a precious commodity, given to every soul. It takes so little to snuff it out, though it requires a measure of maturity "to live life to the end." I shall always cherish a colleague, who during my teaching years, illustrated books, composed music, and taught the value of art. Still active in retirement, nonetheless, he slowly lost the ability and agility to hold a pen, to sketch or draw, compose, or paint. I went to visit him, to be of what cheer I could. His wife assisted him into the living room, where he nodded with pleasure upon seeing me, but the shadows of time lay heavy in his eyes. With phlegm in his throat and his long silver hair in retreat past his brow, he looked up and smiled. "I can't shake your hand," he said, as he held up his twisted fingers. "You know what they say about the Golden Years? Well," he shook his head, "they're not that golden after all." He was a Realist—a saint of the arts and a saint of the soul. Living life to the end is not a childish task.

From the earliest of times, the compliers of the Old Testament had already grasped Pasternak's assessment and assigned it the highest status possible. They enshrined it in the Ten Commandments, immediately following the hallowing of the Sabbath. "Honor your father and your mother, that your days may be long in the land which the LORD your God gives you" (Exod 20:12). Jesus valued it, too, and with disappointment in his eyes, upbraided those who minimized its sanctity (Mark 7:10–13). It is good to be a Realist and recognize the truth. Nonetheless, the Psalmist reminds us of an equal truth we may also cherish—that God loves all his children, yea, to the silent, somnolent, and even bitter end. "O God, who is like thee? Thou who hast made me see many sore troubles wilt revive me again; from the depths of the earth thou wilt bring me up again. Thou wilt increase my honor, and comfort me again" (Ps 71:19b–21).

∼ ∼ ∼

Give the king thy justice, O God, . . . May he defend the cause of the poor of the people, give deliverance to the needy, and crush the oppressor!

Psalm 72:1, 4

Since its founding on May 14, 1948, the nation of Israel has spared no effort in searching for and arresting any surviving officials who sought to crush Jewish people during the period of the Third Reich. And successful they've been!

In the spring of 1961, before crossing the border into Jordan from Israel, I attended a session of Adolf Eichmann's trial in Jerusalem. The courtroom was packed. Delegates of Jewry from all over the world had journeyed to this room to witness and attend this single German's trial. Bald, diminutive, and dressed in modest clothing, with black, wide-rimmed glasses concealing his eyes, Eichmann entered and was seated in a lone chair behind an enclosure of bulletproof glass. The court was gaveled into session, and in methodic style, the prosecutors began to question and listen to one witness after another. With tears and broken voices, they testified to the atrocities that Eichmann and his subordinates had committed. Many of the witnesses wept as they related their stories. One woman in particular rose and, pointing her finger directly at Eichmann, shouted, "Yah! He is the man!" Later, when the accused was summoned to stand and address the woman's allegation, he merely replied: *"Ich war einzig ein kleiner Mann."* "I was only a minor figure." Or, "I was merely a little man, a small fry." The court didn't buy it, and in the end, he was found guilty and executed.

It is somewhat fitting that the Psalter's Book Two concludes with a hymn dedicated to Solomon. Recall, that Solomon was considered the wisest king ever to sit on the Kingdom of Israel and Judah's throne. Book One opened with a psalm on the Torah, the wisdom by which Judaism has sought to live. Now Book Two ends with a psalm dedicated to a king on his coronation day, swearing him in to protect the least advantaged of his country's people. His task: to defend the poor; deliver the needy; and crush the oppressor. It set the standard for all future kings, just as Lincoln's presidency set the standard for all America's presidents since. In each case, integrity, justice, and perseverance symbolize the desired goals.

History is not always kind to kings or presidents or any political leader. But the Psalmist is right to remind us of what good government requires. It is about people, about you and me, and the extent to which we defend the poor, deliver the needy, and crush the oppressor. These are more than metaphors, as they have to do with the integrity, justice, and opportunities we strive to provide for all. O, we could say, "I'm just a small fry in the middle of this vast pond!" But we know that isn't true. God needs us to defend the poor, to deliver the needy, and prosecute oppressors who suppress the poor. Joseph was sold into slavery, but he rose to become one of Egypt's wisest providers; David had only a sling, but his heart made up for what he lacked in resources, as he committed himself with courage to serving God. George Washington lost his first two engagements against the French and Indians, but Congress, nonetheless, chose him to be the commander of their newly declared independent nation. In light of all, it is such a small thing for us to examine our hearts and do all that we can to defend God's Kingdom, wherever we live, as often as possible.

Book Three
Psalms 73–89

8
Plight and Deliverance: Hymns of the Levite, Asaph

> Truly God is good to the upright, to those who are pure in heart. But as for me . . . I was envious of the arrogant when I saw the prosperity of the wicked. . . . my soul was embittered, . . . I was stupid and ignorant, . . . Whom have I in heaven but thee? And there is nothing upon earth that I desire besides thee . . . [For] me it is good to be near God.
>
> Psalm 73:1, 3, 21–22, 25, 28

Once more we enter into the realm of Israel's poetic Writers, its Wisdom tradition, steeped in lyrical song and historical narrative of plight and deliverance. Our task is to love these Psalms as we have loved the Psalms of David. As in the case of the Sons of Korah, the Songs in this present chapter are ascribed to Asaph. According to 1 Chronicles 6:39, Asaph was a Levite priest whom David commissioned to oversee the choir in the days of the Tabernacle. Scholarship is divided, however, as to whether Asaph was an actual contemporary of David's or lived much later. For the soul's perfecting, either will do. Psalm 73 and the following ten psalms flow from Asaph's harp and pen.

"For me it is good to be near God," he writes. The very thought of God's nearness floods his soul with solace, while nudging his conscience to regret his incriminations against the arrogant and the wicked affluent. After all, their fate is worse than his. At least he has God to whom to turn, whereas they do not. He is ashamed that he has harbored enmity at all, or allowed his soul to become embittered. How "stupid and ignorant" he feels. "No, LORD, I don't want to be that way. Stupid and ignorant, envious and embittered!" In doing so, he is speaking to us, even for us. His prayer becomes our prayer. In offering it to God, he is offering it for us.

Artur Weiser in his commentary on the Psalms considers Psalm 73 to occupy "a foremost place among the more mature fruits borne by the struggles through which the Old Testament faith had to pass." More than an intellectual bout with theodicy (how a good God can allow evildoers to prosper while the righteous suffer), Weiser sees it as an existential "confession," whereby the poet wrestles with his *very own faith*, leaving the intellectual question for another day.[1]

Bitterness is, and has always been, one of the more disabling vices we are prone to exercise. It arises especially in times of disappointment, or when berated by others and made to feel sad. It hurts equally when our best efforts are rejected, or someone else is chosen when our credentials were by far superior. It quickly bristles when our motives are attacked as disingenuous or self-serving, when we know that isn't the case at all. To say the least, it leaves us offended. It renders us helpless and, if we stew over it long enough, bitter. Asaph had experienced enough of it. "I want no more!" he finally cried. "O God, how fortunate I am to have thee! And how 'stupid' and 'ignorant' to wallow in spite, when the plight of the wicked is more perilous than mine! For lo, those who are far from thee shall perish; thou dost put an end to those who are false to thee" (Ps 73:27).

In truth, it is difficult not to savor seeds of bitterness when shunted aside. But the voice of God in Asaph's song encourages us to will otherwise. "Take inventory of thyself," God's calming voice whispers. "Your flesh and your heart may fail, but I am your strength beyond your heart and your portion for ever" (Ps 73:26). It is a wise prayer, this Wisdom Song! Like taking God's hand and following his lead through life's billowing sheets of rain and fog.

---

1. Weiser, *Psalms*, 507.

> Remember Mount Zion, where thou hast dwelt. Direct
> thy steps to the perpetual ruins; the enemy has destroyed
> everything in the sanctuary! . . . Yet God my King is from
> of old, working salvation in the midst of the earth. . . .
> Thou didst crush the heads of Leviathan, thou didst give
> him as food for the creatures of the wilderness. . . . Thine
> is the day, thine also the night; thou hast established the
> luminaries and the sun.
>
> Psalm 74:1–2, 12, 14, 16

His litany of woe is bold and upfront. How can the Almighty, the Creator of so vast and starlit a universe as ours, allow his people to be ravaged and their sanctuaries razed to the ground? That is what the Psalmist wants to know. Didn't God himself cleave the Dragon, Leviathan, into numerous pieces—that mythological seven-headed beast whose debris sparkles in the sky? Did he not fling its glistening entrails into the whirling night? "How, then, O God, can you sit by, ignoring the very sanctuary you once dwelt? Its embers glowed to your glory, perfuming your halls with the redolence of incense and myrrh."

His words are powerful, wafting through Judah's broken heart with the mystical aura of ancestral times. It is a legitimate prayer. "Please God! Dost thou not care for thy dove, Israel?"

Our poet, Asaph, sounds like Job, rendering his monologue, his soliloquy of faith, before the silent hosts of God. He resists saying more. After all, God is his "King," his advocate through life. He leaves the stage as he found it: its strobe lights still blinding his eyes. He has met with God. He has poured out his heart. God is his equal, strange to say. Like Jacob of old, he has taken his stand in the Wadi Jabbok and wrestled with God. God lets us do that, wrestling with him, his strong arms pinning back our own. He lets us rail at him all we want. He understands. The poet will live to see another day, to carry the great weight of his existence back up the hill of his destiny, where God waits to mend his spirit and calm his soul. Indeed, when the poet descends in the morning, he will be wearing God's sword, for God has knighted him to be God's advocate. It is he who must wield the sword against the seed of Leviathan who still scoff at God without regard for the poor. Yes, we are that poet! God's love for the world is our sword. Let us take courage and in faith, serve God.

∽ ∽ ∽

> For not from the east or from the west and not from the wilderness comes lifting up; but it is God who executes judgment, putting down one and lifting up another. For in the hand of the LORD there is a cup, with foaming wine well mixed, . . . and all the wicked . . . shall drain it down to the dregs.
>
> Psalm 75:6–8

This is the cup of wrath of which Jeremiah, Isaiah, and Luke write. It pertains to God's judgment against all nations, a judgment which each and all deserve! Yet in the end, it is the innocent Christ who drinks the cup and, tasting its dregs, cries from his cross: "My God, My God, why hast thou forsaken me?" As the cup of wrath, it is no simple metaphor; rather, it is a symbol of that darkest part of the self that sinks to the bottom of the heart. There it stings the lips of man's hopes with its rancid dregs. It is a "mirror" of the soul!

Thank heavens it is God who puts down and lifts up and not false saviors of anywhere else! Judah had its fill of them, from Assyria and Babylon, to Egypt and the wilderness, where conquering heroes trampled fallen Israel with impunity in the name of their gods. "Thou shalt have no other gods before me!" How that sacred mantra redeemed Israel's heart more than chariots or armies!

Now it is we who read Asaph's lines. Who stare into the "foaming wine, well mixed," tempting but bitter. Far better to choose God's cup, divine. "Drink of it, all of you, for the remission of sins."

We pause and read the lines a second time: "putting down one and lifting up another." Thanks be to God that he is our savior and not a fickle Zeus, who holding the golden scales of fate in his hands, watched as Hector's pan sank low, "spelling his doom," while Achilles' rose to Athena's delight. Here was father and daughter, each on opposite sides, yet neither able to save Hector or Achilles. They could only watch the rise and fall of the weighted pans and grieve the death of their favorite mortal.

The nailing down of evil and the lifting up of life constitutes the very essence of Jesus' Passion and Cross. Asaph, like those before him, could not have imagined his verse to carry anagogical insight. One does not have to be a Christian to know that the darkness within must somehow be let out, released, or put to death, if our hearts and minds are to be liberated for life's highest satisfaction. The quadrant of the Cross makes that visible, where Eternity bends to time to lift up the soul and bless it with newness of life.

∽ ∽ ∽

> Glorious art thou, more majestic than
> the everlasting mountains.
>
> Psalm 76:4

That spring our kibbutz guide treated us to a tour of Galilee. Early one morning, Moshe (Moses) aroused our troupe of volunteers and drove us off to visit Hazor. Hazor is situated just north of the Sea of Galilee, near the former Lake of Hullel. Solomon and other kings of Israel kept horses and chariots garrisoned here. Their purpose was to guard the northeastern routes into the fertile "bread basket" of Israel. Remnants of Solomon's stables stand in glorious ruins where huge rock pillars mark the stalls where chariots were stored and horses groomed and prepped for battle. It was a cool morning, and mist still drifted over the site. But something far more glorious loomed in the distance to captivate our eyes—Mt. Hermon.

The sun was just then rising in the east, struggling to break through dark patches of drifting clouds. But over Mt. Hermon, all was clear. Its snowcapped peak glowed with brilliant colors, reflecting the pink, gold, and delicate yellow hues of the clouds as the sun's rays filtered through them. Only, the phenomenon appeared to be floating above the mountain itself, cloaking its shoulders under its suspended halo. The mountain had to be thirty or more miles to the northeast, but it loomed over Solomon's stalls as if it were only a hand's stretch away. It was here—just possibly—that Jesus took Peter, James, and John up its slopes for a badly needed retreat, and here that Jesus was transfigured before them. And, lo, appearing with him were Moses and Elijah, their apparition filling the disciples' souls with fear. For "his garments became glistening, intensely white, as no fuller on earth could bleach them" (Mark 9:3). "And a cloud overshadowed them, and a voice came out of the cloud, 'This is my beloved Son; listen to him'" (Mark 9:7).

As our group stared off toward the mountain, I wondered if, just maybe, Jesus and his disciples' footprints were still embedded there, frozen under layers of icy slush and snow, preserved for time and eternity to discover one day! We all need at least one sacred Mt. Hermon in our private spiritual lives, where we can kneel before Jesus' radiant presence and hear his Father's voice calling to our souls: "Behold, my beloved Son; listen to him." Surely we would. We would bow down like Peter, James, and John, and, if not weep, receive the greatest blessing a heart can ever know: the gift of God's presence in our souls, and the peace of his Son's perfect life illuminating our own.

∼∼∼

> I think of God, and I moan; I mediate, and my spirit faints.... I will call to mind the deeds of the LORD; yea, I will remember thy wonders of old.... What god is great like our God?
>
> Psalm 77:3, 12-13

The Psalmist's pattern of remorse and remembrance, of the present versus the mighty past, the momentary versus the long haul of Israel's history, repeats itself over and over again in the Psalms. Each new memory rekindled faith's hope and renewed the suppliant's courage. Especially, is this so in Psalm 77. "Will the LORD spurn for ever, and never again be favorable?" Then, just as suddenly, "When the waters saw thee, O God, ... yea, the deep trembled" (Ps 77:7, 16). The entire story of the Exodus, along with Israel's forty years in the desert, is rehearsed here. Celebrating and remembering God's deliverance renewed Israel's faith. It provided both solace and inspiration.

Faith has its way of oscillating between the troubled now and the sacred script of long ago, when God's bold acts rescued his beloved. If God did it then, he can do it now, faith reasons. That is our hope and joy.

"Ask, and it will be given you; seek, and you will find; knock, and it will be opened to you," is Jesus' way of rephrasing the same. "For every one who asks receives, and he who seeks finds, and to him who knocks it will be opened" (Matt 7:7–8).

Today's psychologists reiterate the secret, too. The current emphasis on overcoming fearful moments with positive thoughts is not without theological foundations. "If there be any excellence, think on these things," wrote Paul (Phil 4:8); then he provides a therapeutic list of redemptive activities for overcoming depression and sorrow. What are they? Writes Paul: "whatever is true, . . . honorable, . . . just, . . . pure, . . . lovely, . . . and gracious," incarnate! "And the God of peace will be with you" (Phil 4:8–9).

O Asaph! If only you could have known! If only you could have lived to touch the hem of his garment! And yet you did, as you bowed in faith with David, as he clutched the linen drapes, suspended on their golden rings, separating the Holy of Holies from David's longing to know God as God is.

∼ ∼ ∼

> He remembered that they were but flesh, a wind that passes and comes not again.
>
> Psalm 78:39

One has to read this Psalm in its entirety to grasp its profound remorse, yet gratitude for God's steadfastness across the span of Israel's fearful existence. "Full of merit, yet poetically dwells man on the earth." How right Hölderlin was! How prescient Asaph! He knew the truth and would not belie its power, nor betray it. He was the LORD's Heidegger in David's time, reminding his king of life's brevity, finality, and need of authenticity before God. We cannot pretend to be something we are not. God knows our frame too well. He remembers that we are "flesh" and that our lives pass like a breeze, never to return again. That is why time is so precious, each moment filled with challenge and opportunity. It is where God meets us and we meet God, in each inimitable and unrepeatable second of life's trickling hourglass. "Here I am, LORD! I need thee. Take my time, my span of days and moments, and help me fill them with acts of goodness that I may discover your highest joy, both for myself and others." It is a quintessential prayer. We cannot fulfill it without God's grace redeeming us, as he redeemed his people and does all Prodigals who repent and return home.

~ ~ ~

> Help us, O God of our salvation, for the glory of thy name; deliver us, and forgive our sins, for thy name's sake!
>
> Psalm 79:9

While attending a writer's conference in Beaufort, South Carolina, a famous short-story writer and professor of literature shared a humorous moment from his childhood in a parochial Catholic School. With a devilish grin on his face he reenacted how his nun teacher would bite his hand when he misbehaved. He pretended to be in great suffering and, while waving his hand, cried aloud, "Mea culpa! Mea culpa! Maximum mea culpa!" He averred that even the confessor priest would ask, "Is that you again?" We all laughed but we knew what he was alleging.

Contrary to Luther's view that the "righteousness of faith" is scarcely glimpsed in the Old Testament, the Psalms (which opened his eyes to true grace) abound with salvation by grace through faith. For anyone of a contrite heart, salvation awaits his or her search for the mending of a broken and shattered soul. Why is salvation so compelling, and redemption so thoroughly cleansing? Because God's grace receives us where we are—like the psychiatrist's sounding board ear—and refusing to let us go, fills our life with hope and liberty. Well did Asaph sense God's mending power as he, no doubt, soothed the king's conscience numerous times. He goes unsung, this Levite priest, Asaph, yet his presence about the Tabernacle and his inward experience of God's ubiquity must have been an assuring comfort to David. That David singled him out to oversee Tabernacle services makes this observation feasible. It is worth our pondering, as we seek to be Asaphs for others in their hour of need.

My Aunt Evelyn, who was Catholic, would have been diagnosed today as bipolar. Her swing moods were unpredictable, marked by periods of histrionic grandiosity followed by catatonic episodes of withdrawal and solitude. Her rosary was ever with her. Her behavior and rapid mutterings during periods of quietude mystified me as a child. She would rock back and forth with her rosary in her lap, mumbling "Hail Marys" and "Our Fathers" to herself. Observing her, I knew to be quiet. Sometimes she would leave us and go off for long periods to a convent in Ohio. This usually occurred after struggling with month-long bouts of alcoholism, associated with episodes of magnanimity. At her call, a taxi would arrive and the driver hand her a paper bag, containing spirits of alcohol. My grandmother would grimace; then scold Aunt Evelyn and the driver. It was toward the end of her alcoholic binges that she would realize her need for help. These moments of clarity would trigger her trips to Ohio. When she returned she would be humble and grateful to everyone. Her face would shine with a luster of goodness, which would be reflected in her behavior for months at a time. Her countenance would actually be angelic and her demeanor saintly and inspiring.

You or I may never suffer from mood disorders of a serious nature, but grace and faith can heal a wounded heart that looks to God. The writers of the Psalms and Wisdom literature focused on this reality, hiding nothing of the self from God. Little wonder, thus, that their writings continue to appeal to our souls' anguish and renew our hope and expectations. Their writers moaned and cried, wept and bit their lips with bitter insinuation, as if God were responsible, but in the end they praised God and affirmed his everlasting grace and righteous counsel. As we search our own hearts, does Christ's living Spirit not minister to us in a similar manner? In that light, let us also unburden our hearts and praise God for our salvation!

> Thou didst bring a vine out of Egypt; . . . Thou didst clear the ground for it; it took deep root and filled the land. . . . Why then hast thou broken down its walls, so that all who pass along the way pluck its fruit? . . . Turn again, O God of hosts! Look down from heaven, and see; have regard for this vine, the stock which thy right hand planted.
>
> Psalm 80:8–9, 14–15

Though ascribed to Asaph, the historical clues in this Psalm suggest a period later than David's—possibly as late as the declining years of the Northern Kingdom, whose tribes broke away from the United Monarchy after Solomon's death. Isaiah witnesses to this period in his allegory of the vineyard. His purpose was to appeal to Judah's leaders to reconsider their ways. He refers to his allegory as a "love song." Now that God has planted his vineyard, God asks, "What more was there to do for my vineyard, that I have not done in it? When I looked for it to yield grapes, why did it yield wild grapes?" (Isa 5:1–4.) With that tone, Isaiah goes on to predict a numbing hour of devastation that Judah will long remember.

On my grandmother's farm, our two-story granary's east wall captured the warmth of the sun, spring and summer, fall and winter. A huge grape vine covered the entire side of the building. Birds nested in it and, no doubt, mice as well. In the fall, festoons of purple grapes awaited harvesting, hanging in glorious clusters of deep blue and purple-red. Pauline and I would gather the fruit as best we could, but a ladder was required to reach the vines under the eaves. Once plucked, my grandmother, mother, Pauline, and Aunt Evelyn would squeeze the grapes for juice and can numerous jars of jelly and seed-free pulp. If Isaiah could have seen our granary's produce, he would have scolded Judah all the more.

Faith is more than just believing, or reciting ancient creeds and memorized prayers, or singing favorite hymns. Faith calls us to action if it is true faith. "Take my yoke upon you and learn of me," said Jesus. A yoke exists to keep us harnessed that we may not go astray. As a metaphor in Jesus' hands, it steadies us as we pull life's load, plowing as straight a row as possible. After all, it enables us to pave the way for God's seeds of faith and hope, love and courage, to take hold and bear fruit.

In Isaiah's song, God looked for his beloved vine, salvaged from the brickyards of Egypt, to produce sweet and luscious fruit; he replanted it, hoed around it, fertilized, and watered it in patient expectation. But what did it yield? Wilted and bitter fruit, enough to make God gag from its sour lining and tough pulp!

True faith issues in grateful forms of love and action. Such faith has produced cathedrals and chapels worldwide, along with educational institutions, hospitals, schools and improved laws of justice and fairness. In the West, Judaism, Christianity, and Islam have produced magnificent works of art. The same is true of Hinduism, Buddhism, and Zen in the East. The Psalmist longed for God to restore Israel's place as God's vine of hope for mankind. It took another five to eight centuries, however, for God to plant another vine in Judah to fulfill his highest hopes. We are that vine's branches, says Jesus. May we search our hearts and, longing with Israel, produce God's will in all that we do. Justice and mercy, righteousness and love are products of a living faith, actions of a credo at work as well as in worship. What we do is as important as what we believe. That is the heart of this story of a vineyard, of now and of long ago.

"LORD, help us be faithful laborers in thy vineyard and not simply admirers of its vines! To do that we need thy Spirit, alive and zealous, guiding our physical and mental resources, our minds and our hands. To thee, all glory, O God, our Father and Savior Divine!"

〜〜〜

> O Israel, if you would but listen to me! There shall be no strange god among you; you shall not bow down to a foreign god. I am the LORD your God, who brought you up out of the land of Egypt. Open your mouth wide, and I will fill it.
>
> Psalm 81:8b-10

One of the supreme realities of biblical faith is its insistence on the Oneness of God, that he is singular. There are no others. More than dogma, this tenet of faith grew out of the long history of the Hebraic and Israelite experience of a thousand years of wandering and searching for a spiritual homeland. With all life's needs and goals united in one divine source, a soul is liberated from having to serve a multitude of competing energies. To one God and one alone, all one's hopes and sorrows, dreams and conscience are consecrated in wholeness and joy. Once this unity is broken, however, the self suffers a bifurcation of mind and spirit that clouds one's pilgrimage through life's cycles and rites of passage.

The Israelites were tempted to exchange God for both the gods of Canaan and the gods "beyond the river," i.e, the gods of Mesopotamia. Rather than serving the Creator, these cultures' gods represented aspects of Nature, serene yet lustful, cyclical yet sadly incapable of proffering redemption of a self in conflict.

The same temptation faces us today. The gods of varying perspectives, of unlimited self-indulgence, of quietude and unity with Nature, or no standard at all plague our time as they have others. What alone can bring us up and out of these lands of bondage, if not the living God of Abraham and Moses, of Isaiah and Jesus? Why? Because the God of David alone provides that saving grace that liberates a divided self and transforms it into a new being.

All who came to Villemétrie loved wandering its shaded park. I especially loved pausing by its statues of Apollo and Artemis, placed in the center of the park's ivy-wrapped oval crossroads. Reared amid mountains and endless forests, my inner heart has always found renewal in Nature. But our hearts soon transcend Nature's limits once we pass through the veil of life's trials. "What is man that thou art mindful of him?" defines us more than a hunter/gatherer's mystical feelings as he wanders Nature. Nonetheless, even in Nature, the Creator's voice speaks to us through the sunlit canopy of the forest and in the murmur of its trickling brooks. "I am here!" his voice whispers. "Do you recognize who I am? Behold, I am he who delivers souls from bondage and their hearts from despair."

It is a beautiful voice, and Asaph captured it anew in his story of God's deliverance of Israel from its house of bondage. His Psalm celebrated then, and still lauds today, that defining moment when God brought his people out of Egypt to the land that Abraham loved.

> God has taken his place in the divine council; in the midst of the gods he holds judgment: How long will you judge unjustly and show partiality to the wicked? . . . They . . . walk in darkness; . . . I say: "You are gods, sons of the Most High, all of you; nevertheless, you shall die like men, and fall like any prince."
>
> Psalm 82:1–2, 5b, 6–7

Asaph creates a striking, if not dramatic, vision of God in this Psalm. Standing amidst the council of Israel's neighboring gods, Elohim denounces them for their inability to provide justice, while chiding them for their own mortality. Such is the fate of all "gods" invented and reified by mankind. They are no wiser or morally superior than any finite human. They will perish like any prince.

A study of the mythologies of Mesopotamia and ancient Egypt is as fascinating as it is depressing. Fascinating, because we meet so many gods fashioned in the image of man and all his longing; yet depressing because they cannot resolve the anxieties of transcendence, or speak with authority to Tillich's tri-fold fears—the threat of nonbeing, the reality of existential doubt, and the angst of meaninglessness. We want more. We need more than the gods of our anxious searching can supply or offer.

"Be still and know that I am God" provides the most comforting and therapeutic words humankind has ever heard. By quieting the restless mind, God opens before us the possibility of a unified and liberated self. No more do we have to be fragmented by the opposing and jealous levels of the heart. Our ego, haunted by our unconscious self, is cleansed and mended for a meaningful life, empowered to surmount the anxieties of existence, while sustaining us through bouts of hardship and doubt. The courage to be is an inseparable facet of a living faith. All things are possible when the heart is united with God. Goodness, mercy, justice, and love become pragmatic resources, not just idyllic words. Goodness conquers evil; mercy—cruelty and revenge; justice—unfairness and recrimination; love—a mean spirit and broken heart.

Who are the "gods" that rule the council of our souls, our sense of destiny and value? "Let them go," urges the Psalmist, "even if only one at a time, until your soul finds peace in God alone."

∽ ∽ ∽

> O God, do not keep silence; do not hold thy peace or be still, O God! For lo, thy enemies are in tumult; . . . O my God, make them like whirling dust, like chaff before the wind. As fire consumes the forest, as the flame sets the mountains ablaze, so do thou pursue them with thy tempest and terrify them with thy hurricane!
>
> Psalm 83:1–2, 13–15

This is Asaph's last hymn. The editor of the Psalter does not cite his poetry again, this wonderful Levite whom David chose over others. The remaining few psalms in Book Three are ascribed to a variety of composers. But Asaph's last hymn leaves us puzzled. It concludes with a series of poetic denunciations, if not defamations, of the numerous Canaanite tribes around Jerusalem, whom David's army had conquered earlier. Asaph blasts them once again. Why so negative an ending? One might have hoped for a more visionary and edifying hymn to God's grandeur and glory, but Asaph surprises us to the contrary. David's rise to power and supremacy was not so calm as we imagine; his glory was painful in coming and short-lived after his affair with Bathsheba. From within and without, he had to fend for himself, time and again. The story is there in Second Samuel for anyone to read. It is we who have glorified David, falling in love with his dashing spirit during his youthful days, and sorrowing with him during his years of family dysfunction, turmoil, and tribal uprisings that occurred throughout his realm. We love his story and identify with his innocence, his spirit, his courage, his élan, and above all, his faults. But time moves on. Suddenly, we are faced with his declining years, his loss of power, his decrepitude, and his son Adonijah's failure to succeed his father. None of it is necessarily a positive theme, but realistic for certain. That is why the Psalms remain relevant and a "mirror" of the soul.

plight and deliverance: hymns of the levite, asaph

Asaph was unafraid to tell it as it was; and with all his spiritual and literary gifts, he preserved Judah's story of trial and heartache, of petulance and hope. Throughout Israel's plight and God's deliverance, he exalts the sufficiency of God and reassures us of the everlasting, redemptive ubiquity of God. His understanding of our human condition humbled even him, and, lest we perish from our own embitterment, he floods our hearts with the knowledge of God's forgiveness and power to transform human lives. Well did he serve his earthly King, his friend—David of Judah—while serving his Heavenly King with talent and grace.

"Our heavenly Father, hear us as we search our hearts, regretting the false gods we know we have worshiped. Forgive us for lapsing into self-pity rather than claiming thy promises of wholeness; for craving thy love while denying support to others; for elevating ourselves rather than helping our neighbors. Help us to grasp thy hand, while opening our hearts to thy mercy and power; cleanse us of sin and empower us anew with the knowledge of thy nearness and everlasting peace. In thy holy name, we pray."

9
God's Steadfast Love

> Even the sparrow finds a home, and the swallow a nest for herself, where she may lay her young, at thy altars, O LORD of hosts, my King and my God. . . . For a day in thy courts is better than a thousand elsewhere. I would rather be a doorkeeper in the house of God than dwell in the tents of wickedness.
>
> Psalm 84:3, 10

Attributed to the Sons of Korah, this lyrical hymn guides us past the innervating exigencies of Aspah's era into the restful courts of YHWH's temple. The same is true of the remaining five psalms in Book Three. They are devoted to the healing balm of *hesed* love and the sound of the choirmaster's lyre. Psalm 84 in particular contains two of the Bible's most often quoted verses: the one concerning the tiny sparrow and the nervous swallow, finding a home and building nests by the altars of God; the other, the doorkeeper in the house of the LORD who preferred his anonymous position over any career he might have otherwise selected. Both metaphors fill the heart with comforting thoughts and divine reassurance.

All religions honor mankind's periodic necessity to be alone, to be as close to God as possible. It allows the soul to experience one's deeper self, that sacred chamber of mystical silence that God has created for the heart to know. Hinduism values its sadhus, or holy men; Buddhism its arahants; Zen its Masters of Enlightenment; Judaism its kabbalists and Hasidic rabbis; Islam its followers of dance and light; Taoism its rustic enclaves beside the rocky brooks of Nature; and Catholicism its celibates and members of religious orders. Even Protestantism encourages seasons of spiritual withdrawal, morning and evening quiet times, nurtured by prayer and Bible study. In one form or other, we all seek refuge in the sanctuary of God, whether in his house or in our hearts.

Such was the case of André's Centre de Villemétrie. Though the community existed to provide weekend spiritual solace for groups from Paris, its days in between belonged to the quiet nurturing of each frère. Once each brother completed his daily tasks, the rest of his time was his to invest as best he deemed. Most of us focused on reading French literature and history, along with taking quiet walks through the Center's park. Its oak alleyways and linden trees, gentle paths and limestone walls provided a solace that speech can rarely match. Such walks, then and now, create oneness with God, a sense of his holiness guiding each step and expectant thought. So too, the alleyways of the soul beckon the heart forward as it offers its self to God. Birds sing; woodpeckers drill somewhere off in a neighboring forest; while the tiny sparrow and swooping swallow seek a home in the shadows of God's natural "altar." Here, we the doorkeepers are blessed to welcome each and every restless thought.

"O God, how unfathomable thy ways! How kind a balm thou hast preserved for each of us to discover and enjoy! A Paradise in a single flower; thy Kingdom shining in the darkest hour! Thy face in the mirror behind our own! Thy sanctuary in every heart! Receive us, LORD, and cleanse our hearts and make them fit for thee to dwell!"

∽ ∽ ∽

> LORD, thou wast favorable to thy land; thou didst restore the fortunes of Jacob. Thou didst forgive [*se-ath*] the iniquity of thy people; thou didst pardon all their sin . . . Steadfast love [*hesed*] and faithfulness will meet; righteousness [*zedek*] and peace [*shalom*] will kiss each other.
>
> Psalm 85:1–2, 10

Note the sequence of God's forgiving action and hope for every soul: *forgiveness* first, as it flows from God's *steadfast love*, which in turn makes possible *goodness*, thereby enriching the soul, creating *righteousness* and *peace*. There can be no peace when the soul is captive to its darker nature, wrestling with subconscious foes. They simply must be coaxed from their realm of darkness and forgiven. In the end, all our doctrines of guilt and redemption hinge on God's sequence of grace, transformation, and peace. Then do works of righteousness and sanctification become possible. It is a process, as Judah lived to witness. From the loss of their nation to the restoration of their hopes, God never forsook them, as he led, forgave, and returned them to their homeland.

What happened to Israel can happen to us. For we too wrestle with dark suppressions and archetypes of our unconscious. They erode our sense of self and require recognition and release to make us well. It may take years for the process to run its therapeutic course, but if we open our lives to God's holistic love, hiding nothing back—whether wholesome or bad—the restoration of a humbled self can lead to a higher good and inner peace.

～～～

> Incline thy ear, O LORD, and answer me, for I am poor and needy. . . . Gladden the soul of thy servant, . . . For thou, O LORD, art good and forgiving [*tov we-selah*], abounding in steadfast love [*hesed*] to all who call on thee. . . . There is none like thee among the gods [*ca-elohim*] O LORD, nor are there any works like thine.
>
> Psalm 86:1, 4–5, 8; designated as a Psalm of David

Note how the Psalmist links the predicates "good" and "forgiving" with God's unfathomable *hesed*. Then he turns to God's preeminence over all mankind's "gods," whose works are inferior to YHWH's. It is this word *tov*, however, that captures our attention, as it is the identical word that God used when he observed each day's created wonder and pronounced it "good." God's goodness and faithfulness were ever uppermost in the Psalmist's mind as he composed this hymn. It suggests that some Israelites were still worshiping the gods of Canaan, or the older gods "beyond the River," that is, the gods of ancient Mesopotamia. As gods they were fascinating and alluring, as the *Gilgamesh Epic* makes so clear; yet, they were unable to cleanse a suppliant's heart or bestow peace of mind. Even more alarming was the neighboring Ammonite god, Molech, into whose gaping, ember-glowing mouth newborn babies were tossed to appease the machinations of the keepers of this myth. The curse lasted long into the time of Jeremiah, who wept over it. Even to the time of the Phoenicians, who founded Carthage and whose practice of child-sacrifice sickened her nemesis, Rome! Yes, the latter had their faults, but once the Roman Empire conquered the city of Carthage, they sowed salt the length and breadth of its streets so nothing ever could grow there again.

As we read the Psalm, its tacit question seizes us, too. Are we still worshiping some phantom of the past, some pain or hurt or broken dream we can't let go of, whose domination enchains our lives rather than liberating them? To think that a glowing Molech may still indwell our hearts should act as a sufficient cause to repent of all mistaken goals. These "gods" are unworthy of our time, of a single moment's brief allegiance, in comparison with the liberty and goodness that God's lovingkindness bestows. It means that our hearts can be changed, too, our lives transformed by the good news of God's salvation, offered so freely in this lyrical song. As Moses Maimonides reminds us: "No evil comes down from above."[1]

"O LORD, help us bend our knees that we too may sing with David to the glory of thy name! May we ever search our own souls for signs of secret *elohim* who feign would steer us along life's path only to break our hearts with shame! For like the Psalmist, we too are "poor and needy," nor are we ever beyond want of thy cleansing love and guiding hand. In thy Son's name we pray, Amen."

---

1. Maimonides, *Guide*, 452.

∼ ∼ ∼

> On the holy mount stands the city he founded; the LORD loves the gates of Zion more than all the dwelling places of Jacob. Glorious things are spoken of you, O city of God... And of Zion it shall be said, "This one and that one were born in her"; ... The LORD records as he registers the peoples, "This one was born there."
>
> Psalm 87:1–3, 5a–6

Once again, the Psalmist brings us to the City of God: to the gates of Zion that God loves. O to have been born in its glorious environs! Such was the longing of every Israelite. Of course, not all could claim this fortune; nonetheless, God's salvation extended to those outside its walls as well.

The Psalmist mentions Rahab (Egypt), Babylon, Philistia, Tyre, and Ethiopia. Their names suggest a post-Exilic period, when Judah's Diaspora pined to visit their one-and-only spiritual homeland: the inimitable City of Zion.

We too have been born outside God's city's walls, yet never beyond God's register of those whom he loves. Like the temple's performers, singers, and dancers of verse seven, we too, belong to God. With them, God listens to our hymns of thanksgiving and joy. "All my springs are in you!" they sang. For mankind's hopes are only quenched by the springs of God's sparkling fountain that overflow to dispel our anxiety and cleanse us from sin.

It is interesting to note that Augustine saw in the reference to Babylon "the city of this world." He writes; "By Babylon is meant the city of this world; . . . all the unholy belong to Babylon, even as all the holy to Jerusalem: . . . Jerusalem is the city of the saints; Babylon of the wicked," nevertheless, Augustine praises God for his salvation that extends to the wicked through Christ's death, thus justifying and qualifying us for citizenship in the City of God.[2]

O the difference between the City of God and the City of Babylon! To which do our hearts belong? The Psalmist urges us to choose the former and let the latter go. "For nothing evil comes down from above."

---

2. Schaff, *Augustine*, 422.

> I cry out in the night before thee.... For my soul is full of troubles, and my life draws near to Sheol. I am reckoned among those who go down to the Pit [*vor; bor*]; ... like one forsaken among the dead [*ba-methim*], ... like those whom thou dost remember no more ... Thou hast put me in the depths of the Pit, in the regions dark and deep.... Is thy steadfast love declared in the grave, or thy faithfulness in Abaddon?
>
> Psalm 88:1, 3–6, 13

And so the lament continues to its last throes of hopelessness in vs.18. For the Hebrew people, death represented the opposite of life, life being the gift that God alone gives mankind. The realm of the dead, or Abaddon, existed independent of God; where even remembrance of God ceases; and where one's lifeless spirit is no longer under one's power.[3] One of the best descriptions of the realm of Sheol is found in the *Gilgamesh Epic*, Tablet VII. The hero Enkidu is dying, and with his last few breaths he says to Gilgamesh:

> Some fierce and threatening creature flew down at me and pushed me with its talons toward the horror-filled house of death wherein Irkalla, queen of shades, stands in command. There is darkness which lets no person again see light of day. There is a road leading away from bright and lively life. There dwell those who eat dry dust and have no cooling water to quench their awful thirsts.[4]

Even more compelling are the words of Sidura, the bar-girl who sits by the river that leads to death:

> Remember always, mighty King [Gilgamesh], that gods decreed the fates of all many years ago. They alone are let to be eternal, while we frail humans die as you yourself must someday do.[5]

---

3. Bucke, *Interpreter's Dictionary*, Vol.1, 803.
4. Jackson, *Gilgamesh*, Tablet VII, 43.
5. Ibid., Tablet X, 63

At one time or other we have all felt the cold draft of mortality whisper in our ear, "I am never far away." It is one of those discords Tillich lists, which he calls the "threat of nonbeing." My father longed for death during the last two years of his bout with prostate cancer. The latter began as a diagnosis; then slowly spread throughout his body. When not medicated, he would greet each of us with a smile, though obviously fighting back pain. But, once under medication again, he would hallucinate and beg us to pick up the pencil he had dropped so he could complete his teacher's assignment to name the capitals of the states. So cruel a torment in itself! He would writhe and turn, struggling to sit up just to take sips of water. His soul was already on the edge of Abaddon, teetering toward the Pit from whence none returns. When time came for him to slip away, we knew in our hearts that Dad was safely in his Father's care.

How spent or old, lively or frail we may be, Psalm 88 is more than metaphorical. When hurt, rebuffed, frightened or lonely, we should not be surprised that Abaddon surfaces to haunt our fitful nights, or taunt our tears and troubles. However great our pain, Korah's psalms are a welcome boon, especially Psalm 88, attributed to Heman, the Ezrahite. Why? Because it contains the truth about life; Heman refuses to back down or lie. According to 1 Chr 6:33–47, the author may have been the son of Zerah and one of the leaders of the temple musicians during Solomon's reign. In 1 Chr 25:1–5 he is described as a seer who prophesied when induced by music. Whichever, he was a realist and understood those melancholic moments that sweep over life.

The magnificence of the Psalter lies in its encompassing range of fears and emotions, along with the joys and troubles that we experience. There are no questions, problems, dreads, or disorders that God forbids us from bringing to his attention. All are welcome; all acceptable. Who can forget Psalm 55:22: "Cast your burden on the LORD, and he will sustain you." That is a promise that neither life nor death can cancel or take away.

"LORD, encompass us, too, with your loving kindness and patience to hear and bear our trials and sorrows. Like Heman of old, we too have cried in the night and moistened our pillow with tears. We too have feared your silence and borne life's darkness, afraid that you have turned your face from us. Forgive these doubts of our troubled hearts and buoy us once more with your eternal love and healing mercy. In your Son's name, Amen."

∽ ∽ ∽

> I will establish his line for ever and his throne as the days of the heavens. If his children forsake my law ... then I will punish their transgression ... but I will not remove from him my steadfast love [*hesed*].
>
> Psalm 89:29–30, 32–33

Psalm 89 recalls God's covenant with David at a time when one of his successors had returned from defeat in battle. The Psalmist—an evasive Ethan the Ezrahite—pulls out all the stops that Israel has come to associate with God. He does so in order to convince God of how much they need him. God's loving-kindness, justice, established works of creation over the chaotic forces of Rahab, down to his everlasting fondness for the house of David are called up in historical succession to remind God of his past acts in their behalf, and to reassure themselves of their place in God's scheme of nations. What God is like Thee, supreme over the "heavens" the "earth" and "the world?" they ask. It is one of those grand roll calls of God's mighty acts of history, sung in the hope that God will lift Israel once again to her place of ascendancy over the godless and idolatrous nations around her.

We cannot blame them for doing so. We have equally sought to win God's favor in one form or other, especially when desirous of attaining a dream, a goal, a coveted possession, or position we'd love to have. Just as often we turn to God in times of trouble and despair, praying for God to mend our wounds, our illnesses and sorrows, sometimes reassuring him of our sincerity and our promises not to waver.

As always, we owe thanks to the Psalmist for his forthright presentations, though in this Psalm he seems unaware of its relevance to himself. Remember, we are still in the era of what Luther deemed, "the righteousness of the law," though from time to time, "the righteousness of faith" surfaces from the poet's soul to find expression in his pen. One suspects that Luther caught a glimpse of it, too. Nonetheless, the beauty of the Psalms resides in their invitation for every heart to pour out its soul to God, regardless of one's station before the presence of God's Spirit.

Perhaps it is helpful to recall the deeper meaning of *hesed*. According to Maimonides, *hesed* evinces two meanings. One refers to the kindness we offer anyone, deserved or undeserved; the second has to do with showing kindness over and above what we owe someone. As he explains:

> Loving-kindness is practiced in two ways: first, we show kindness to those who have no claim whatever upon us; secondly, we are kind to those to whom it is due, in a greater measure than is due to them.[6]

Ethan seems to utilize loving-kindness in the second manner, primarily.

Maimonides' explanation sheds light on our own walk of faith. Obviously, he considered *hesed* to be a virtue to "*practice*," not just an "attribute" to be assigned to God. It is meant for us to exercise, to put into usage and good works. To be kind to those who have no claim on us is a virtue to admire. And to show a greater measure of kindness than what is expected or owed equally surpasses any general meaning we may ascribe to kindness.

When we consider all that God has done for us and for mankind, from the mystery of creation to the establishment of the house of David, down to our time today, *hesed,* as a *form of action*, fosters a rejuvenating ethic. It is what the Good Samaritan put into practice; what St Francis adventured; what inspired Florence Nightingale; and what Eli Wiesel captured in his memoirs of the Holocaust. The question becomes, where do you or I fit in? Are we doers of God's *hesed* or simply admirers?

"O LORD, hear our prayers anew! Where we have luxuriated in thy steadfast love but have neglected loving others, forgive us. Inspire us to be faithful and true. Help us to become practitioners of thy *hesed* grace and not simply receivers, content to remain secluded in our self-enclosures. Open our hearts that we may care for others as thou dost care for us. To thee be honor and glory, till we rest in peace with thee!"

---

6. Maimonides, *Guide*, 646.

god's steadfast love 143

∼ ∼ ∼

> How long, O LORD? Wilt thou hide thyself for ever? ...
> Remember, O LORD, what the measure of life is, for what
> vanity thou hast created all the sons of men! What man
> can live and never see death? Who can deliver his
> soul from the power of Sheol?
>
> Psalm 89:46–48

Few hymns approach death with the honesty these verses do. "Our measure of life!" "What man can never see death?" "Who alone can deliver him?" A modern branch of theology known as Process theology doubts that God can know anyone's measure of life as depicted here. In the mind of Process theologians, omniscience is a mistaken attribute to assign God. The purpose of their belief is not to take anything away from God but to protect both God and our freedom of self-determination. God knows our thoughts as they occur; he longs for each of us to become the best we visualize; to live as long as possible; to be as creative and novel as we can, to be interactive and helpful, joyful and successful, both for ourselves and others. Then when death comes, far from ceasing to be, our individuality is preserved in the indelible memory of God's greatness and love. Within the realm of God's divine memory our uniqueness is honored for eternity. Such especially is the view of Charles Hartshorne, as well as a facet of the Greek Orthodox Church's funeral incantation: "Eternal is the memory of God." To be part of God's eternal memory is to be drawn up into God's paradise, forever. Will we enjoy reciprocity with God as we step into that great light? The Process School thinks not, but why yield all of God's surprises to them?

The Psalmist is all too aware of life's transience, its vanity and brevity. He knows of its mortal summons to be prepared when life's Captain calls us to board his craft for the final voyage. Where are tomorrow's mornings now, when last we hugged a child, or kissed our spouse? Gone are summer's breezes, autumn's grandeur of silver and red; winter's swirling snow and Frost's downy flake, along with spring's blossoms of dogwood and satin-white magnolia. Gone! Gone into Tillich's stream of nonbeing that bears all life away! Yes, it is good to remember the greatness of life and not be ashamed to call God's attention to our mortal frame.

"What man can live and never see death? Who can deliver his soul from the power of Sheol?" (Ps 89:48) With these words, the Psalmist is already entering Kubler-Ross's 4th stage of grief and dying. You may recall her famous five stages of death in her book on *Death and Dying*, published in 1969. First came denial, second anger, then bargaining, followed by depression, and lastly acceptance. Our Psalmist appears already to have agonized through her first three. Now depression and a glimpse of acceptance fill his heart. He is almost bargaining with God. "Why have you made us so?" he asks, "suited only for vanity and destined for Sheol?"

Remember, the Psalmist knew only of this present life. It took the coming of the Maccabean Era to expand Israel's faith. But how wonderfully the Psalmist put the question of nonbeing to God. In doing so, he crafted a prayer for us that we too may use when the reality of nonbeing and the shock of death confront us. Many are ready when the Captain calls; just as many are not. We never know "our measure of life," or whether by old age, disease, or accident we shall be summoned away. It is good to have this prayer to cling to. It allows us to speak freely and openly and pleadingly with God when life's shadows lengthen and death draws near. "O God, help us to be bold and calm, as you shelter us with thy wings."

The Psalmist looked to God in gratitude for solace. He found God's love sufficient beyond his fear of Sheol, or even Siduri's wistful words to all who crossed the river. "Help us, too, O LORD, to trust thee with all our heart; for thou hast brought down thy holy Son for us, whose words of peace far outstrip Siduri's: 'He who believes in me, though he die, yet shall he live and whoever lives and believes in me shall never die' (John 11:25-26). May we, the living, never cease to believe in thy kingdom's power, O God, nor ever cease believing in Thy Son, now and as far out on the horizon as thy light shines! As thy servant John Donne put it: 'Death be not proud.' Nor may we, O LORD!"

∽ ∽ ∽

Blessed be the LORD for ever! Amen and Amen.
Psalm 89:52

This brief verse of Psalm 89 brings to a conclusion Book Three. It also contains a doxology for all that has gone before. Its simple verses allow us to pause as well, and reflect on all that has transpired in our own lives. Are we able to say "Blessed be the LORD for ever!" or are we still nursing wounds and sorrows we can't let go of, burdens and disappointments we should have laid aside long ago, or setbacks and heartaches that still weigh heavily on our soul? Few lives are idyllic to the end. But, O to let go and find that peace of soul that God provides for each of us! What a joy that would be!

Jesus offered a cure for his age, though hardly an easy one, for he understood our human frame. Said Jesus, "do not be anxious about tomorrow, for tomorrow will be anxious for itself. Let the day's own trouble be sufficient for the day" (Matt 6:34). His therapy of "one-day-at-a-time" is echoed in every modern psychologist's counseling setting, or on every psychiatrist's couch, as he or she attempts to enable the patient to gain a deeper insight of the self, accepting each day as it comes. Faith, hope, and love strengthen us to do that too, along with the wisdom of the Psalms. To see life from God's aspect of eternity, while being protected under the shadows of his love, buoyed by his *everlasting* mercy, and guided by his righteousness opens the way for the heart to walk forward in gratitude and praise. Whatever remorse we carry is forgiven; whatever wrong pardoned, whatever bitterness assuaged by the balm of Christ's Cross. Still the greatest therapy of all, is Jesus' own definition of love: "But I say to you that hear, Love your enemies, do good to those who hate you, bless those who curse you, pray for those who abuse you . . . And as you wish that men would do to you, do so to them" (Luke 6:27, 31). Then may our souls sing with the Psalmist: "Blessed be the LORD for ever! Amen and Amen."

Book Four
Psalms 90–106

10

Obtaining a Heart of Wisdom

> For a thousand years in thy sight are but as yesterday when it is past, or as a watch in the night. . . . So teach us to number our days that we may get a heart of wisdom.
>
> Psalm 90:4, 12

The writers of the Book of Proverbs valued wisdom [*hokmah*] more than silver or gold or anything else. Nowhere do they actually define wisdom in a declarative statement, but they knew in their hearts from years of experience that "the fear of the Lord is the beginning of knowledge," and that "fools despise wisdom and instruction" (Prov 2:7). Our days are like a miniscule star that makes its glowing debut, then disappears amid the shimmering Milky Way and those distant galaxies, millions of light years away.

The quotation from Psalm 90 carries a somber, yet wonderful consolation in and of itself. Why? Because we know in our souls it is true. It is both poetic and existential. It has the wisdom of Heidegger's insight about it and the poignancy of Hölderlin's night-priests chanting their hymns in a time of the absence of God.

How transient we are! Our days are like a vapor, a mist on a mirror and then no more. *Einmal und nicht mere*! As for wisdom, quite often we fail to discover it until we've become "fools" ourselves, breeching life's time-tested "instruction" that took eons of regret to establish. It is the way of all flesh. Not even Augustine escaped it, as we noted earlier (Pss 38 & 51), nor Jesus' Prodigal Son. Yet in both cases, God bent down and lifted each to salvation. The same can happen to us.

Having been reared on a farm, in the midst of the Knobs, on the edge of the Appalachians, my grandmother saw to it that I was "instructed" in the way a young man should go. Her injunctions were simple, but wise for our life on a farm. Some rested on superstition, e.g,, "Don't throw your hat on a bed or it'll bring bad luck." Others, however, possessed the ring of truth. "Don't ever put on airs." Pretense to her represented the height of conceit. In turn, a conceited heart concealed an evil spirit, which could never be trusted, nor could its machinations ever be sounded. No. We were to be just who we were. "Yes ma'am; no ma'am!" Nothing more needed to be said. Another she repeated was: "A bird in the hand is worth two in the bush." Why cast away a beloved certainty for an unknown phantom? Pushing the envelope, to her, would lead only to sorrow, and goodness knows, we had experienced more than our share of distress and grief. I can still see her smile as she rocked back and forth, as we poked the hissing logs in the fireplace. Similar was her favorite: "Don't count your chickens before they hatch." I agreed with that, because once when peeping at a nest under a setting hen, she pecked the devil out of my hand. Of course, what Granny meant was: "Don't be rash, or bullheaded." It was her way of counting the cost. Yes, conservative advice, but we had so little as it was. "Never look a gift horse in the mouth." If given anything, accept it with politeness; know when and how to be courteous. If the gift is something you don't need, you can always give it to someone poorer. And there were always poorer people on the farm, tenants who came by the kitchen door after work, humble and dirty. They'd ask if there were anything else they could do. You could see how tired and hungry they were, and always my grandmother or aunt gave them something to eat, biscuits, or fried chicken, or pork chops, whichever we had. They waited patiently by the screen, for they knew how limited our own resources were. "Shoosh! Virtues fit only for farm life, and beggars at that!" you might think. But, no! These were virtues of the heart, born from the wisdom of the soul, in a time following the Depression, on a farm that still hadn't recovered from Reconstruction, let alone the Civil War, that had impoverished all. Sayings such as, "Nothing ventured is nothing gained," would come later.

Even Socrates despised "pretense," because he knew that wisdom begins on that very day, in that very hour, that we acknowledge that we don't know what we wish we did, thus launching a quest for what can be known when we pursue it with all our heart, mind, and strength. Wisdom is a form of humility, insight, and discernment, and the savvy to know when to act or fall back. It is the recognition that we are not always sufficient unto ourselves; that there are larger truths to be learned and goals to be pursued that keep life human. That we do not climb the hill of destiny alone, as Gabriel Marcel put it. That our hearts will forever be restless until they rest in God, as Augustine discovered! It is what Reinhold Niebuhr came to express in his simple yet profound serenity prayer: "God grant me the serenity to accept the things I cannot change; the courage to change the things I can; and the wisdom to know the difference." May it be our prayer too.

∽ ∽ ∽

> For he will give his angels charge of you . . . On their hands they will bear you up, lest you dash your foot against a stone.
>
> Psalm 91:11a–12

Jesus' quotation of this famous verse is found in Q and repeated in both Matt 4:6 and Luke 4:10–11. It appears in each Evangelist's story of Jesus' "Temptation" following his baptism. For reminders, "Q" refers to an unknown author's collection of Jesus' sayings found in Matthew and Luke. They are instrumental in providing in-depth knowledge of Jesus' life and teachings. In both Gospels above, the Tempter tests Jesus' comprehension of his mission, urging him to use miracle and wonder to win converts. Jesus refuses. "No." He will not stoop to the Tempter's level of using God. Yes, Jesus' works will point to himself as God's Suffering Servant, sent as a ransom for mankind's sin, but they may never substitute for the heart's leap of faith that we must each make on our own. As Jesus said to Thomas: "Blessed are those who have not seen and yet believe" (John 20:29b). Even the disciples had to make their own leaps of faith. According to Kierkegaard, they enjoyed no advantage over us, for they equally had to determine how to respond, though Jesus stood directly in their midst.[1] Remember that many who witnessed his miracles were among the first in the crowd who cried for Pilate to crucify him.

---

1. Kierkegaard, *Philosophical Fragments*, 111–139.

For some, faith comes as gently as a breeze; at no point having to struggle with doubt or unbelief. In the Reformed Tradition, faith is inseparable from growth and maturation as a child of the Covenant and as a member of the household of God. All along, one's faith is guided until one is ready to affirm what his or her parents pledged on the occasion of their infant baptism. But that is the ideal and not always the journey for everyone. It is individual for each of us, and no one needs to disparage another's way. As a child I recall those many arduous Saturday nights, spent in memorizing the correct answers for tomorrow's Sunday School Catechism Class. Poor Pauline suffered through the questions and answers with me. But I was determined to earn my silver stars. I suppose André would have smiled at the thought. Just to look into his face was to realize the depth of his own leap, which had come with great suffering and trust, before he walked away from his pulpit in Le Midi of France to become a wandering servant, offering communion and baptism to the excommunicated and un-churched of southern France.

Still, the Psalmist's words have survived the vicissitudes of time, to taunt and test us, if not to guide and console us. Yes, in countless ways, God's unseen angels bear us up on their celestial wings—not only to protect us—but also to rescue our frightened souls after we have fallen and bruised, not merely our bodies, but our souls and the hearts of others. Yes. The Psalmist's words are meant for us, too, lest in our fallings and failures we lose heart. On their wings they bear us up, even when our souls are heavy and our eyes wet with tears. "LORD God! Here am I. Sin and all. Sores and wounds! Anguish and suffering. Remorse and bruises! Bear me up, O Living God, on thy holy angels' wings, and mend my soul, anew."

～ ～ ～

> It is good to give thanks to the LORD, to sing praises to thy name, O Most High, . . . The righteous flourish like the palm tree, and grow like a cedar in Lebanon. . . . They shall bring forth fruit in old age, they are ever full of sap and green, …"
>
> Psalm 92:1, 12–13a, 14

For many years there were two cedars of Lebanon on the campus of Erskine College. One flanked the southern end of the college's seminary building, while the other the northern end. They stood lofty, towering above McQuiston Hall's roof and eaves. Conical in form, they provided shade in the summer with their stratified limbs, and graced the winter months with their lacey, evergreen boughs. They were the gift of a missionary of long ago.

Somewhere in my mind, I recall cedars of Lebanon in Israel, if not to the north of our kibbutz, at least around and about the Jordanian Historical Museum of Antiquity, or its Museum of Natural History, located then in the Jordanian quarter of old Jerusalem. Shadows of one in Christian cloisters in New Jerusalem also beg to be remembered. Whatever one's religion—Jewish, Christian, or Muslim—they represent the majesty of the Most High and the beauty of Holiness. "Come!" they whisper to all who pass by, "behold, and give thanks to God!" The same is true of the palm, spreading its serrated fronds for all to see, hinting that water for the thirsty is nearby; but, alas, the latter is so ubiquitous, thriving in almost every temperate zone, we pass it, scarcely noticing its glory or fruit.

As a college youth, I shall always remember my summer between my freshman and sophomore years, when assigned to work with the US Forest Service in the Toe-Cane River District of Western North Carolina. I was a Forestry Major at the time, and our district incorporated the valleys and mountains between Mt. Mitchell to the east and Roan Mt. to the west. A glorious area to say the least! Neither tree species of Psalm 92 grew beneath the hickory, pine, oak, and basswood canopies, but lonely stands of hundred-year-old American Chestnuts occasionally hugged the backbone of sun-bright ridges; then leaped across rhododendron filled ravines to challenge any wily logger to fell their bone-white trunks. Still in old age, they witnessed to the majestic hand of their creator.

Somewhere amid the climes of life, Nature herself puts God's question to us. "Behold, my hand and handiwork in you. Yes, you! Did I not create this all for you as well as for itself? Where, my child, my son, my daughter, is the green growth of glory I long from thee? I long in thee? I long for thee? I long as long as old age itself longs of thee! O my favorite floral of all creation, rise and lift thy heart to me, as I have filled thy heart with mine!"

> The floods have lifted up, O LORD, the floods have lifted up their voice, the floods lift up their roaring. Mightier than the thunders of many waters, mightier than the waves of the sea, the LORD on high is mighty!
>
> Psalm 93:3–4

Arthur Weiser identifies many of the hymns in this chapter as "enthronement psalms," or hymns celebrating the annual renewal of a king's enthronement. Such a view was popular in the 1950s and early 60s when the Old Testament was considered to possess a unique theology of its own. The School of Biblical Theology championed this theory, though other foci are in vogue today. Many interpreters still find The Old Testament Library, as it was called, immensely resourceful and supportive of faith.

What captures our hearts, however, in this brief psalm is its celebration of God's triumph over the darkest powers of chaos. Borrowing from the Mesopotamian myth of Marduk's victory over the dragon, Tiamat, which Marduk slew—symbolized in the Psalm by the roaring waters—the Psalmist proclaims that the LORD, the sole and true God of the universe, reigns exultant over every chaotic power that would attempt to replace his order and goodness with bedlam and turmoil.

From a spiritual perspective, the Psalmist takes us one step further. Do our lives contribute more to the chaotic and heartbreaking developments that add to life's confusion and desperation, or are our lives dedicated to promoting God's goodness and righteous ordering of life? We are part of one or the other: always stirring up uproar, hoarding grievances, longing for revenge; or seekers of peace, forgivers of sin, and menders of wounded hearts. The LORD'S victory should make us think. Do we fancy ourselves more in the guise of a Tiamat, or a servant of YHWH's grace?

Uproar has hurt many people, so many times. The Psalmist calls us to put Uproar in its place? "O God, help us to do so! To be part of thy healing hand that stills the roaring waters! That loves thy mighty greatness, thy beauty in the temple of thy holiness, which thou has planted in our hearts!"

obtaining a heart of wisdom 155

> Understand, O dullest of the people! . . . He who teaches men knowledge, the LORD, knows the thoughts of man, that they are but a breath. . . . If the LORD had not been my help, my soul would soon have dwelt in the land of silence.
>
> Psalm 94:8, 10c–11, 18

We know the above is true, however disparaging to contemplate at first. To think that our thoughts are but a breath against the long trajectory of time, let alone the eternity of God, seems to devalue the brevity of our own mortal days. That our intellectual and literary achievements are slated to pass away, we can understand. For one day our sun's surface will swell as its fuel is depleted, and our planet will vanish in the fiery flares of our star's silent death. How could it be any other way? Yet it creates pause to ponder such an ineluctable end.

God is God; we are not. His thoughts are eternal; ours but a sigh. There should be strength in that, not despair. At least the Psalmist does not condemn the *content* of our thoughts, as if they were as empty as the vanities Qoheleth[2] laments. His contrast, rather, rests on the distinction between time and eternity; between mankind and God; which of necessity puts the value of our lives and our thoughts to the question. We cannot escape it.

Still, what an insensitive disapprobation the Psalmist hurls toward mankind: the "dullest of the people!" "Such a condescending slur!" we are wont to think. But the Psalmist knew then and still today how to capture our attention. We feel trapped by his words; nonetheless, we fulfill them whenever we isolate ourselves from God and rely on the fidgety angst of our own resources. Think of it! The finite expirations of humankind! What are they against faith's "that than which none greater can be conceived?"

When we step outside the Bible, we discover an ancient, well-worn trace of poets and philosophers who have pondered the same. Take Homer for example. His heroes and their mighty deeds never escape the

---

2. Author of Ecclesiastes.

anguish of mortality and the evanescence of human hope. It is one thing to *vaunt* our thought, to rely on our "breath," while another to *record* the ephemeral passage of human loss and passion, its dreams and achievements. Socrates, Shakespeare, Goethe, and Nietzsche, all confirm the Psalmist's truth. Faulkner's *As I lay Dying* and Hemingway's *For Whom the Bell Tolls* equally attest to the same.

Far from experiencing a melancholic moment on some forlorn morn, the Psalmist addresses both the grand and petty aspirations of the human race. We are mortal, he reminds us, defined by that end which cannot be "outstripped," as Heidegger maintains. We arrive on the scene of life's wonder, to dream, achieve, love, and grow old. There is nobility in that alone, for life is sacred in God's eyes. But it is only the extent to which we allow God to claim us that our souls are saved from the inevitable Pit of chaos, and our hearts redeemed from the "land of silence"—that taciturnity of mute and forgotten souls. "Which will it be?" asks the Psalmist. "A life that yearns for the wisdom of God, for his love and presence? Or a life that settles for something less?" God does not want that something less to define us, or any of his hands' creation. It is our redemption and joy that he wants us to savor, our fellowship and reciprocity that God seeks.

"O living God, how surely we need thee. Like the Psalmist, we yearn for thy help, knowing that without thee, alone we go down to the land of silence, where all breath ceases and thoughts come to rest. We thank thee for those whose poetry and insight remind us of our brevity, whose prose and lyrics record our longings amid the transitory journey of our lives. Help us, O LORD, to cling to thee and cherish no wisdom but thine. Fill our hearts, O God, with thy highest thoughts that we may fulfill thy highest joy."

∽ ∽ ∽

For he is our God, and we are the people of his pasture,
and the sheep of his hand.

Psalm 95:7

The bucolic scene rose before us, visible far ahead on the road. We had left Burgos earlier that morning and were in route to Madrid. Stark hills, purple in the distance, and rolling white pastures fell off quietly toward a river below. The Basque shepherd's black cap and red bedroll captured our attention first, as he herded his flock of bleating sheep down a slope and across the highway. We were the sole traffic that morning, and we knew that the ancient pageant unfolding before us we might never witness again. The sheep's shaggy undercoats dragged in folds along the highway, then up the crest of the orange embankment they struggled for footing as they separated and went their way. We had stopped the car to wave to the shepherd, but his mind and eyes were focused on his flock as they wandered out of sight toward greener fields.

We could have been in David's time, a scene the Psalmist witnessed. The guiding hand of God, the people of his pasture, the sheep of his hand! We are not sheep, of course we know. Nor like rag-wrapped shepherds do we lie down in rain, strung from soft clouds! But the metaphors! The symbolism that the Psalmist employs!

Life for many of us will never be simple again; never pastoral, rustic, except when we seek it from time to time. Even I can't go back to the farm as it was in my grandmother's day. It is still there, safe in my brother's hands, its pastures now home to turkey and deer, but all around housing developments threaten to claim it, along with its traceable sheep and cattle paths, former fields of wheat and corn, and its patches of green tobacco. Such rural tranquility did fill our days with satisfaction and quiet evenings, of rocking on a porch, or happy laughter about a table, and, in the bitter wintertime, pleasant hours beside a glowing hearth.

We may not be able to go back to that; nor have many known it at all. But the thought of God as our Shepherd, and we the sheep of his hand, creates its own tranquility and peace. The sense that all is well is what the Psalmist is celebrating. That can happen when we trust God, abide in God, and accept his never-dying love and guidance. Like the shepherd that morning south of Burgos, God's sole intent is to guide and guard the lives of all who entrust themselves to him. Hardly an easy task for God or us!

We could say so much more about this Psalm, about God and the shepherding his Son offers each of us to claim. To open our hearts is a wise place with which to begin, whether morning or evening, as we turn to him.

～～～

> O, sing to the LORD a new song! Sing to the LORD all the earth. . . . O, worship the LORD in the beauty of holiness. . . . Let the heavens rejoice, and let the earth be glad; let the sea roar, and all its fullness; . . . For he is coming to judge . . . the world with righteousness, and the people with his truth.
>
> Psalm 96:1, 9, 11, 13

We can see them now, the Levites and Priests, dressed in their white linen and bright blue-and-white-striped shawls as they walk in procession before the temple. And the people, bearing their offerings, singing to the Levites' lyre, stepping happily in cadence to their drum. The renewal of life again! The order of goodness over plight; of holiness over blight; of joy over sorrow; of hope over flight!

O, sing unto the LORD a new song! For he is coming, yes, coming, even to you and to me. Let us join their glad parade bearing our offerings too. "O how we need thy blessing, LORD! Thy loving kindness and righteous order! Thy hope for us and thy hope for all! Help us always to choose goodness over wrong; forgiveness over fury; goodwill over malice; love over bitterness and spite; kindness over uproar; generosity and mercy over avarice and a stingy heart!"

O LORD how good it is to sing to thee and let thy mercy fill our hearts!

∽ ∽ ∽

> Let all be put to shame who serve carved images, who boast of idols. Worship Him, all you gods.
>
> Psalm 97:7; NKJV

Judaism, Christianity, and Islam, all three revere Mt. Zion. None espouses the worship of idols, though each sanctions symbolic representations in reverence for what is ineffable and divine. Judaism has its Wailing Wall; Christianity its Cross; Islam its Dome of the Rock under the Mosque of Omar. Here Abraham brought his son, Isaac, to offer him to God in obedience to the divine voice that commanded him to do so. All three religions trace their spiritual heritage to this man and his faith in the Absolute who claims our total heart. There are no images capable of depicting God, he whom none greater can be conceived. Yet Judaism loves its prayer shawls and tassels, Christians their crucifixes, rosaries, and crosses, and Islam its mullah's cap and gown and crescent banner.

In the East, revered symbols of Brahma, Vishnu, and Shiva also abound; along with Buddhism's yellow robes, begging bowls, gilded stupas, and statues of the Buddha, not to mention Zen's wistful temples and pleasant gardens to soothe and guide the soul. Who among us has not found peace of mind wandering through restful gardens or meditating beside stonewalls and quiet ponds?

During the Reformation, Protestantism accused Catholicism of worshipping idols; thus its early founders opposed stained-glass windows, relics, votive candles, the Stations of the Cross, and statues of Mary. Since the Enlightenment, however, that boisterous old lion has been put into its cage and only rarely do we hear its roar. Its cry was replaced by a call for "ecumenism," to venture beyond stagnant dogmas to celebrate unity with Christ.

The world's religions are rich with symbols, meant to point the devotee toward the inner and transcendent, for which the outer and material is but a glimpse of higher glory. Is does us little good to bash another's faith. If I reserve the right to denounce another's, I only set a precedent for him or her to denounce mine. God is above all that. It is for God alone to decide who belongs and who doesn't, who loves and serves him and who shies away. Wouldn't you rather have God be your judge and redeemer rather than someone else? The Buddha, if you're a Buddhist; Vishnu, if you're a Hindu?

That is why the Psalmist's verse 7c captures our attention. "Worship him, all you gods." True, the Psalmist may have had in mind only the gods of the Fertile Crescent, as those were the only gods he knew: the gods of the Mesopotamians, the Hittites, and the Egyptians! But today the Psalmist's verse extends to all religious persons. "Behold, God! Whatever your religion, whatever your culture, whatever your race may be! Love God and God only and your fellow human neighbor as yourself. And leave to God all else for God to judge." Therein lies God's mercy and righteousness for all.

～～～

> The LORD has made known his salvation; his righteousness he has revealed in the sight of the nations. He has remembered his mercy and his faithfulness to the house of Israel; and the ends of the earth have seen the salvation of our God.
>
> Psalm 98:2–3; NKJV

The Psalmist was scarcely a provincial. His Psalm shadows Isaiah's famous praise of Cyrus (Isa 44:28; 45:1) and Ezra's recognition of the same (Ezra 1:1–4). They both knew of the Edict of Liberation, which Cyrus the Persian decreed upon overthrowing the Babylonian Empire. His Edict was unparalleled in history, for it permitted all former exiles of Babylon to return to their conquered homes, rebuild their temples, and live in peace again. Isaiah's Chapters 44–46 proclaim God's hand in Israel's liberation and hail Cyrus as YHWH's champion of this momentous deed, though Cyrus hardly knew the LORD by name. The Edict was proclaimed in 537 or 536 BCE. This places the Psalmist's hymn quite sometime after Cyrus' historic event. It signals the rise of David's house of Jacob once again. Beyond the unpredictable and staggering horrors of history, YHWH's prophets and temple singers saw the mending hand of God, sweeping evil from the earth and saving mankind out of God's love, out of his *hesed* and *zedek* zeal.

obtaining a heart of wisdom 161

There is comfort in knowing that God's providence still guides our fearful world. Wherever grace and equity, mercy and fairness rule, we can rejoice knowing that God is nigh. When both are absent, then just as God called Cyrus to rise up and be his champion, God looks to us to rally and promote his healing order, to announce the acceptable year of his presence, and its good news of salvation for all. That may not require our carrying banners, chanting slogans, or marching in protest in city streets. For some, that is the norm, but not for all. God's rule of love and kindness, of liberation and joy, can begin with a friendly greeting to a lonely neighbor down the street or in a hospital hall. It includes forgiving someone whose words have long burdened your soul; or by asking forgiveness of others whom you've wounded. It consists in providing food, clothing, and shelter for the wretched and the poor, for in our time their number grows rather than abates. It embodies listening to a friend's shattered dream, or comforting him or her when tearful of soul. Whatever the form, such deeds engender liberation, flowing from God's cup of hope and joy. And, yes, such adventures are not easy. Often they are awkward, especially if we are shy. And, yes, they do require faith and courage. But if we take God's hand, his way of salvation will strengthen and fill our hearts with joy as we go.

Indeed, "let us come and bow down before the LORD, our Maker; for he is our God, and we are the people of his pasture, and the sheep of his hand." He is still the everlasting Father, wonderful counselor, Prince of Peace, whose shepherding never fails, "who came down from heaven for us and for our salvation," as the Nicene Creed captured it so poetically for all the world to know.

~ ~ ~

> The LORD is great in Zion, . . . Exalt the LORD . . . and worship at his footstool—He is holy.
>
> Psalm 99:2,5; NKJV

Most of us value at least one sacred place, one quiet cove of the heart, or a mending wall where we go for reflection and renewal. Mine is still the farm and climbing that hill that looks out across the land where I was reared. Far off to the east rises Whitetop Mountain, and to the west, lie the long and rugged ridges of the gray Appalachians. Ruminating amid the once-prolific apple orchard on the hill, and staring down on the rusted, tin-roof barn, granary, and house we called home, I reunite with all I treasured as a boy, especially my grandmother. With her smile, her one good eye, her gray hair tucked into a frizzed bun, and white apron drawn about her waist, she welcomed my every step from room to room, from fireplace to kitchen, until I scampered out to play or feed the chickens.

We all have memories of someone we love, or loved, and someone who loved us. They become our heart's truest source of what is good and pure. We need such memories, along with sacred sites of peace and calm, of what was once our heart's fresh home to keep our spirits warm and gentle. The saddest part of living occurs when all we treasured is no longer retrievable. The farm will one day go but not the homey temple the farm instilled in a young boy's soul. The same is true of you. Somewhere a memory rushes in to soothe and calm the heart: sometimes with tears, sometimes with jokes and inappropriate grunts and groans from granddads and uncles. It is all part of the fabric that decorates the secret tabernacles where our hearts retreat and God awaits us quietly to take us up when sorrow and loneliness overwhelm our need for peace.

Of course there is a difference between a heart's retreat, to which from time to time we seek, and the hidden inner holy place where God in silence dwells. In all our search for solitude, there is no substitute for the secret and the holy "space" that God alone can fill. His is the peace, the highest order of holiness and wisdom by which to live.

~ ~ ~

> Serve the LORD with gladness! Come into his presence with singing! . . . Enter his gates with thanksgiving, and his courts with praise!
>
> Psalm 100:2, 4

We hardly need to close our eyes to imagine the regal procession that the Psalmist describes. The people lined along the quays; singing with the temple chorus, as they wend their way toward the city. They enter its gates with thanksgiving and approach God's courts with jubilation. Then the procession stalls, at least momentarily, outside the outer courts as the congregants look on, and the priests and Levites, elders and leading men walk slowly toward the lattice, fenced-in inner courts and gleaming sunlit edifice of the temple. No one may enter the Holy of Holies save the High Priest, and he only once a year during Yom Kippur. Still, the drama runs high as eager eyes drink in the holy sites and sounds of lyre and horn, knowing that God is nigh and that all the earth need hush its soul and worship God in silence.

Scholars may never know whether religious pageantry preceded or took root after the royal processions of kings, their triumphant victory marches, or their enthronement festivals became popular. Nietzsche denigrated priests and their betrayal of the princely, nobler, valiant class of men of action and power. The separation between church and state is nothing new; however, for millennia, gods and kings, priests and nobles ruled their empires of gain and loss, united in a bond of God, King, and State—in that order. Fears of theocracies still abound, for mankind's proclivity to play God has always created its share of tyranny and abuse.

As for marches and festival parades, who among us does not enjoy the "boom" of a big bass drum, a Homecoming Queen throwing flowers from her float, or the patriotic Marches of a military band on the Fourth of July or Veterans' Day? While in France, I was honored to witness the national excitement that seized the crowd as elements of the Foreign Legion marched past—their black boots proudly shining as they paraded in perfect unison, with guidons fluttering along the Avenue des Champs Elysées. It was July 14, 1960.

But let us return to this sacred psalm we've often sung in our liturgies. Behold the robed minister or priest as he enters the nave with his entourage and processes down the central aisle, following the children bearing candle, cross, and Bible. And as you sing, listen to the choir's voices as they lift your spirit, and walking past you, each member takes his or her place in this hall of worship. Far from emasculating what is royal, noble, and valiant, entering God's courts with praise and hymns of thanksgiving silences what is violent, rude, and catastrophic. It fills our hearts with faith and love, hope and transformation. And while the organ's prelude, anthems, and joyful fugues reverberate among the rafters, God's cherubim once more descend on silent wings to mend our hearts and heal our wounds, and call our souls to action.

"O precious God, our strength and redeemer, how good to enter thy gates with songs of joy, and thy courts with hymns of praise and glad thanksgiving!"

> I will sing of mercy [*hesed*] and justice [*zedek*]. To you,
> O LORD, I will sing praises. I will behave wisely in a
> perfect [*tom*] way. Oh, when will you come to me? I will
> walk within my house with a perfect heart.
>
> Psalm 101:1–2; NKJV

Much was expected of Judah's kings. This Royal Psalm permits no exceptions, as the Temple Choir's voices make clear. *Hesed, Zedek, Tom:* Mercy, Justice, Integrity! Without the three, does justice reign at all? The Temple Fathers put the question to the king at every enthronement festival. It was part of his recital, a facet of his inaugural speech from year to year: "I, King of Judah, Son of David's house and Israel's lineage, pledge, O living God, to serve thee and thy holy people with mercy, justice, and integrity." No easy expectations to fulfill! No wonder the Court Historians deem so few "perfect" in their annals. YHWH wanted each king's best, just as he, in turn, pledged his best—his everlasting love, his righteous order of peace and goodness, and lifelong loyalty. His promise still endures, unbroken and undimmed down to our own time. Love, justice, and equanimity are inseparable qualities of God's integrity. O kings and peoples of the earth, how slow we are to learn! "Oh, when will you come to me?" is more God's refrain than ours.

Our age greatly needs the Psalmist's triple attributes as much as any gone before. Can any power ever weary of electing the ablest leaders to guide its institutions? Cynicism is the root of social suicide and moral rot. God's will is that we spare ourselves such indifference and collective decay.

Equally, we ourselves, as private souls and individuals, need God's crowning three. Mercy, justice, and integrity are ours for which to pray as well. No meditations of the Psalms would be complete if we recluse ourselves from the mirror of our personal and national despair. "Have I been just, have I been kind, have I been honest? I know I can't be 'perfect,' but I can be fair, or seek to be; I can show mercy, if I so choose; I can be true and good and just, if only I attempt to be. Yes, the good I would I often can't attain, nor the evil I would flee, escape" (Rom. 7:19).

Nonetheless, God blesses our efforts to bind up our neighbor's and our nation's wounds. Even if only one soul at a time!

Yes, God! We need thee! Fail not to come to us, for what are we without thee, O LORD?

11

The Right Hand of God

Hear my prayer, O LORD; let my cry come to thee! . . . For my days pass away like smoke, and my bones burn like a furnace. . . . I am like a lonely bird on the housetop.

Psalm 102:1, 3, 7b

Some of us never overcome all grief. Like the Psalmist's lonely bird, our inner thoughts are there, exposed for all the world to see. We are that bird on the rooftop. Only God's loving presence can bring reprieve.

There lived an elderly man, whom I came to admire, who was yet sad and inconsolable. Years separated the moment of his soul's default from his present paraplegic condition. Nonetheless, he bore his existence with passive yet courageous acceptance, while greeting family and friends with a smile from his bed in his nursing home. Early in his marriage, he lost his wife—a cataclysmic event as great as the plunge of any brilliant dying star. He never got over her loss, though occasionally he would speak of it. It was just there, like the lonely bird on the Psalmist's rooftop.

My wife and I would visit him to be of what cheer we could. He would look up from his laptop, his full head of gray hair dangling in his eyes, while he smiled beneath a white moustache bunched above his lips. Confrontational, he loved politics! "Well, what do you think of this or that?" he'd ask before I could take a chair. He was an old-time Liberal, left of center. He considered his opinions grounded on the inviolable truths to which he clung. Nothing I said could break his steel-hardened convictions that he was right. "Liberals are open-minded and tolerant!" he'd avow, "supporters of reason, you know," he'd stare through his hair with a twinkle in his eyes. I'd let the bait go and pick up a photograph of his granddaughter. She was a youthful, Meg Ryan look-a-like, with short blonde hair and a loving smile.

Actually, the old man was brilliant. It was just that being confined to his bed created a shrinking world of contact. Slowly he grew more opinionated and a bit acerbic and obtuse. Yet he charmed the hearts of visitors and staff alike, and wrote insight-filled columns for the home's weekly paper. From sheer memory, he'd offer advice on everything from poets to opera, film stars to cuisine, and the breaking news of national scandals and global strife. His wit would cheer you, but his unsolicited advice made you bite the tip of your tongue. Still, he remained an anomaly to everyone's regret, since he couldn't let go of the loss of his wife, nor find the wherewithal to seize upon a new and open door. Thus he remained a victim of unhappiness to the moment of his violent last gasp. Like all of us, he was a child of God. He was like the suppliant in this Psalm, bearing his lonely life with silent sighs and downcast eyes for God to hear and see—even when visible to others.

Of the many insights Psalm 102 offers, it comforts us to know that God longs to console us, even in our sadness and despair. The repair of a broken heart constitutes one of God's central works of love. It constitutes a formidable aspect of operation in his repair shop, where his Carpenter Son daily mends shattered and contrite hearts.

"O God, grant us thy strength to labor equally with love and skill in the workshop of the heart, both for those we love, as well as all who cry to thee."

~ ~ ~

> Hear my prayer, O LORD; let my cry come to thee! Do not hide thy face from me in the day of my distress! . . . My days are like an evening shadow; I wither away like grass. . . . He has broken my strength in mid-course; he has shortened my days. "O . . . thou whose years endure throughout all generations."
>
> Psalm 102:1–2a, 3a, 11, 24

This is now the 5th Penitential Psalm. Once more, we race against time to Augustine's cell. Death is only days away as he rereads and reflects on the seven Psalms. We shall come to his musings, but first, the thought races through our mind that, if not now, one day we too shall require someone to peg the Psalmist's verses on the cells of our heart. So bound to time are we! So far away its ending seems when we are young and in our spring! Much closer as the light grows dim and time's "evening shadow" makes its debut in the winter of life's dry "grass." But let our hearts be bold, as Augustine's equally was! After all, this is God's Word, or at least mankind's prayer of that universal hour we shall all share, when God's descending angels light to bear us up to Paradise. How can that not happen when our souls are gathered into the right hand of God "whose years endure throughout all generations"? Let us cling to this Psalm! Let us love it as if God's mighty hand penned it for us alone to read.

But back to Augustine and his meditation on the Psalmist's words, "Do not hide thy face from me in the day of my distress!" Yes, Augustine retorts, "But did God not hide his face from his very Son? Did the Father not hide his face from his own Christ?" His point—Neither you nor I are the first, nor shall we be the last, to know distress and suffering! In fact, anticipating John Donne's "No man is an island," Augustine rises in poetic form to state that wherever mankind has suffered, and shall suffer in the future, all of us suffer, too. We are not unaffected by humankind's suffering, wherever it occurs in the world. But just as Christ endured his Cross and rose to set us free, so too our sufferings can come to us as opportunities to serve God and our fellow man. Thereby shall all generations yet to come know and find their perfect peace in God.[1] True, Augustine was a Neo-Platonist and was influenced by Plato's concept of the Good and its power to lift us upward; yet he was a realist and knew how prone to pride and human deception all of us are. Thus he hailed God's Word and the Son of Man's cross as the only anodyne for all our sin.

---

1. Schaff, *Augustine*, 495.

> I am like a vulture (or pelican) [*pe-eth*] of the wilderness, like an owl [*cosh*] of the waste places; . . . like a lonely bird [*zephor bovev*] on the housetop.
>
> Psalm 102:6–7

Few Fathers of the Church excelled in the usage of the allegorical and anagogical methods of interpretation as Augustine of Hippo. Augustine saw in the verse above three types of mankind as well as three stages of Christ's redemptive activity. He was a master of exploring Scripture and applying it meaningfully to his time. His insight is worth recovering for ourselves.

For Augustine, the pelican is a bird of the Nile, a bird of the wilderness, representative of a lost mankind, not even aware of its concupiscence and fallen condition. To that extent, the pelican represents you and me, especially in our vagabond and lonely stage of unconsciousness of our true existence. The owl represents the soul that inhabits deserted ruins where once houses, homes, and city walls stood, where people dwelt, alive and with joy. We are that owl, bereft of life's pulse and purpose, living amid the death of our own souls. As for the lonely bird, which Augustine identified as a "sparrow," it represents risen man, saved from life's ruins and years of wilderness wandering. Thus the sparrow on the housetop represents joy and the promise of our salvation.

As for Christ, the pelican represents Jesus' own wilderness experience and temptation, which he mastered in service of God. The owl, Christ's abode in the ruins of our soul's death, symbolized by his Cross and his broken cry: "My God, my God, why hast thou forsaken me?" As for the "sparrow," it represents the Son's resurrection to new life, by means of which he leads us to heaven.

How convincing Augustine's method was, we can only guess. But from an existential viewpoint, Augustine's interpretation speaks to our own angst of uncertainty, to our fear of meaninglessness amid the wasteland of our own days, and our longing for worthwhile existence. The Psalmist knew that only God can quell the heart's searching and fill our life with love and goodness, courage, and the will to live.

∿ ∿ ∿

> Bless the LORD, O my soul; . . . The LORD is merciful and gracious, slow to anger and abounding in steadfast love . . . For, . . . as far as the east is from the west, so far does he remove our transgressions from us.
>
> Psalm 103:1, 8, 12

While staying with the American School of Oriental Research—when the Hashemite Kingdom of Jordan controlled the West Bank and Old Jerusalem—I'd wander down past the Dome of the Rock to reflect in the shade of the Al-Aqsa Mosque. Here East and West met on the holy site of Zion, atop the Temple Mount, resting on the support walls that Herod built during Augustus' reign. Judaism's Wailing Wall remained hidden but accessible down a dark alley behind the Dome of the Rock. I went to the Mosque to meditate and admire its high vault, polished columns, and Persian carpets. Beggar boys were prevented from tormenting tourists outside Al-Aqsa, which made it a haven for me, but once leaving the area you were on your own. I still remember the gang of little boys taunting me for "baksheesh" (coins or gratuity), who hurled dried pieces of dog offal as I ran back toward the Suq (market place). There East and West met again as the shopkeepers watched and laughed before chasing the boys away. I sat and drank tea and munched on honey cakes with one of the merchants as his wife brought out bolts of embroidered cloth, threaded with streaks of silver and flecks of gold. I bought several yards from a beautiful bolt for my mother and several curios for my father back home.

Here Judaism, Christianity, and Islam dwelt in peace, at least moderately, before the wars of conflict brought that respected unity to a close. "As far as the East is from the West!" We in the West think of Jerusalem, Israel, Palestine, and Jordan as oceans away, a distinctly different culture from our traditional Judeo-Christian past. But such global distances of foreign lands and unique religions melt like sinking icebergs in our current millennium of instant access to all things, everywhere. Perhaps our Psalmist, if he had lived today, would have written: "As near as the East is to the West, does not God love all?" Yes, even Muslims, Arabs, Hindus, Buddhists, Shinto Japanese and Confucian households; Tibetans, Dali-Lamas, Zen masters, and Taoist priests. "Well, only if they're converted!"

you might object. No! "As far as the east is from the west, so far does he remove our transgressions from us." Why not allow God to decide who is "us," and who isn't?

Yes, the Psalmist's faith and his ancient story, as well as Christ's passion and cross, cry out to be told. And tell it we have and still do! But "as far as the east is from the west," or "as near as the East is to the West," begs also to be heralded. It confirms the good news of One God for all the world to serve and love, throughout all cultures and above all strife. Is that not the wisdom of Israel as well as the credo of every faith? It is worth pondering in our age of discord and religious strife.

"O LORD, truly make us instruments of thy peace, of thy everlasting *hesed* and righteous *zedek*, by means of which thy love transforms the world. In the Son of David's name, Amen."

∽ ∽ ∽

> Bless the LORD, O my soul! . . . In wisdom, thou hast made . . . thy creatures. . . . These all look to thee, to give them their food in due season. When thou givest to them, they gather it up; when thou openest thy hand, they are filled with good things. When thou hidest thy face, they are dismayed; . . .
>
> Psalm 104:1, 24b, 27–29a

So few Psalms praise God to such full length as this one, focusing entirely on celebrating God's providence over all his works. No part of God's salient order is left unsung in this tribute to God's Creation—from its heavens to earth, from its mountains to the sea, from the frolicking Leviathan to every creature of prey, down to none other than man himself, from his vaunted glory to his days of decline and decay—all, all of it, is praised as the magnificent work of God's munificent hand.

In Luther's translation of the Psalms, he opens this, and the preceding hymn, with the words: "*Lobe Den HERREN*," on the basis of which Bach composed the music for one of Christianity's most popular hymns. Whatever your tongue, it is likely you have sung *Lobe Den HERREN* in your church, chapel, or cathedral.

> *Lobe den HERREN, den mâchtigen König der Ehren;*
> *Lobe den HERREN, der alles so herrlich regieret.*
>
> *Praise ye the LORD, the Almighty, the King of creation! . . .*
> *Praise ye the LORD, who o'er all things so wondrously reigneth.*

André's favorite hymn was: "O Morning Star, how fair and bright!" Standing together before the communion table, huddled in our stiff blue blouses, we'd sing the hymn à *cappella*, no matter how freezing cold it might be. With no heater in the chapel, our voices comprised our major source of warmth and consolation. Even our fingertips, cheeks, ears, and toes burned with cold. Nonetheless, the hymn's allegretto pace and Advent grace warmed our hearts.

> *Brillante étoile du matin, Que fait lever l'amour divin,*
> *Pure et sainte lumiere,*
> *Répands dans nos coeurs ta clarté,*
> *Viens dissiper l'obscurité, Que regne sur la terre.*
>
> O brilliant Star of morning light,
> With love divine thou shinest bright—pure and holy.
> Come fill our hearts with clarity, dissipate obscurity,
> And end its reign of terror.[2]

Yes, with a few liberties, but we live in a time of captive hearts, for ours is an era, quick to forgive ourselves, but fast to fault others. Our proclivity toward personal impunity belies our age of sin's obscurity and self-indulgence. Where God constitutes the core of our belief system, then God's grace humanizes our relationships and magnifies our awe of his universe. Without God to praise for his creation's grandeur and glory, as well as life's struggle to survive and succeed, then whom would we praise for its beauty and wonder, and where within find solace for a happy and worthwhile life? Are humanism, agnosticism, atheism, and neo-paganism the better answer? Some would argue, "Yes," surmising that the religions of the past are dead! But our Psalmist and mystics, along with years of religious heritage, boldly proclaim, "No!" "*Lobe den HERREN*" is as endemic to the heart as the Big Bang and the story of Evolution are reasonable to the searching mind.

Yes, it is good to come into God's presence with hymns of praise and glad thanksgiving. It is uplifting and cleansing to acknowledge our

---

2. Author's translation. See Catherine Winkworth's translation in most any hymnal.

plight and mortal misgivings while clinging to God's grace and goodness, praising him all the daylong. Every culture in one form or other has done so, whether in meditative silence, or to the trembling rattle of tambourines, or the solemn moans of rams' horns, or to the pleasant OMMM of pink-and-pearl conch shells as their soulful tones drift across the Ganges. In turn, may we search our own hearts and awaken each morning with songs of praise to God! *Lobe den HERREN!*

༺ ༺ ༺

> Thou dost cause the grass to grow . . . and plants for man to cultivate, that he may bring forth food from the earth, and wine to gladden the heart of man, oil to make his face shine, and bread to strengthen man's heart.
>
> Psalm 104:14–15

For all the memory of Israel's years of misery and Exile, the Psalmists and their editors never forgot the joyfulness that God intended mankind to savor. Today's psychologists, counselors, and psychiatrists confirm that depression and unhappiness were never meant to be life's highest goal. Adult tantrums, coupled with anvil-hardened attitudes, were never meant to define our mortal essence. Whether we lean toward cognitive therapy, or Jung's subconscious archetypes of anima and animus, we were born to enjoy intimacy and bounty. One does not have to be a hedonist to cherish Edward Fitzgerald's translation of Omar Khayyam's vision of happiness:

> A Book of Verses underneath the Bough,
> A Jug of Wine, a Loaf of Bread—and Thou
> Beside me singing in the Wilderness—
> Oh, Wilderness were Paradise enow!

Or feel compelled to repress his solemn verse concerning our mortality:

> The Moving Finger writes, and, having writ,
> Moves on, nor all your Piety nor Wit
> Shall lure it back to cancel half a line,
> Nor all your Tears wash out a Word of it.

Such truth the Psalmist endorsed over and over again. We are God's. We are the people of his pasture and the sheep of his hand. He prepares tables for us in the presence of our enemies; he anoints our heads with oil; our cups run over. God wants us to be happy and joyful, strong and glad of heart, rich of spirit and soul. Yes, a few choose to become Anchorites, sadhus, or monks and vestal nuns for life. That they do so deserves to be honored, but many who came to Villemétrie prized a single weekend with André and little more. Indeed, those days were filled with joy and contentment, laughter and enrichment, along with glasses of French wine and loaves of crusty bread to slake natural appetites!

Earlier that summer, when the Center was then located at Senlis, Friends of the équipe purchased a 19th-century chateau south of Paris for André's new home and retreats. A brother Jean and I were dispatched to prepare the chateau for the arrival of the Order. Jean and I accepted our commission with excitement yet humility, for we knew that André expected our very best. To our joy—late one hot afternoon—we discovered a musty underground cellar, filled with dusty racks of hundreds of grit-coated bottles of yellow and pale red wine. With unbounded delight we began opening one after the other, only to discover that each had aged sour and turned into a distasteful swallow of murky mouthwash. Being young and undaunted, however, we dusted off our clothes and returned upstairs to breathe the fresh air of the estate's grand park. After work that evening, we consoled ourselves with a glass of wine from a bottle of Vin du Maroc, which André had sent along with us. Then we selected a memory verse for the next day.

Yes! God means for us to enjoy life, to regale in its bountiful and diverse blessings, and to love him, and allow him to love us in turn.

∼∼∼

> When thou givest to them, they gather it up; when thou openest thy hand, they are filled with good things. When thou hidest thy face, they are dismayed; ...
>
> Psalm 104:28-29

Since the Reformation, theologians have referred to the "works of God's hands" as a figure of speech. The mighty acts of his right hand display the effects of his grace; while those of his left represent his disappointment with Israel's apostasy, as well as his disfavor of the godless cultures that tempted and tested their faith. Imagine if you will the works of God's right hand, versus the works of his left! It is an engaging method of picturing the Deuteronomic Historian's themes that undergird most of the Old Testament. In the eyes of biblical scholars, the term "Deuteronomic Historian" refers to the author of the biblical books of Deuteronomy through 2 Kings. If not their author, his views govern the viewpoint from which the story is written. Briefly, as long as Israel is faithful to the Covenant, all goes well, but once Israel turns away, then things go terribly wrong. Once they repent, however, God gathers them anew and bestows his blessing on them once again. This may sound simplistic, but nothing could be more profound.

When we turn to the Scriptures, we never meet "the left hand of God," per se. Not that it isn't there! It is very much implied. According to the Deuteronomist's theological theme, it is quite apparent that God's right hand symbolizes his guidance of his people, consisting in a host of blessings. Among these are God's deliverance of Israel out of Egypt and into the Land of Promise, while marshaling them to drive out their Canaanite enemies. He calls forth a legion of Judges to establish the tribes in their land; then chooses David and others to secure their birthright. All this closes with his summons of a league of Seers and Prophets to remind them of God's love, and the love he longs from them in turn. However, even God's people are only people. Their personal wills are strong. Israel rebels time and again. So with "God's left hand," or his "face turned away," he allows Israel to reap the regret they have elected to bring on themselves. Yet, he loves them and listens for their cry, and when they repent, like the Prodigal, he awaits their return with open arms.

That is the work of his "right hand," along with the work of his "left hand." For God, the latter constitutes a sad, yet reluctant gesture by which he allows us to reject him in our quest for self-fulfillment. With patience he waits for us to repent and turn to him once more. Which will it be? The question has never changed, has it? It applies to us as much as to Israel, to the age of Constantine as well as Aquinas, to the era of Luther as well as Nietzsche, to the time of Heidegger as well as our own.

How true the words of the Psalmist were and still are! When God opens his hand, we are filled with good things. But when he is forced to withdraw his goodwill, we reel with shock and tumble into sorrow. "O

176 By the Waters of Babylon

LORD, take our hand! Clasp us with thy strong right arm, lest letting go we slide into that silent land of death's dark well and perish evermore!"

∼ ∼ ∼

> He is the LORD our God: . . . He is mindful of his covenant, . . . which he made with Abraham, his sworn promise to Isaac, which he confirmed to Jacob . . .
>
> Psalm 105:7, 9, 10a

Every religion has its founder, along with its first and second generation of disciples who shape its foundations. One thinks of Jesus' life, his passion and resurrection, and the letters and travels of Paul that established the core of Christian beliefs as we know them today. In a similar manner, so emerged the Hindu story, from its earliest era of animal sacrifices, leading to its hymns of the *Rig Veda*, the esoteric teachings of the *Upanishads*, and to the epic verses of the *Bhagavad-Gita*.

In the case of Israel, it all began with Abraham, whom God called to leave the land of his fathers and journey to the land that YHWH would lead him. Others before him had made the journey, especially along the river beds and wadis that run from Mesopotamia to the Canaanite corridor, but none traveled west with the promise that the LORD had made to him: that God would bless, sustain, and choose him to found a people whom God might call his own. Thus he went, journeying entirely on the adrenaline of his faith and the awareness of One whom he could not dispel from his thoughts. The call next fell to his son, Isaac, and then his grandson, Jacob, who wrestled with God all his life, as Israel herself would do, down to modernity's groups of contemporary Jews.

It is not ours to question the great migrations of faith's followers to the lands of promise that God's universal Spirit has assured them. Their content of faith might be a different issue, but not their leanings of the heart. The Bible makes it quite clear that it was Abraham's trust in God that became the foundation of his salvation, not the primitive content of any religious residue he brought with him from ancient Babylon. Sarah's willingness for Abraham to have heirs through her handmaiden Hagar was part of that religious tradition, along with the ceremonial trappings of ritual blood covenants, capped off by antagonists reciting the so-called

Mizpah Benediction: "May the LORD watch between you and me, while we are absent one from another" (Gen 31:49). The story's context makes it sorely clear that the covenant to which Jacob and Laban agreed was uttered as a warning, not as a blessing.

Other great traditions preserve equally intriguing heritage stories. The relationship between Lao-tzu and his Taoist successor Chuang-tzu may never be known, but the challenging and comforting message of the *Tao-Te-Ching* and Chuang-tzu's *The Inner Chapters* speaks with unmitigated consolation to anyone who opens their pages and allows the spirit of truth to minister to their hearts. The same holds true of the Buddha's earliest teachings and those first conclaves of monks who preserved his sayings and elevated them to contemporary relevance. One could go on and on, from the puzzling koan of the Zen Masters to Buber's *Tales of the Hasidim*.

God is the LORD our God, as well as the God of all nations and people and all cultures and civilizations that cry to God and lift their hearts to him. It is our faith, our trust, our love and longing for him that he longs to receive from us. Even at that, we are saved by grace, by his everlasting loving-kindness and his commitment that our lives should be preserved to his glory and our own. It has never been the other way around. It is always God who calls us first as he did Abraham, if not the Buddha when still a prince and pampered boy. It is God who blesses and forgives us first, then sends us on our way to live in the joy and courage of his *hesed* love and *zedek* righteousness, which never fail.

"Almighty God, how gracious thou art and how grateful we are for all thy loving kindness and salvation granted unto us. Fill us with overflowing joy to be members of thy universal kingdom, chosen, established, ordained, and sustained by thy grace and mercy. In thy Son's name, Amen."

> So he saved them from the hand of the foe, . . . But they soon forgot his works, . . . and put God to the test. . . . They sacrificed their sons and their daughters . . . to the idols of Canaan; and the land was polluted with blood. . . . Nevertheless he regarded their distress, when he heard their cry . . . and relented to the abundance of his steadfast love.
>
> Psalm 106:10, 13, 37–38, 43–44

Once again the Psalmist presents us with the Deuteronomist's four-fold theme, first of God's faithfulness, second of Israel's apostasy and sin, third of their repentance and regret, culminating fourth, in God's forgiveness and renewal of the Covenant with them.

The sacrificing of children to appease the Canaan gods of fire and furnace—Molech being the supreme immolator of innocents—still shocks the modern mind. That such ever occurred sickens us to the pit of our civilized stomachs. We touched on the subject in our meditation of Psalm 86, but that the Psalmist repeats God's horror and disdain of the practice witnesses to its fascination among the returning Exiles and their bordering neighbors. But the practice is far from dead. The Taliban's attempted murder of the Afghan child, who wished only to study and gain an education, qualifies as much as any act of repulsion, equal to any ancient rite of child sacrifice. That the men of this cult continue to oppress their daughters, especially, and do so in the name of Allah, the Almighty and Merciful One, saddens every civilized soul. Would that they could heed the word of the Psalmist.

But they are not the only subjects to commit modern-day atrocities against children. Whenever and wherever adult parents neglect or abuse their offspring, the Deuteronomist's charge of abomination should shock our sensibilities. We have all witnessed parents, both mothers and fathers, who act out their adolescent grievances late into maturity. Psychologists refer to such behavior as "adult tantrums." Counseling sessions and medications are often prescribed to assist such parents to understand and correct their behavior, lest their tantrums provide unwanted modeling for their children to emulate. Their outbursts do not have to be ineluctable, nor driven by emotion rather than intention. So often, however, the change never occurs; thus the state must step in and remove these little ones from their homes. I have been to hospitals and mental wards where these "innocents abused" are kept under lock and key behind metal doors, both to protect them from themselves and to prevent them from harming each other. Such abused children revert to heartbreaking behavior, defecating on themselves and smearing it on windows, biting the hands that heal them, or looking up sadly into your eyes until your own soul weeps. Even when abused, they still long for their mamas and daddies. I have sat with the latter who equally grieve for their little ones.

How do we treat our own children? How do our children treat theirs? When broken and brought to their knees, the Israelites cried to the LORD, and he lifted them up and showed them his mercy again. So must we as parents and adults desist from acts of abuse; and, by God's grace, love the children whom God has entrusted to us. Let us search our hearts and re-offer them to God, correct our modeling of the innocents committed to our care; provide and shelter them, and educate and rear them in the Spirit and Compassion of God Most High. May God renew and strengthen our faith and labor to that end.

Let us now unite with the Psalmist in bringing Book Four to its conclusion, praying with him: "Blessed be the LORD, the God of Israel, from everlasting to everlasting! And let all the people say, 'Amen!' Praise the LORD!" (Psalm 106:48)

Book Five
PSALMS 107–150

12
Psalms of Encouragement and Gratitude

> Some wandered in desert wastes, finding no way to a city to dwell in; hungry and thirsty, their soul fainted within them. Then they cried to the LORD . . . and he led them by a straight way, till they reached a city to dwell in.
>
> Psalm 107:4–7

IN THE MID-1930S AND up through the late-1950s in Southwest Virginia, tenants journeyed from farm to farm, seeking a home in which to dwell. Cold and hungry, ill-clad and thirsty, they'd appear in old Fords or on foot in the graveled drive beside granaries, begging for work and shelter in which to live. Many arrived at my uncles' farms, as there were few means of employment for most, who, being unskilled and poor, could not afford to leave the county. Uneducated and barely literate—the men clothed in soiled bib-overalls, their wives and daughters in faded flour-sack dresses, their children barefoot and stringy-headed—it was heartbreaking to turn them away. Even when signing them on, the full extent of their poverty and the condition of their sour bodies and unkempt hair demoralized consciences. All told, my grandmother had one family of tenants, my three uncles a total of seven, and a neighboring great aunt, two. I often played with the children, and together in the evenings we'd ride the big draft horses down to the creek for water. No one went hungry, but, in time, all left the farms as the South rebounded slowly. None of the old tenant houses is still standing, though the boards of a rotting well are visible where they've sunk into the dank ground, along with a broken fence gate, and the faint trace of ruts where dogs and wagons once rested or were parked. "Finding no way to a city in which to dwell, cold and hungry their cry came up to LORD!" proclaims the Psalmist.

When first arriving in Paris, I witnessed the same. It was the winter of 1959. The city had yet to sandblast its monuments and cathedrals, and their ancient stone buildings glared down black and cold. Huddled under archways and bridges, and curled up in black coats over the subway's filthy grates, the poor sought warmth and shelter wherever they could.

Today such poor indwell our own cities. They beg for handouts along our busy streets. Rightfully, merchants call the police and file court actions to have them removed. Nevertheless, they make it back, seeking food and shelter, sleeping in unlocked doorways, curled up behind steep concrete stairwells in downtown parking garages, ever dwelling in the city, with no city of their own. Their presence strains our hearts as well as our charitable institutions' budgets. The goal remains to rehabilitate them; feed, clothe and shelter them, without emasculating their ability to become contributing and proud citizens again. It is a work that never ends, a task before every generation called to act justly and show mercy to *les misérables de nôtre temps*. We must not give up, nor yield to apathy, nor cease to preach good news to the poor. It is every generation's task to do.

Of course, the Psalmist's "homeless"—with no "city" in which to dwell—were the tribes of Israel, before the era of Zion. But spiritually, he is addressing us as well. We too are sometimes wanderers, lost in life's vast concrete deserts, seeking a "city" in which to dwell, poor of spirit and frail of faith, weak in courage and low on hope. Even upon arriving in the "city," we are more often fascinated by its glow and glare, tempted to live by the values of mankind's "City on Earth," than eager to serve God's kingdom first, with our eyes on the "City of God." It is a singular calling of the greatest cause, to seek "God's City" instead of concupiscence and lust, to embody his grace and righteous love above power and avarice or pride and indifference of the poor.

"O God of all mankind—rich and poor, powerful and meek—we thank thee for thy gracious kingdom, and, above all, for thy help in enabling us to strive in faith, to act with hope, and exercise thy righteous zeal, emboldened by thy everlasting love."

> Some went down to the sea in ships, ... Then they cried to the LORD ... and he delivered them from their distress.
>
> Psalm 107:23, 28

The rescue of the Nigerian cook, who "went down to the sea," one hundred feet to the bottom of the ocean for three days, made international headlines when the story was finally released. Like biblical Jonah, he gasped for breath in the tugboat's belly, kept alive only because of a trapped air bubble in his tiny cabin. With a sense of glum bearing down on his heart, he shivered, as the air grew thinner with each passing hour. With only a flashlight and Coke tucked in his briefs, he awaited his fate as the long dark hours slipped by. His wife had sent him verses of the Psalms, which he read and reread as the batteries lasted. He cast his lot on God to save him. And save him God did! Yes, in the form of three strong Dutch divers. Working for a salvage company on that murky morning of March 29, 2013, they were astonished to discover the live cook. With hopeful joy, they braved their way into his cabin, placed an air mask over his mouth, before pulling him out into a decompression chamber.

We must never underestimate the deliverance of God, whatever its form, whenever it occurs! We too can be saved from the darkness of disconsolate despair when life's thundering waves draw us down into the sea's black lonely night. It happened to Jonah; it's happened to others, whatever their peril, whatever their sea. It happened to Jesus, wrapped in grave cloths and sealed in Joseph of Arimathea's tomb, on that Sabbath night his disciples would never forget.

"O LORD, we bow to thank thee for the rescue of the young Nigerian cook and the brave men who brought him up and back to praise thee. Help us, too, to clasp thy strong right arm, until thy waves and billows pass over us and we are safe again with thee. Amen."

~ ~ ~

> O grant us help against the foe, . . . With God we shall
> do valiantly; it is he who will tread down our foes.
>
> Psalm 108:12–13

I have always admired the State flag of Virginia, with its emblem of Lady Virtue standing with her left foot on the chest of a defeated tyrant. Beneath the latter the State motto reads: "*Sic Semper Tyrannis*," "Thus to all Tyrants." Its motto is surely one we have quietly prayed from time to time when confronted by the petty "tyrants" who would bully us and direct our lives, if we'd let them. As an attorney friend of mine once acknowledged, "Every family has its angry few and dysfunctional siblings who despise each other. I have had to represent them in countless cases and bitter law suits." He should know, as one of his own kin declined to visit him when he was hospitalized and not expected to live. We all know of cousins who have treated each other with similar indifference, even sons and daughters who hate their parents. Little wonder that YHWH commanded Moses to phrase the fifth commandment: "Honor thy father and thy mother," instead of, "Love thy father and mother." Even God suspected that mankind was incapable of the latter.

This all sounds so negative, so fault-finding and unworthy of a meditation, but the greatness of the Psalms lies in its disturbing, yet therapeutic perspicuity, and capacity to enable us to accept the truth about ourselves. That includes our loved ones—especially when the latter are difficult to love and unloving themselves. Even the brothers of the équipe grumbled about Americans and their profligacy, wastefulness, and, yes, the size of their feet! With great laughter they dubbed my left foot "Queen Mary" and my right one "Queen Elizabeth." A size 13-A was unimaginable to them. Only oafs and fairy tale giants possessed such *pieds*.

There was a physician in the mountains, whom I often visited, who nay-said everything and anything I brought up about our rural parish and its needs. Not once did he design to darken our church's door, but when I asked him one winter for his help, he stopped, became quiet, and spoke of other matters. Later, however, he came to church, smiled when I saw him, and gave the equal to several of our tithing flock. Sometimes those who oppose us actually admire our work. It's just that, in their mind, life's deck of cards has not dealt them a gaming chance. The challenge of the Gospel remains unchanged: "Love your enemies; do good to those who hate you; bless those who curse you; and pray for those who despitefully use you" (Luke 6:27). As hard as that is to fulfill, it includes our families as well: mothers, fathers, sisters, brothers, children, aunts, uncles, cousins and cousins once-removed.

"O LORD, hear the voice of our supplications, above all when it extends to our families and those whom we need to seek and long to love."

~ ~ ~

> Be not silent, O God of my praise! For wicked [*rasha*] and deceitful [*tertath*] mouths . . . beset me with words of hate, and attack me without cause. . . . For I am poor and needy, . . . I am gone, like a shadow at evening; . . .
>
> Psalm 109:1–3, 22–23

One has to read the entire verses, 3–22, to appreciate the genre of this lament. It is more like a malediction; indeed, a curse. The Psalmist exhorts God to expend maximum retaliation against the *rasha* and those of *deceitful* conduct who have beset his life. Scholars note that the tone of his violent language was not unusual during the Psalmist's era. During that period, a counter-curse was required to nullify the power of an enemy's curse. In addition to an eye for an eye, and a foot for a foot, the *lex talionis* sanctioned a curse for a curse. Such declamatory and virulent language catches us off guard unless we remember the culture of the B.C. Era. After all, it predates Jesus' Sermon on the Mount, in some cases anywhere between five hundred to a thousand years. The practice, however, is not necessarily biblically inappropriate. Sometimes the most humble and pious religious people have to fight fire with fire, as the adage goes. Evil is what it is, and the Psalmist knew he could not let it pass without exposing and denouncing it.

One of my mentor pastors during my seminary days perfected the usage of denunciatory speech. I say, "perfected" because he filled his sermons with terrifying threats of vindictive opprobrium against anyone who owned rental property in the city's ghetto but which they neglected to keep up. "That is the surest path to Hell!" he once thundered to everyone's aristocratic shock. People loved him, however, because his heart was anchored in the mercy and justice of God, and because he wasn't afraid to call a "spade" a "spade." He was tall, manly, wore sweaters over his broad shoulders and smoked a pipe whose bowl was fashioned in the shape of an ugly head with silver rings in its nose and ears. He delighted in smoking the pipe in front of visitors to his office. In that way he was a maverick. He'd look them in the eye, wink toward his secretaries, then exhale a stream of rank gray smoke from his nostrils. The Psalmist would have loved him, if not Jesus. He was more bluff than gruff, but he knew how to command a congregation's attention when they needed to hear the Gospel. No mouse of the scrolls was he! In fact, seminarians referred to the good preacher as "the Charlton Heston of ministry."

To preach the truth in love has never been easy. As Nietzsche once attributed to Schopenhauer, "the task of philosophy resides in the pain of telling the truth." The same holds true of the biblical message—that "the fear of the LORD is the beginning of knowledge" (Prov. 1:7), and only the foolish of heart fail to seek it. Jesus expressed it in his own inimitable way, "Seek ye first the kingdom of God," and life's essentials will fall into place (Matt 7:33).

One doesn't have to address the subject of poverty, however, in the manner that the good Preacher did. In contrast, André addressed the subject from an entirely different perspective. Rather than denouncing his Parisian guests for ignoring the plight of the poor, André placed himself in their stead, taking on the poverty of the poor through the eyes of Christ. He devoted a series of meditations to the subject based on Jesus' words in Matthew 25:31–46. "I was hungry and you gave me food, I was thirsty and you gave me drink, I was a stranger and you welcomed me, I was naked and you clothed me, I was sick and you visited me, I was in prison and you came to me" (Matt 25:35–36). Hearers of André's sermons left the chapel humbled and more aware of their Christian duty in the same way that the proud "Charlton Heston's" congregation felt aroused to do better. If the latter were a Heston, André was more like a Boris Pasternak. In truth it takes both. The shocking voice of the prophet, as well as the prayerful psalms of the poet! Sometimes, God looks to us to be both: a prophet and a therapist, an activist and saint. It should fill us with joy to serve the LORD God with mercy and justice, peace and love, until the shadows of evening o'ertake us, and he lifts us into his eternal arms. Amen.

∽ ∽ ∽

> The LORD says to my lord; "Sit at my right hand, till I make your enemies your footstool". . . . The LORD has sworn and will not change his mind, "You are a priest for ever after the order of Melchizedek."
>
> Psalm 110:1, 4

In his *Commentary on the Psalms*, Wiser clarifies verses 1 and 4 concerning their meaning for post-Exilic Israel. The verses stand as "oracles," or pronouncements, that God is establishing David's House and his successors as his divinely appointed *vice regents* over the state, and his *high priest* over its religious institutions. Melchizedek was a Canaanite prince and priest who ruled over Jebusite Jerusalem in ancient times, especially during the period of the Patriarchs (Gen. 14:18). Wiser suspects that the Psalmist's oracles were meant to limit the power of the priesthood by investing it under the power of the king.[1]

Both the New Testament and the Church's earliest theologians interpreted the two passages as anagogical forerunners of Christ's role as priest and king. This unification of both offices, however, was and is nothing new. Rome bestowed the dual offices on Augustus, recognizing him as *Emperor* and *Pontifex Maximus*, that is, the Empire's highest priest regarding the reading of auguries to discern the will of the gods. During the Middle Ages, Pope Innocent III declared himself the indisputable head of the Church as well as the titular head of the State, by means of which he ruled through the kings and princes of Europe, whom he alone had the power to place or remove. Henry VIII of England claimed the two offices for himself, as does the present royal family through Parliament and the House of Lords. The Dalai Lama of Tibet enjoyed both offices prior to the Chinese invasion and occupation of his homeland. Many of his followers still recognize him as their rightful political leader and the incarnation of the Spirit of the Compassionate Buddha. Traditionally in America, it has been the practice of Presidents to call upon the nation to pray in times of peril and uncertainty, even calling on the nation's citizens to join in acts of prayer and thanksgiving on Thanksgiving Day.

---

1. Weiser, *Psalms*, 694–695.

The Psalmist's oracles represent a long and venerable tradition. Granted they are vulnerable to cronyism and abuse; nonetheless, they witness to our need for sound and just government as well as need for therapeutic institutions of healing and hope. In the end, there exist no substitutes of either. Though often presented as something of a tongue-and-cheek retort, Jesus' famous statement about rendering unto Caesar the things that are Caesar's and unto God the things that are God's remains mankind's hallmark of hope for oneself and one's nation, one's children and the common good of all.

"O God may our own prayers of thanksgiving and commitments to justice ever be pleasing to thee, O LORD MOST HIGH!"

∽ ∽ ∽

The works of his hands are faithful and just; all his precepts are trustworthy, they are established for ever and ever, to be performed with faithfulness and uprightness.

Psalm 111:7-8

Scholars remind us that Psalm 111 is an acrostic psalm. Each line begins with a successive letter of the Hebrew alphabet, i.e. *aleph* through *taw*. Such poetry requires linguistic skills beyond the level or interest of many poets. It reflects the intricacies of the Hebrew language; it also underscores the desire of the psalmists to praise God through poetry rather than prose. In that respect, they were forerunners, if not contemporaries of the Greek playwrights who discerned the same. Language is one of the consummate achievements man has acquired since learning first to speak in symbols that expressed his yearnings and love. All speech carries with it an ancient sense of sacramental awe and joy. That is why Heidegger's respect for Hölderlin's poetry constitutes an essential aspect of his understanding and creation of the value of philosophy. Philosophy represents mankind's poetic quest of the mystery and meaning of existence. The language of science also represents a form of the quest in the guise of empirical and mathematical metaphors. Together, we are all on the same track under the watchful eye and care of God. His life-giving works are "faithful and just" phenomena for us to seek and discover. Indeed, we should praise the LORD for all his works, as well as engaging our minds with joy in serving him. As the poet Noa Daniels has put it perceptively:

> All life is a revelation
> through images and observation.[2]

Beyond the power of the Psalmist's poetry to nudge our hearts, however, lies a truth all religions sponsor—our universe reflects an underlying orderliness, despite a few wayward comets, as well as a longing for a moral center that is perceived by all cultures despite differences in language, time, and history. Each feels driven to acknowledge a moral imperative—a wisdom appropriate to its religious or cultural perspective. The Psalmist refers to the phenomenon as, "all his precepts are trustworthy," and "established for ever and ever." That sense of conscience is more than a mere perspective of time and place; rather it is grounded in the common core of humankind's nature. We live best when our hearts, minds, and creative energies recognize that our humanity is an inseparable extension of the wisdom, power, and love of God in our hearts. May we rejoice in believing so!

∽ ∽ ∽

He has caused his wonderful works to be remembered.
Psalm 111:4a

For the Hebrew people, the "wonderful works" of God centered particularly about the events of their deliverance from Egypt and their miraculous passage through the waters of the *Yam Suph*, or Sea of Reeds. Even more so, their experience included the Covenant that God made with them at Mt. Sinai, the long years of wandering in the Sinai and Negev and finally their victory over the Canaanite tribes. The latter especially enabled them to take up residence in the land of their fathers, of Abraham and Jacob. This memory never faded. It became seared forever on the souls of those who survived and returned from Israel's Babylonian Captivity. Theologians refer to these events as the "mighty acts of God," through which Israel's allegiance was won to God and sealed with his

---

2. Noa Daniels, *The Common Ground*, www.smashwords.com/profile/view/Noa-Daniels. Used with permission.

eternal blessing. Indeed, many of Judaism's sacred festivals are connected with these stupendous events.

The works of salvation, however, are not the only means by which God steals into our lives and commands our allegiance. For many years Aquinas' Fifth Way, or Argument from Design, was held in high opinion. He reasoned from the deductive principle that "from effects we may search for like causes." In his mind, this "Fifth Way" demonstrated that an intelligent designer had to be the Principal Cause behind the universe, since inanimate reality could not have designed itself. Last century's British philosopher, R. J. Tennant, embraced this view, maintaining that the universe itself clearly displays a divine artificer. However, Tennant went one step further. He argued that the *beauty* of the universe—its awe inspiring stars, galaxies, and the planet Earth—imply a Designer who values *beauty,* in and of itself, else the phenomenon of aesthetics would make no sense in a world without God. Beauty would be superfluous.

Modern scientists, especially Hawking and Dawkins, dispute this view. They do so on the basis that neither the universe nor Earth requires an intelligent designer to account for either's appearance. The Big Bang and Evolution provide sufficient empirical evidence to mute Tennant's teleological view. Perhaps fore-sensing such a movement explains why Goethe complained about his own era that: "the age of the beautiful is over; ours is one of emergency and implacable demands."[3] Again he wrote from his home in Weimar: "things here [are] so . . . confused that one scarcely knows a single person who is content with life."[4] Still, anyone with eyes to behold the beauty of the universe without, and who ponders the mystery of mankind's restlessness within, will find Thomas's Fifth Way and Tennant's Teleological Argument of value. Certainly the Psalmist did, as well as Jesus in his praise of the lilies of the field, which outshone Solomon in all his purple raiment.

Foreign visitors to America remember with awe the grand works they have seen: from the Grand Tetons to the Okefenokee Swamp; from the Yellowstone to the Grand Canyon; from Mount McKinley to the white sands of Biloxi; from the wildlife of Denali to the bald mountains of the Presidential Range; and from the bays of Lake Superior to the snowy woods of Maine.

3. Ludwig, *Goethe,* 252.
4. Ibid., 283.

These scarcely exhaust the world's list, let alone pay tribute to the creative powers that the LORD God has inspired in man: from the Great Wall of China to Egypt's Pyramids; from Homer and Hesiod's works to the dramas of Shakespeare and Goethe; or from the art of Giotto to the Impressionist works of Renoir and Van Gogh. We each have our list, our journals filled with notes and cards, drawings and stamps from around the world; and now iPhone and iPad pictures preserved in computer files. All, all of it, yes all of it, bears witness to the Artist of artists and our longing and yearning to be artists, too.

"O LORD God, how can we ever forget thy wonders and the works of thy hand? May we ever be lovers of thy Beauty and Truth and artists ourselves insofar as our special talents burn within us! Amen!"

∽ ∽ ∽

> Blessed is the man who fears the LORD, who greatly delights in his commandments! . . . Light rises in the darkness for the upright; . . . The wicked man sees it and is angry; . .
>
> Psalm 112:1, 4, 10

As my grandmother aged, lost sight in both eyes, and underwent the amputation of her left foot, she never grew bitter, nor sank into remorse. She always saw the light in each day's arrival and faced dusk with courage and gratitude. I shall never forget visiting her the last time I would see her alive. I was a freshman in college and had come to Abingdon to visit her. She was seated on the edge of her bed, propped up by a pillow. She looked up at me in her gentle way as I entered the room. I announced my presence, at which she bade me come to her side and kneel beside the bed. As I did, she ran her fingers through my hair, her hands over my face and ears, lips and mouth, and pressed my head against her chest. "Oh, Benny Boy!" she exclaimed, "How wonderful to hold you again."

Hers was the kind of experience that members of Israel's *hakamim* would have applauded. Remember, Israel's Wisdom Writers fell into two distinct schools—those who celebrated Israel's belief that service to God results in riches and blessing, long life and joy; versus Israel's more pessimistically inclined writers who contended that life is hard, filled with hurt and anxiety, and numerous uncertainties that gnaw at the soul. In each school, faith alone and loyalty to God constituted the underlying pinnings that support human existence. Psalm 112 reflects the former school, while Job's sorrows and Ecclesiastes reflect the latter school. The Psalms' stress-filled laments and tender prayers of confession reflect the latter as well.

Most of us are a fusion of optimism and pessimism, though on occasion we fall into the slough of what Nietzsche called, "the loneliest loneliness," or, "the greatest weight." The Bible acknowledges that both joy and sorrow weigh on our human souls, and that God waits in patience to bear us up, either way.

In truth many of us are shy, prefer quietude to crowds, and silence and time with ourselves to arguments we'd rather not start, whose only end arouses emotions and ill feelings. My Aunt Evelyn was of the latter persuasion and passed countless hours sitting in front of the fireplace, shuffling her deck of cards and playing Solitaire. When, afterwards, she withdrew to the parlor, with Rosary in hand, I knew to slip outside and comfort old Trixie—our bird dog.

An equally great number of folk can't help but seek and enjoy company. Rather than cultivating aloneness, they prefer the warmth of companionship and friends. They enjoy conversing, laughing, and sharing experiences with one another. It isn't always a matter of being an introvert or an extrovert. Our hearts experience joy and woe, cheer and sadness, as they are irreparable and existential modes of human life. One thing we do know, however—that an unbounded and unlimited ego that soars to the heights of a lawless self, burns out in the end from the excessive fires of concupiscence and voyeurism. The same is true of an unchecked pessimism that innocently enough begins in skepticism, then slips slowly into withdrawal and seclusion, if not cynicism and the scourge of fatalism. Fatalism, cynicism, and skepticism reduce our capacity to take command of our own lives and render them useful and worthwhile. Yes, the Psalmist is right: "Light rises in the darkness for the upright," whereas the "wicked sees it and is angry."

"O God, brace us in our moments of joy and depression ever to seek thy face; to long for thy healing hand, thy righteous ways of everlasting grace that we may become all that thou dost desire for each of us to attain!"

> Blessed be the name of the LORD from this time forth and for evermore! From the rising of the sun to its setting the name of the LORD is to be praised!
>
> Psalm 113:3

The Psalmist never tired of reworking the cosmological myths of his time into occasions to praise God. The Greeks and Egyptians especially favored myths involving the rising and the setting of the sun as facets of divine activity. In ancient Greece it was Apollo, the son of Zeus, who rides the chariot of the sun across the silver sheen of the sky to provide light and warmth for mankind. In Egypt, it was the god Ra, or Re, who from his orbital advantage point, observed humanity's mortal trial along the Nile and blessed the earth with sunshine, mist, and light. For all the fascination associated with both religions, however, Zeus remained preoccupied with, and often stymied by, his fellow/sister/offspring Olympians; while in Egypt, the sitting pharaohs of the Middle Kingdom, who represented the incarnation of Ra, seemed unable to rule themselves, let alone provide equity and mercy for residents of the Nile. The latter was true in Israel, when kings of the Davidic line turned their peoples' eyes away from YHWH to serve the gods beyond the River. The Psalmist knew as much and thus pressed his case for his people's allegiance to the LORD and none other. It is he and he alone who keeps the human heart from failing and who remembers the poor and needy in the land.

Well might the Psalmist ask: "Whose light enlightens your lives from the dawning of each morning to the setting of the orange-red orb? Whose love and grace commands your thoughts and steps, or bears your burdens when you are weary, disconsolate or lost? Who lifts you up when you fall down, or redeems you from your own chaos? Who extends his hand, though marred with scars, and bids you bind your heart to God?" Remember, the Psalmist knew how to be direct, this Psalmist of Abraham, Jacob, and Moses. "O God, our sure Redeemer, in spite of all our faults!"

> What ails you, O sea, that you flee? ... O mountains, that
> you skip like rams? O hills, like lambs?
>
> Psalm 114:5-6

The imagery could not be clearer! Nor its metaphors more to the point! What God has done for Israel, Nature equally peals! From the sea that yields to Moses' rod, to the hills that skip like lambs—to thunder, lightning, and fleece-white rain—all confirm God's mighty hand! It is God and God alone who saves, leads, guides, and makes the hard flint soil yield its springs to slake the traveler's thirst. We are that sojourner, that wanderer of then and now, pressed between life's rising seas and mountains white and tall. Behold! The hand of God is here, to stay the lapping dark sea's waves and guide our steps through cliffs and hills.

> The heavens are the LORD's heavens, but the earth he has
> given to the sons of men [*beni-atham*]. The dead do not
> praise the LORD, nor do any that go down into silence.
> But we will bless the LORD from this time
> forth and for evermore.
>
> Psalm 115:16-18

Three of the Psalmist's pre-Exilic tenets leap from this text to vie for attention: 1) the elusive sons of men, 2) the eternal silence of the grave, and 3) both in juxtaposition to Israel's faith in YHWH. We, who are strangers to the House of David, Aaron, and Ezra, constitute that mass of residual humanity that descended from the loins of Adam and Eve, but were never part of the Hebrew people's journey with Abraham and Lot into Canaan. We represent mankind in general, that universal seed of the earth, that primordial man that swelled out of Africa to populate Europe's Ice-Age-caves and later tilled its fields of grain—from Sumer to Ethiopia. We constitute universal man, while Israel represents God's holy and particular people. Or so believed the writer of Psalm 115. It is we who go down to the grave in silence, the resting place of all mankind. We are that creature writ large—the designer and creator of our own destiny, to whom the earth has been given to name and rule. We cannot fault the Psalmist for what appeared so clear to him. Nor can we fault modernity when the truth applies to us.

As for the "sons of men," or literally in Hebrew, "the sons of Adam," two things require our recognition. The phrase represents two classes of mankind separate from the House of Israel. We have already recognized part of this. One has to do with that class of humanity whose urgent concerns eclipse any ultimate concern for the Eternal in their hearts. This is not offered as judgmental but to recognize the truth, even the truth about ourselves. The lust for life, its joys and goals, as well as its means and ends, often take precedence over man's "ultimate concern." When our hearts are set on the trajectory of self, first, and its alluring benefits, then profligacy, Philistinism, and boredom check our spiritual development and its joy of knowing God. Every son of Adam knows the same. It symbolizes what Friedrich Schiller once called, "a sterile loneliness." The second class identifies those who recognize their "loneliest loneliness" for what it is, but have yet to yield their hearts to God. It is their "greatest weight," if not ours. We know it points to God alone who can fill life's empty spaces. It happened to Augustine, St. Francis, and Albert Schweitzer. The latter, recall, gave up his chair of New Testament Theology to become a missionary-doctor, just as Jesus gave up whatever career he might have had to serve and heal his nation's poor. There are no guarantees. No promises even of a life after this one; at least not in the Psalms. Just the joy of knowing that when God's love reaches out to us, it is time to deny ourselves, take up our cross, and follow his Son.

Yes, all mankind are mortal and go down to the land of silence, none exempt. But the Psalmist reminds us that those who love the LORD and serve the LORD are embraced by his eternal kindness as none others have been, or shall be! That is a hope that fills us with joy *now*, not just a goal to reach at the end of history.

13

The Quintessential Grace of God

I love the LORD, because he has heard my voice and supplications. Because he has inclined his ear to me, therefore I will call on him as long as I live.

Psalm 116:1–2

THERE ARE RELIGIONS THAT do not espouse prayer. Rather, meditation fills the gap when their followers' thoughts are sore bestead and inner self ill-reposed. This is true even when they feel at peace with the world and themselves.

But, what of prayer? What may we say of ourselves? Especially when our hearts are broken and overwhelmed with disappointment and remorse. Some hold that silence is the heart of prayer, a holy meditation before and with God. Even Jesus held as much. Yet our hearts cry out, if not with words, at least with thoughts when we turn to God. That is why the Psalmist's verse boosts our hopes and rekindles light in our inner soul.

If the Psalms have taught us anything, they have taught us that prayer provides those extraordinary moments in which time and eternity become one. In that sphere of time, God meets us heart-to-heart, soul-to-soul, and lifts us into his holiness by his grace and silence.

Of course the title: "The Quintessential Grace of God," is laden with philosophical abstraction, but in our hearts we know that God unites all universals in himself, supplying all that is essential. Within the mystery of our self-consciousness, God's Spirit inclines his ear to hear our supplications and bestow his therapy of calm. To whom else can we go to be heard to the depths; to pour out our thwarted aspirations, our tears of disconsolation, and hours of lonely isolation? What other love than God's will bear us up and fill our hearts with serenity and repose? Little wonder that the Psalmist's verse opens with his praise of *hesed*, followed by his cry of joy, "therefore I will call on him as long as I live."

Many are the books on prayer that sound the Psalmist's theme: God is here, in our hearts, transcendent and immanent, ready to listen. In truth, psychiatrists, counselors, and psychologists are also prepared to hear our "prayers"—and we are wise to seek them when at odds with ourselves—but they are as human as we. Our benumbed thoughts, depressions and moods often unnerve them and arouse their inconsolable grief. Their minds wander, too, and old hurts return to haunt them. It is called "transference," a subtle yet normal psychological phenomenon. Only the wisest and most experienced of counselors can hear us with dispassion and reflect back our anxieties and fears. Such secular sessions relieve our trauma and enable us to embrace more cognitive strategies.

But it isn't just strategies, or cognitive attitudes, that the soul longs to receive. It is hope, encouragement, and strength, a renewal of the inner being that the soul pines to receive. Indeed, it is to know God himself. That is prayer's true longing. Moreover, the mind requires its repose too; its subconscious probed, coaxed up into the light and healed. Nonetheless, the soul requires the same. We are not just physiological beings, subject to blood levels, oxygen, and the neural activity of the brain. No. We are far more. We are the dust of the earth, which YHWH bent down, cupped in his hand, and into which he breathed his living spirit. From, "Now I lay me down to sleep," to, "Our Father which art in Heaven," we were fashioned in God's image for fellowship with him, for that rich reciprocity that only prayer can nurture and mend. Otherwise we sink into the Pit of our own weak and fevered souls. But through prayer, we are enabled to return to the sphere of our daily lives, strengthened and inspired to love and help others.

> A Brief Excursus: Quotations adapted from Peter Forsyth on Prayer

"The worst sin is prayerlessness. We are left by God for lack of seeking Him. The Saints left their fellowmen but did not always find God. He who finds God also finds his fellowman. Only living prayer keeps loneliness humane. Our egoism retires before the coming of God, and into the clearance there comes with the Father our brother. When God fills our heart He makes more room for man than the humanist can find. Not to want to pray is the sin behind sin. And it ends in not being able to pray.

"Prayer is the assimilation of a holy God's moral strength. To feed the soul we must toil at prayer. We must pray even to tears if need be. Prayer is not mere wishing. It is asking—with a will. Our will goes into it. It is energy. Thus prayer is, paradoxically, both a gift and a conquest, a grace and a duty. Every duty is a gift, every call on us a blessing. The task we often find a burden is really a boon. When we look up from under it, it is a load, but those who look down to it from God's side see it as a blessing."[1]

∽ ∽ ∽

When I was brought low, he saved me.
Psalm 116:6

The Psalmist knew how brash it is to come before God as if he owed us something—especially an answer in response to our frantic prayers. That he inclines his ear to us is a blessing in itself. Just to be heard, to be understood, to kneel before his countenance in silence and trustful rest is to know the calm and serene gift he gives to every heart. But such does not always come without travail, without struggle and a wounded heart. Listen to the Psalmist as he summarizes his case. "The snares of death encompassed me; the pangs of Sheol laid hold of me; I suffered distress and anguish. Then I called on the name of the LORD: . . . The LORD preserves the simple; when I was brought low, he saved me" (Ps. 116:3–4, 6). Once again it is the story of a broken and a contrite heart, a story in which pride and lofty reserve have no part. We are so slow to learn and quick to beg God's favor.

As a young pastor I remember a still younger man who went off to Vietnam. He was frightened, as were so many, but he hid his fear behind his youthful face and muscled limbs. "I'll be fine," he assured his mom, who prayed daily for him until his return. Tanned and muscled even more, he came by the office one morning late, a bit embarrassed and white about his lips. He pulled up a chair, wrung his hands, stared out the window; then he looked back at me. "Sir, I did some awful things," he began, "and saw awful things. Things I never meant to do." He paused.

---

1. Forsyth, *Prayer*, 12–13.

"I wasn't always good. I went to places and did things. I hurt myself and others. I didn't mean to, but I did." He moved about uneasily, staring back out the window, then down at his hands. "Preacher, I met a girl I want to marry, but I'm not clean inside, if you know what I mean. Will you pray for me, sir? My Mama doesn't know, nor does hers. I want to change, if I can." And so we prayed, and several months later I officiated at their wedding.

Sometimes we have to be brought low, especially those of us who think we're clean and good and know far better. As Zen Masters have taught for centuries: "You can't pour fresh tea into a cup that's already full." It's what Jesus meant when he said, "You can't pour new wine into old wine skins." We have to have a new and open heart.

"When I was brought low, he saved me." Let us cling to these words as if to none other. Let us love God's Word as if we knew none other. "O God of purity and unconditional love, we've not been clean ourselves. Forgive us and cleanse our hearts anew. May we never forget thy Son's bruised brow, the blood about his crown of thorns, or twisted bleeding hands and feet."

~ ~ ~

> Precious [*yaqar*] in the sight of the LORD is the death of his saints [*qadosh*].
>
> Psalm 116:15

If we were asked to make a list of our favorite Psalms, no doubt 116 would show up among the top ten. Time and again, as a young minister, I read Psalm 116 to the widowed and the widower, to the cast down and those recovering from illness, grief, or pain. I would sit on the radiator by a window in a hospital room, or pull up a chair next to a patient's bed. Sometimes I would hold the patient's hand in my own and read the words of the Psalm. Never once did any hand let go, or anyone refuse to hear the words. I preached them at funerals, read them to grief-stricken mourners in parlor waiting rooms, and read and reread them to the lonely in nursing homes. I read them for the soul to hear, for worn and weary parishioners to savor, as well as for myself, for I needed to hear them, too. They were ours to lift before the living God as the cup of our salvation;

ours to call upon the LORD and pay our vows in the presence of one another, yea, in the courts of the house of God, in the muted light of our own sanctuaries that played upon the scarlet reredos, behind the golden cross pinned to the wall.

There is more here, too. The words "precious," [*yaqar*], or "saints," or [*qadosh*], also pique our interest. Precious means "prized" as well as "special," and "uniquely valued"; saints means "beloved" as well as "cherished." Contrary to thought, it does not mean "holy," as the Latin word *sanctus* implies, which interpreters employed to translate the Greek word ʻ*agios*. Beloved carries a different meaning altogether. It is closer to the Greek word ʻ*agapétoi*, meaning "beloved," which the Apostle John favored when addressing Jesus' followers (1 John 4:1, 7). Prized in the sight of the LORD are his beloved who die trusting in him! What greater consolation could we ask?

Still there is more. It has to do with that secret whilom tie between God's beloved and the great unwashed that the Psalmist calls *ha-beni-atham*—"the sons of men or Adam." Are they not also beloved in God's eyes, perhaps not as a class, but as individuals? Universals are abstract, empty as Immanuel Kant declared. Only particulars, or individuals enjoy existential import, or that miraculous reciprocity for relationship and love that God created and called Adam and Eve.

And so when the Psalmist speaks of God's looking down upon the "sons of men," and longing that they might look up to him, God's gaze would be empty, unless his gaze were to fall on individuals, with distinct hearts and faces, spouses and children, dreams and hopes, as well as troubles and despair. We are part and parcel of universal humankind, in all the mystery of our yearning and being, but in the eyes of God, we are each a soul, an individual human whom God created a little less than himself (Psalm 8). As our text teaches, we are that "precious" individual in God's sight and "beloved" as much as any son or daughter of biblical Adam and Eve. As Paul put it: "It is . . . the children of the promise [who] are reckoned as descendants" (Rom 9:8). Blessed then are all who cry: "O LORD, I am thy servant; I am thy servant, the son of thy handmaid" (Ps 116:16).

"O God, we pray thee to accept us as thine own, not just as a son or daughter of thy universal and abstract *sons of men*, but as thine own son or daughter. Indeed, Father, we know that thou dost, thanks to thy beloved and precious Son, who came down from heaven for us and for our salvation! Otherwise, what choice do we have but to wander down "life's labyrinthine broken ways," as Goethe penned it years ago?

∽ ∽ ∽

> Praise the LORD, all nations [*goyim*—"heathen" in Luther's translation]! Extol him, all peoples [*'ah-mim*]! For great is his steadfast love [*hesed*] . . .
>
> Psalm 117:1-2a

Luther devoted an entire book to this brief Psalm of only two verses. Yes, dedicating it to a noble, to a Knight by the name of Hans von Sternberg. It is one of Luther's "middle" works, written in 1530. That the Psalm contains less than twenty-two words was inconsequential to the Reformer. His point was to praise von Sternberg for supporting the Reformation. In Luther's mind, nobles who did so exemplified the *'ah-mim* who recognize the priority of God and Scripture over the teachings of the Pope, Canons, Decretals, or the Church's blasphemous priests. He minced no words. Throughout the little book, Luther denounces "Jews, Turks, sophists, and reason itself." Still fired up so close to his discovery of the "righteousness of grace," he wanted to emphasize that forgiveness flows from God *alone*, not from mankind's words, deeds, efforts, and cooperation. For Luther, the latter is without virtue. It is God's righteousness alone that cleanses and redeems man. Idolatry, factions, and errors have always plagued the *goyim*, or "heathen" as far back as mankind can trace religion.

In spite of Luther's thunder, his point is well taken. Just whose side are we on? To what extent do we take credit for our spirituality, or private progress during quiet retreats with God? No saint wants to minimize God's grace or cheapen it. It is simply a facet of the soul's journey as we turn our hearts toward God. In truth, we are the *goyim* whom God has come to summon, love, and justify. None of the latter is for us to claim. God has come to save us all. Our works, efforts, deeds, and words will fade in time. Only God's steadfast love endures forever. That is why the Psalmist calls us to praise God, and not our proud or muddled self-sufficiency. I suspect von Sternberg got the point and drew strength from Luther's little book. The Church of the high Renaissance enjoyed its day and is now gone. But the temptations it faced are now ours. Let us thank Luther, as well as the Psalmist, for his call to praise God alone. Amen.

∼ ∼ ∼

> Out of my distress I called on the LORD; . . . The LORD has chastened me sorely, but he has not given me over to death. . . . The stone which the builders rejected has become the head of the corner.
>
> Psalm 118:5, 18, 22

Complex and enigmatic is this Psalm. Though not attributed to David, it might have been, for Nathan sorely chastened him upon Uriah's death. Sitting in ashes and torn robe, David prayed for forgiveness, which God granted him. Like the young man returning from Vietnam, his conscience had chastened him sorely. Luckily, the young veteran returned home, alive from that pitiless and political mire of America's jungle rot and death. As a stone rejected by his inner heart, God's presence in his soul pulled him through, inspiring him to seek a humble and more perfect life.

Both David and the veteran loom as mirrors for us. Sometimes our conscience fails to do what consciences across the years have done for the human heart and that is to shock us to our senses again, and bring us back to home and hearth. Socrates tells us that his conscience never told him what to do, but whenever he was uncertain, it whispered what not to do.

What is this stone that the builders rejected but which became the head or cornerstone? Is it not our soul, which we surmised would never do? Such moral despair, only God can heal. He healed Paul's, who had persecuted the church until his conscience flung him from his horse. It took Jesus' voice to revive Paul's soul and transform him into an Apostle. It happened to a princely youth of wealth, adventure, and ease, who passing by the soiled poor became St Francis. It happened to Mother Teresa, who during her years of doubt became an angel of hope for trashed and thrown away infants. She picked them up, cleaned them off, fed and nurtured them—these little stones whose wretched mothers, for reasons we can only mourn, abandoned them in dirty gutters.

"O heavenly Father, so touch our hearts never to reject another. But to lift them up and tend each one as thou hast loved and nurtured us! O living God, the hope and praise of all!"

~ ~ ~

> Thy word [*dabar*] is a lamp to my feet and a light to my path.
>
> Psalm 119:105

Deber or *dabar* may well be the most magnetic, theologically charged word of the Hebrew Bible. Only *hesed* and *zedek* approach its significance in terms of revealing the greatness of God. God's *Dabar*, or Word, is what goes forth from his soul in all his willful vision, and creates all that is visible and invisible, all that is known or can be known. And at the center of God's *dabar* burns his loving kindness and his cleansing moral order. It took time, but by the period of the Psalms, God's *dabar* became Israel's Torah—the heart of God's gift for humankind's true fulfillment. And so it ruled all Judah's history until, in Christianity, God bent down and nailed it to a cross. No greater love or understanding of how to live sprang so quickly into existence and spread its light and hope across so vast a dark and pagan Europe.

"Thy word is a lamp to my feet and a light to my path" appears midway in the Psalter's longest hymn, containing no less than 176 verses. A commentary in itself, Psalm 119 praises God for all his wisdom and soul-illuminating truth. Whatever definition of God a religion may hold, the verses in this Psalm of praise apply. With God's word as a lamp unto our feet and a light along our way, we are able to fulfill even Hölderlin's dream of persons of merit dwelling poetically upon the earth. It is in the light of God's light that we see all else with genuine clarity. It is in the light of his light that we see our angst, our anger, and despair for what they are—the absence of God's presence in our hearts. How his word of truth and love abate our common woes, our lusts, our fears, our disappointments, and all our foiled hopes! Only in the light of God's light do we finally recognize his redeeming love and righteousness for what they are: our path toward peace and wholeness again.

14

Songs of Ascents

> In my distress I cry to the LORD, that he may answer me;
> ... Woe is me, that I sojourn in Meshech, that I dwell among the tents of Kedar! Too long have I had my dwelling among those who hate peace.
>
> Psalm 120:1, 5–6

PSALMS 120–134 ARE KNOWN as "Songs of Ascents." They refer to the crafted hymns, sung by Israel's pilgrims on their way to Jerusalem to celebrate the great festivals of the Covenant. Psalm 120, in particular, appears to be a lament of a Post-Exilic Israelite who lives too far away [in northern Arabia] to make the sacred ascent to worship at the Temple. His dwelling site is peopled by warrior tribes, who know nothing of YHWH's love and righteous ordering of life; thus his lament.

His poem-song cuts into our hearts as well. Does our dwelling sphere encourage or disparage our ascent to God's holy hill? We are not talking here about a "spatial place" per se, or a site of distance far away. No! We are talking about our souls and how often our hearts ascend in prayer to God's sphere.

In his Chapter 15 of *The Guide for the Perplexed*, Maimonides provides a stunning interpretation of our ascents in obedience to God's eternal revelation of himself. His text is Genesis 28:13, the story of God's appearing to Jacob in a dream during his flight from Beer-sheba to the land of Haran. Says the text:

> And he dreamed that there was a ladder set up on the earth, and the top of it reached to heaven; and behold, the angels of God were ascending and descending on it! And behold, the LORD stood above it . . . (Gen. 23:12–13)

Maimonides' point is that God stands *above* the ladder, beyond even the angels who ascend and descend, looking to God for their own enlightenment and down to earth where we alone are called to apply it.[1] Any person may "ascend" this ladder, as all hearts long for God's everlasting and eternal wisdom. But we, and we alone, in Maimonides' mind, are charged to *apply* it, which is the meaning of "descend." Yes, there's a bit of Neo-Platonism and Plotinus in his interpretation, but also the Psalmist's brunt biblical truth: "The fear of the LORD is the beginning of wisdom." We who are Christians in our fumbling "ascents" are blessed to know God for his humble "descent" in the form of his Son, born in an innkeeper's manger in the village of Bethlehem.

As always, the Psalmist's verses put us to the question. When was the last time we made our "ascent," with trembling hands and heavy feet, up God's holy ladder, in prayer, mediation, or simple silence, knowing that God was waiting there for us, already present on the bottom rung?

∼ ∼ ∼

> I lift up my eyes to the hills. From whence does my help come? My help comes from the LORD, who made heaven and earth.
>
> Psalm 121:1–2

The old cosmology of the Ancient Near East maintained that the heavens, with all their clouds and moisture-bearing rain, rested on the four great columns of the earth's geographic points, specifically the mountains. Thus shrines were built on mountains and the highest hilltops to pay homage to the gods. In Canaan, these heights became associated with numerous lush-green groves where priests and consorts reenacted the lustful union of their local gods, the Ba'als and Ashtaroth. Such fertility rites were held in high regard in a land desperate for rain to make the soil arable. To

---

1. Maimonides, *Guide*, 46.

what extent these well-intentioned rituals determined Israel's own earliest shrine sites remains for scholars to debate and sort out. That Abraham worshiped God under the names of El-Shaddai and El-Olam and made sacrifices to the same on Israel's hills, journeying to Mt. Moriah to offer his own son, suggests that he was acting in the best culturally accepted manner to praise God at the time. Our task is to understand the practice and be humble before God.

It is no secret that the Cherokee revere the mountains of East Tennessee, or that the Lakota and the Sioux defended the Black Hills with all their heart. They were not about to let Custer slip away after invading their sacred ground. His decision to relax the injunction against miners panning for gold in the Dakota hills was tantamount to signing his own death warrant.

But it is not the hills that the Psalmist calls us to love, but the LORD God. It is he who created their sylvan skyline and majestic glory, as well as the pastures and fields of his fecundate earth. Still, we are drawn to the hills, their shade in the summer, their colors in the fall, their snow-white domes in the winter, and their white and pink blossoms of laurel in the spring. Such beauty lifts our burdened minds from things below to God above, to the highest order of his gracious empyrean. Did God suspect as much when he began to forge slabs of granite out of the molten magma to create his first hills? Did he long for the time when we should evolve to marvel at the beauty of his hand? To think that the Himalayans are still rising in syncopation with the magma's movement to the moaning rumble of the earth's continental plates is a sacred phenomenon to ponder!

From whence cometh our help? It is the inescapable question of all mankind. In terms of *locale* or place, it was Mt. Moriah for Israel, that sacred site which later became Zion, the apple of God's eye. For Christians, it remains the hillock, Golgotha, barely steps away from the Temple's torn curtain the week of Jesus' passion, crucifixion, and resurrection. For Islam, it is its Dome of the Rock that points its people to the heavens, to which Mohammed journeyed on the night of his dream from Moriah's rock, as well as the Ka'aba, housing the holy stone that fell to earth one ominous night. Buddhism has its stupas and mountains, so also Hinduism its tiered temples to Vishnu and Shiva. The Olmec, Incas, and Mayans, built pyramids to the sun with thigh-steep staircases hard to climb in order to reach a sacred copula. There, Aztecs ripped hearts from horrified breasts and offered them to their soulless gods.

How humbling the Psalmist's version, in which the God of heaven and earth keeps our hearts intact for love and joy; who provides us shade from life's burning blaze when we are weak and broken; who guards our life from evil's sway, and keeps our going out and our coming in from this time forth and evermore. "Thanks be to thee, O God. Amen."

∽ ∽ ∽

> I was glad when they said to me, "Let us go up to the house of the LORD!" . . . Jerusalem, built as a city which is bound together, to which the tribes go up, . . .
>
> Psalm 122:1, 3–4a

Few passages are quoted as often as the above, especially at the opening of worship services. To "go up to the house of the LORD" inspires the heart with anticipation, empowering the soul in its quest for hope and salvation.

Anyone who has ever clambered up the steep steps of Paris' "Sepulcher of the Sacred Heart" knows the joy and aesthetic awe that captivates the soul once reaching the top. The cathedral before you and the view of Paris around you create their own phenomenon of ascent as your senses struggle to take it all in. "O to give thanks to the LORD for both his steadfast love and righteous will for the world!" However mystical the experience—whether grace-filled and calming, or breathtaking and emotional—those who ascend to this "house of the LORD" never forget the moment of their first close-up view of the cathedral or its panoramic sweep of Paris below.

There are additional "ascents," too, that bring us into the presence of the holy. Never once has the *National Geographic Magazine* failed to take its readers to the summit of some natural wonder or religious shrine of gongs and bells without reawakening the lonely heart. The Psalmist knew our own need to be lifted up. How often with prayers of repetition the soul yearns for God's upward call and enfoldment in his eternal arms.

Of course, an "ascent" does not always require a physical motion. The "ascent" is as spiritual and metaphorical as it is literal and psychological. God offers it to us as an invitation to enter, once again, into that quiet enclave within our hearts where he who sees and hears in secret blesses us with his presence and grace. Actually, a "descent" from secular heights to the "little brown church in the vale" can awake fevered hearts and feed famished souls as effectively as the rose windows of Notre Dame, or the stain-glassed portraits of Jesus kneeling at Gethsemane. Anyone who has ever made the descent from Jerusalem, down past the Kidron Brook, to the Roman Catholic shrine of the Garden of Gethsemane, can vouch for the same. Intensely hot outside, but cool within, the sanctuary's narrow windows of glowing blue and white crosses lift the soul immediately into God's secret sphere of the Holy.

The pilgrim's path to sacred shrines energizes the soul; nor must we ever denigrate the heart's trek for such. The experience assuages our sense of obligation, while expressing our gratitude for what God has done. It is part of one's private and personal act of humility before God. It is a facet of our individual call to fulfill a measure of discipleship, which we hope will be pleasing to God. Did not his own Son say: "If any man would come after me, let him deny himself and take up his cross and follow me?" (Mark 8:34b) In no way do such ascents belittle God's gift of grace; rather, our "ascents" are his way of reaching down to us. Our "ascents" provide a way for self-examination, leading to the realization that only God's "descent" alone saves us.

~ ~ ~

> To thee I lift up my eyes, O thou who art enthroned in the heavens! . . . Have mercy upon us, O LORD, . . . for we have had more than enough of contempt.
>
> Psalm 123:1, 3

The young professor who dropped by my office remarked that he'd never be able to forget the smirk on the world-class scholar's face when the committee on which the latter served favored another candidate over his application. "Not that I wasn't qualified," he moaned. "I've even out published the person they selected. But it was the way he looked at me," he stated. "He had cocked his head just so, you know," he re-enacted the scholar's dismissive gesture. "You know what he said to me? He said, 'You've got your niche, haven't you? Why not go home and be happy with it?' The condescension on his face was devastating. Even he couldn't mask his contemptuous appraisal of me. I vowed then and there that I would never permit his haughty leer to curtail my call to scholarship. If I may be so bold!" Nor did the young man, whose work went on to receive international acclaim.

Contempt is an eviscerating experience, both to overcome as well as suffer. The philosopher Sartre devoted an entire chapter to the subject in his *Being and Nothingness*. In his now recognized groundbreaking study of phenomenology, he called attention to what he identified as "the Other." We are not just beings-for-ourselves, but we are beings who also relate to others, and for whom the phenomenon of the Other relates to us. Like it or not, it is possible for the Other's glance to reduce us to an "object" rather than a person. When that occurs, the Other's "look" unleashes a series of destructive modes. We can be made to experience shame, fear—even slavery—by such a glance, claims Sartre,[2] and rightly so. For that is precisely what the young professor experienced by the so-called world-class scholar's "glance."

What Sartre called the "look," our Psalmist simply catalogs as "contempt." If we should ever fall prey to it, it is essential to recover ourselves as quickly as possible. It goes for the jugular. It says more about the person dismissing you than it says about you. But at the time of the cutting remark, or immolating dig, one's heart reels back, uncertain as to how to respond. Israel suffered it often; so did Judah. The nation as a whole chose to pray, to lift its collective soul to God whose reign o'er all the earth alone knew best how to judge and preserve Israel. Biblical scholarship denotes such prayers as "laments."

The world can make you lament; it can make you draw back, feel insecure and afraid to venture up the hill of your own calling toward new horizons. The Psalmist fell back on God's mercy, and in God's strength, found marrow to renew his own. Jesus bore Pilate's inquisition in John's Gospel with quiet solemnity. He could have sneered at his persecutors, glared back at them with the fire of his holy glance, or insisted on his right to subpoena witnesses. He could have mocked the crowd, ridiculed them from the treasure house of his command of scripture. But he didn't. He could have towered over them as Sartre's Other. Rather, he stood in silence against those whose breasts brimmed with contempt and hate. Condescension cannot overcome contempt, nor anger hate, nor jealously spite, nor pride self-love. Only a forgiving heart that is buoyed by eternal

---

2. Sartre, *Being and Nothingness*, 268–278.

love can transform the world. In time that's what the young professor had to do: simply forgive the world famous scholar who should have known better.

Not an easy task, is it? It wasn't for Israel; it wasn't for Judah; it wasn't for God's Son, nor was it for the Psalmist, or those few remaining priests whose memories went back to the splendor of Solomon's Temple. The Psalmist is talking about love. Psalm 123 points us to the highest rung to which we can ascend this side of Eternity, and that is love. And that is for us to inculcate, too. Love.

∼ ∼ ∼

> If it had not been the LORD who was on our side, . . . when men rose up against us, then they would have swallowed us alive, . . . then over us would have gone the raging waters.
>
> Psalm 124:1, 3, 5

Israel never forgot her fear of the primal chaos that ruled over the watery *tehom* or frightful abyss that haunted the Sumerian myths of Rahab and Tiamat. The Psalmists knew, along with Israel, how real life's chaotic seas of terror become unless God is there to expel the darkness. Mankind favors the darkness over light, chaos over clarity when his deeds are evil, for, like Adam and Eve, he awakens with remorse from his evening slumbers gone sour.

The Psalmist does not wish that to happen to you or to me. Nor does the living God who inspired him. But we have to want God to be on our side, or else we do chose darkness. Even when God is on our side, we still succumb to darkness. "I can will what is good but cannot do it," Paul lamented. "Woe is me!" he abjured his soul. He knew Luther's "righteousness of the law" condemned him and that only Christ's "righteousness of faith" could save him, though he knew nothing of Luther. Only if God is on our side can we escape the darkness of Rahab's shards or overcome them in our lives. The darkness is there. There's no escaping that. If God had not been on Israel's side, where would Israel be today? If God were not on your side, or my side, where would we be today?

"O LORD God, how we need thee on our side! Our souls cry to thee by day and our prayers ascend even in our sleep. We pray thee, LORD, to guard our soul, our going out and our coming in, for we know that the waters of *tehom*—that void and restless pit—are ever present. We thank thee, LORD, with all our heart that in our darkest hour thou art nigh, within, without, and all around, for thy Name's sake. Amen."

∼ ∼ ∼

> As the mountains are round about Jerusalem, so the LORD is round about his people, from this time forth and for evermore.
>
> Psalm 125:2

Standing on the Mt. of Olives brings unimagined joy to anyone beholding Jerusalem for the first time, especially from that advantage. As you look westward toward the City of David and down and out across the Kidron Valley—toward those massive stones that Herod and later Suleiman placed to shore up the southeastern corner's wall—you are simultaneously awestruck and humbled. From the Mount's view, the walls bespeak of a time and place too holy ever to forget. In the late spring, a plot of ripe dark wheat grows west of the road that borders the shadows of the pink-and-yellow polished granite. The Dome of the Rock equally glows in golden splendor in the molten midday sun. Tombstones tilt eerily on the steep slope beneath the Eastern Gate, and all across the city, minarets and Christian spires bestow a sacred calm of long ago, still girdled "round about" the City.

During the fevered decade of the 1960s, attending presbytery meetings in old Norfolk Presbytery had its moments of rapture amid the season of America's political sighs and numerous sorrows. Singing the great hymns of the Church before the Moderator's gavel came cracking down—surrounded by God and his faithful saints of old—brought encouragement and spiritual wisdom to the attendees' commitments of time and loyalty. As we sang shoulder to shoulder, I found especial strength in one of the closing hymns:

> Glorious things of thee are spoken, Zion, city of our God;
> He whose word cannot be broken, Formed thee for His own abode;
> On the Rock of Ages founded, What can shake thy sure resolve?
> With salvation's wall surrounded, Thou mayest smile at all thy foes.

One does not have to climb the Mt. of Olives or live surrounded by hills or mountains to appreciate the Psalmist's soliloquy. God's grace surrounds us every day, and his protective arms of love and justice await our personal embrace. Mankind will never rise to the level of perfectibility to which our noblest wills aspire, but surrounded by God's promised presence and guided by bold faith, we, too, like David's city, can become a beacon of hope and light for our time.

∽ ∽ ∽

> When the LORD restored the fortunes of Zion, . . . our mouth was filled with laughter. . . . He that goes forth weeping, bearing the seed for sowing, shall come home with shouts of joy, bringing his sheaves with him.
>
> Psalm 126:1–2, 6

As a child on the farm, my favorite season was spring. With the arrival of Spring, yellow-bright jonquils filled the barren spaces between the yard's cedar fence posts, and nearby dogwoods formed graceful white borders about the pasture opposite the front porch. The first blades of wheat covered the hills with their green carpet, and woolly sheep with mud-red flanks came down from the hills with their sturdy lambs, bleating for food and water, still wanting to nurse.

I loved going to church and singing to the top of my lungs, "Bringing in the sheep!" I had no idea the revered hymn was actually devoted to "bringing in the sheaves." We never danced around with "sheaves of wheat" in our hands, like pagan worshippers of ancient times. We let them grow into tall tan shafts before harvesting their tawny heads of grain. So, yes, I was shocked when as late as my first year of seminary, and singing once again to the top of my lungs, I glanced down to realize the word was "sheaves," not "sheep." "Hey, there's a mistake here!" I wanted to blurt. "This hymnal's got it wrong!" Luckily, I kept quiet, glanced about, and fell into silence. It's supposed to be "sheep," not "sheaves" my crushed soul objected with a wounded pout. To this day, I still think "sheep" whenever singing the hymn. Why would anyone want to cavort around waving sheaves? Aren't sheep far more precious in Jesus' eyes? Isn't he remembered as the "Good Shepherd"? Whoever praises him for being the "Good Miller"? The good and the bad grow together, he warned. You will always find tares among the stalks of wheat. Don't be misled, he advised. God will know what to do when the harvest season arrives.

In retrospect, whether "sheaves" or "sheep," the Psalmist is thanking God for new beginnings. He is thanking God for the Israelite's liberation from bondage from their Babylonian Captivity. Life is good! Yes, there is a time to weep as well as a time to plant; a time to brood as well as a time to laugh; a time to sow as well as a time to reap. Life is like that. It has been that way for centuries. It is inseparable from our fallen human condition, which God fully comprehends, which is why his arms are ever open and his love eternal.

∽ ∽ ∽

> Unless the LORD builds the house, those who build it labor in vain [*sahweh*]. Unless the LORD watches over the city, the watchman stays awake in vain. It is in vain that you rise up early and go late to rest, eating the bread of anxious toil; for he gives to his beloved sleep. Lo, sons are a heritage from the LORD, . . . (Psalm 127:1–3a). You shall be happy, and it shall be well with you. Your wife will be like a fruitful vine; . . . your children . . . like olive shoots.
>
> Psalm 128:2–3

Psalms 127 and 128 are tandem psalms, the latter following the precepts enjoined in the former. Both are Wisdom Psalms, added by the Psalter's editor as an element of the piety associated with attending the festivals in Zion in front of the "house" that YHWH built. That house represented more than the Temple, or the city of David, or even the hoped for Messiah to come. All of that is embraced under the metaphor of the "house that the LORD builds." For the Wisdom Writers, without God as the foundation of any "house," all else is built in vain [*sahweh*]. Strive as you may, neither your vigilance, nor labor, nor home life, nor rest will abate the "anxious toil" that defines existence.

In Hebrew, as in English, a life that comes up "vain" is "empty," "ineffectual," "void," if not "worthless." Who can ever forget Socrates' self-defense before the Athenian Assembly? "O men of Athens.... are you not ashamed of heaping up the greatest amount of money and honour... and caring so little about wisdom and truth and the greatest improvement of the soul?"[3] The Wisdom Writers acknowledged the same, whether they lived before or after Socrates. Perhaps "worthless" is too strong a predicate, but "empty" and "ineffectual" certainly are not. We were created to enjoy more than a life defined by "vanity," or devastated by "anxious toil," especially at the expense of neglecting the improvement of the soul.

The Danish philosopher Søren Kierkegaard analyzed the human condition in a similar manner in his work, *Stages of Life's Way*. He identified three stages, of which only the third fulfills human existence satisfactorily. They are the aesthetic, the ethical, and the religious, not that we don't participate in all three at one time or other or even seriatim. For Kierkegaard, the first two always leave us "empty," if not burdened by a sense of the "void." He defined the aesthetic stage as a life of *immediacy*, lived for the now, without thought of lasting or binding relationships. The ethical pursues the dutiful and legal; it is a life lived in conformity with *requirements* and social duty. It shoulders a more responsible weight of the common good; yet, it too can result in an "empty" life, attained without fulfillment of the heart's personal ache. Only a life ventured in devotion to the Eternal can safeguard the heart from the soul's collapse in pursuit of the first and second stages.[4]

Kierkegaard's insight is mirrored visibly in Psalms 127 and 128, where the ethical, subservient to the religious, and the aesthetic, subservient to the Eternal, finally contribute to a balanced and fruitful life of many sons, a loving wife, and a happy household. Yes, it may be overly optimistic, a universal glimpse of what individual families can strive to attain, but in the Wisdom Writers' tradition, it was far preferable to a wasted existence of "anxious toil." As is always the case, such wisdom puts us to the question, too. At which stage of life are we? What foundation

---

3. Jowett, *Apology in Dialogues*, I, 412–413.
4. Kierkegaard, *Stages*, 476–480.

undergirds our "house"? Beyond our aesthetic and ethical pursuits, what part does God play in our lives?

"O LORD, who rulest over all stages of life and surely lovest us at whatever stage we are, come and lift us by thy grace to thy highest longing for each of us that we may find our perfect peace in thee. Bless our love of life, our passion for joy and fulfillment. Strengthen our desire for meaningful employment, a happy family, and a duty to improve the self, as we equally care for others. In your Son's name, Amen."

∽ ∽ ∽

> May all who hate Zion be put to shame
> and turned backward [*achor*]!
>
> Psalm 129:3

Achor, or *achorannith*, without any ambiguity, means: "to turn away," and that in the most aggressive and humiliating manner. All who hate Zion will meet that fate. Granted Babylon, the Romans, the Inquisition, Pogroms, and the Holocaust humbled God's people, nevertheless, Jewry survived. The Mishnah and the Talmud became their new homeland, their spiritual Zion and City of David. Not even the Romans could take that from them, nor Hitler's attempt to eradicate Judaism from the face of the earth. Judaism prevailed against his gates of terror. Nor can mankind destroy those whom God loves, even in humankind's proudest hours of vanity or denial of God. The Psalmist is not speaking here of "walls" per se, or just any "city on a hill," not even Jerusalem. No! He is addressing the Reality of God, whom no evil can ever crush out of the human heart. All who attempt to do so, do it to their own dishonor. The Greatness of God is unassailable. It is like his Son's reference to the Church, against which not even the Gates of Hell can prevail.

Having said all this, however, an equivalent disdain for those who despise the "house of the LORD," is equally of no avail. Jerusalem's ancient Temple is gone, along with its sacred candelabra, now depicted on an inner panel in the shadows of Titus' Victory Arch. Hate has never overcome hate. Only love and forgiveness open life's gates to goodness. Remember the German youth who journeyed from their homeland to work on Israel's kibbutzim. They came as a sign of their generation's commitment to peace and order. As descendants of Germany's nobler past, of its era of Goethe, Beethoven, Bach, and Wagner; Luther, Schleiermacher, Schweitzer, and Bonhoeffer, they wanted their lives to make a difference; they wanted to atone for the "shame" of their fathers; they wanted to demonstrate a spirit of embracement and renewal.

As we search our hearts, the Psalmist's message of God's enduring love and providential care—through good times and evil—is offered to us once again. May we open the gates of our own "house," our own secret chamber wherein we long for redemption, for God to enter and dwell in our hearts, forever!

∽ ∽ ∽

> Out of the depths [*maamaqqim*] I cry to thee, O LORD! LORD, hear my voice! If thou, O LORD, shouldst mark iniquities, LORD, who could stand?
>
> Psalm 130:1–3

We have come to the sixth Penitential Psalm—one we have all prayed at one time or other. Not just Augustine. "Out of the depths I cry to thee, O LORD! Let thy ears be attentive to the voice of my supplications!" Frequently in the Psalms, the "depths" refers to the primeval waters that the ancient world feared. Such is the case in Psalm 46. At other times, the reference is to the biblical Pit that the fallen equally dread, or to the silent land of Sheol—that final resting place of all BCE souls. Here, however, the "depths" represent something totally more complex—that inconsolable disquietude, or "loneliest loneliness," of which Nietzsche foretold, when we descend into the fearful and fragmented fathoms of our soul, and there encounter that emptiness that only the Eternal can fill.

For Tillich, this Psalm played a sentinel role in support of his designation of God as the Ground of Being, that beyond which we cannot go and which underlies all existence. The "depths" bring us to this Ground; it confronts us with the truth about ourselves in all our finitude and anxiety. It startles us with the realization that the true and only anodyne for the soul's void is faith in God. What the "depths" confirms is that God is inescapable. We cannot avoid God anymore than we can avoid experiencing the "depths." It remains one of Christianity's principal core beliefs:

to know God is to know how bankrupt the self is. In turn, to know the self is to know how thoroughly we need God's grace.

That is why the third verse follows with perfect consistency. "If thou shouldst mark iniquities . . . ?" The Psalmist knew that to know the self is to know how much the heart requires God. Concomitantly, to know God is to realize how shattered our lives are, yet how redeemable when at our lowest ebb we turn to God. "If thou shouldst mark iniquities, who could stand?" Here is Luther's "righteousness of the law," satisfied by nothing less than God's "righteousness of grace." What the Psalmist preserves for each of us is the truth about all mankind: that the self before God—in the very throes of its loneliness—is closer to God than when it feels secure and above reproach. Such insight allows the Psalmist to withdraw in peace, as well as in renewed hope for himself and for his chastised nation. His plea for Israel to "hope in the LORD" expresses equally his desire for the fractured community of Israel to find courage again, in order to be about the things that matter most.

∽ ∽ ∽

> But I have calmed and quieted my soul, like a child quieted at its mother's breast.
>
> Psalm 131:2

While pausing during a lunch break—high in the Toe-Cane River District's mountains of North Carolina—Reedy and I watched as a young doe emerged from the forest with her tiny speckled newborn. The little fellow followed its mother as closely as it could. She twitched her ears and peered in our direction. We froze where we sat against a fallen log. Her tiny nimble offspring wobbled on its flimsy legs as it wagged its white tail and nudged her underside to nurse. Slowly, the doe picked her way across the half-logged clearing, guiding her precious fawn to the safety of flowering rhododendron and young buckeye undergrowth. Never once did the little fawn suspect our presence or sense itself in danger from the hunter/gatherer instinct of our human world. Years later, while hunting with members of a hunt club on the edge of the Dismal Swamp, I recall how saddened I felt when a member shot a speckled fawn that was racing wildly from pursuing dogs. No doubt its mother fell too, as nine deer were harvested that morning.

Innocence would carry no meaning in a world without harm. The Psalmist's metaphor of the child nursing at its mother's breast was meant to celebrate the joy and blessing of entrusting our lives to God. Our lives are so infinitesimally insignificant against the sprawling glory of the immensity of the universe's innumerable stars. All one has to do is view those glowing spirals of heavenly spheres to realize the breadth and depth of God's phenomenal universe. How it all drifts like sparkling ice deep beyond and deep within the silent blackness of the night sky! Yet in that bright and cold domain, God's love descends to each of us to guide and nurture our finite souls.

It is a good Psalm, one to cherish, to value, and love.

"O Heavenly Father, never let us drift so far from thee, as to lose our way in the wondrous forest that thou has planted for thy children everywhere. Keep our soul and wandering heart ever close to thee. Guide our steps through dark and light, through fear and pleasure, that we may all our life cherish Thee!"

∽ ∽ ∽

> For the LORD has chosen Zion; he has desired it for his habitation: "This is my resting placed for ever; here I will dwell, for I have desired it."
>
> Psalm 132:13–14

Remember, the Wisdom Writers never claimed inerrancy for themselves or for their writings, nor did the Psalmists or their final editor(s) assert as much. Based on God's loving kindness and his desired righteous ordering, they responded to his grace with fulsome honor. Nor did they fail to cry to him in seasons of lamentation and sorrow, or fail to praise him in times of thanksgiving, nor did they hide their sins and deserved reprobation. To love and revere God was the alpha and omega of their poetic dwelling, as well as their legacy to us. Not a mountain, nor a city, nor a place, other than the quiet citadel of the heart—that is where God dwells. All the rabbis have known that, as well as Jesus in his homey statement about the silent and secret closet where God awaits our broken and hungry soul.

You are Zion; I am the Zion that together forms the habitation where God's love and kindness, encouragement and mercy dwell. We carry within our hearts all the relics of forgiveness and salvation that any pilgrim could ever long to know, thanks to God. Through our hands and labor, our thoughtfulness and effort, God extends his grace and mercy to the world. We are the frontline of his quiet offensive to reclaim humanity, his holy ambassadors, whether we realize it or not. Ascend to Jerusalem, lay flowers on the steps of Buddha's Golden Pagoda in Bangkok, or sit in silence before the meditative gardens of a Zen temple; but the holiest place to find God is in the act of showing love to anyone who needs it, whether in the hour of their greatest weight, or loneliest loneliness, or in the depths of their loss and sorrow, bewilderment and need. It is all there in Matthew 25:31–46. That is where you will find God and where God dwells. In you! Yes, in you and me, notwithstanding his eternal transcendence. For whenever and wherever we welcome his presence in our hearts, he reaches out to others, inspiring us as we reach back to him.

May that Zion forever thrive and promote God's peace!

~ ~ ~

> Behold, how good and pleasant it is when brothers dwell in unity! (Psalm 133:1) Come, bless the LORD, all you servants of the LORD, who stand by night in the house of the LORD! . . . May the LORD bless you from Zion, he who made heaven and earth!
>
> Psalm 134:1, 3

To love one's brother by day, and to stand vigil by night in the house of the LORD, captures the sentiment of the Psalmist's hope in this last "Song of Ascents." Something of the essence of religion is encapsulated here: to stand vigil day and night with one's brother/sister as well as with God—especially at night. It speaks directly to the heart as well as our human condition. It was an endemic part of Israel's annual ascents as they went up to pay tribute to the living God. This unity of brothers and sisters, committed to each other and to the heartbeat of their nation—all under the guidance and love of God—was a cherished revelation to Jacob's sons, which none wished to disavow.

Where is such unity today, such commitment to God and his steadfast love and righteous ideal for all? The Psalmist is not necessarily speaking here of conformity, but of unity. You can have unity without conformity, justice and still cherish liberty. We need not blame God, or each other, nor anyone else but ourselves for unity's demise in our time. The pendulum of left and right, change and tradition, swings ever to and fro, so also the Juggernaut of challenge and recoil. All of it shapes our personal history, our actions, destiny, and highest thought. To that extent, Hegel was philosophically right. Time moves on, just as Heraclius' rolling river defies our stepping twice into its restless stream. Nonetheless, somehow, this quiet recognition of humankind's unity and guardianship of what is holy, stirs our fallen souls. Yes! The Psalmist is correct! Utopias are a dream; reality a different matter; but God's desire for our peace and wholeness trumps all cynicism. Thankfully, by his grace, it calls us to a higher standard of hope and salvation. It can begin today, both in the solitude of our souls and in our care of one another. It can be ours by day and by night, "like the dew of Hermon, which falls on the mountains of Zion!" (Ps 133:3)

"O God, may we open our hearts to thee! May we welcome the dew of the joy of thy salvation! May it fall upon us as thy anointing oil of old emboldened Aaron and thy holy people to love and serve thee! May we too rise up to do thy will! Amen!"

15

By the Waters of Babylon

> He it was who smote the first-born of Egypt, both of man and of beast; who in thy midst, O Egypt, sent signs and wonders against Pharaoh and all his servants.
>
> Psalm 135:8–9

IN SO MANY RESPECTS, the Waters of Babylon during the Exile re-echo what happened along the River Nile. Sometimes God has to forestall one power in order to redeem another, humble one in order to save another, crush an oppressor in order to liberate the oppressed. It is the story of all humankind, preserved even in the Hebrew Bible. Can you name a nation that came to power that wasn't challenged in time, or crushed by another nation coming to power that didn't fear a similar fate? The kingdoms of this world are like that, yet God's "signs and wonders" endure to transform and salvage lives.

Pharaoh, the plagues, and the odious story of the dying frogs, gnats, cattle, and humans alike—bloated and floating in the waters of the Nile—capped by the hardening of the powerless pharaoh's heart, combine to form searching metaphors applicable to our self-understanding. One could well exclaim: "O Egypt, whom God had to 'smote' to bring you down, to bring you to your senses! How your plagues symbolize my own fallen pride-bloated self, floating in a sea of fear and sorrow, blind to God's 'signs and wonders!' Indeed, how right Calvin was to find in you a mirror of my soul!" A bit too much, the mind balks, but not the captive or oppressed heart! Only God provides man's ultimate salvation; he alone our highest liberation from our self-determining efforts gone awry.

While enjoying a tour break amid attending an international conference on Calvin (held in Hungary), a passenger on our bus fascinated me with his knowledge of Mediterranean geography, history, culture, and lore. Since we were seated together, I asked him his nationality and professional background. He answered the second part first. "A business man," he replied. "As for the first inquiry," he smiled, "your President recently dropped a little gift outside our Leader's tent." The latter was in reference to President Ronald Reagan's decision to bomb Muammar Gaddafi's headquarters in order to shake up his regime. The point: a hardened heart neither serves mankind, nor generates peace and goodwill. As stubborn as Gaddafi was, he got the message; and in the end, his own people turned against him.

"O LORD of all time, Creator of heaven and earth, search the hidden places of our souls, lest our own resistance should threaten to undo our life and hope. Free us from all rancorous inner plagues, whose morbid end is self-decay and death, that we may be liberated to love and follow thee all the days of our life, treating our neighbor with dignity and respect. Amen."

~~~

It is he who remembered us in our low estate, for
his steadfast love endures for ever; . . .

Psalm 136:23

Egypt, the Exodus, the years of wandering in the Sinai and Negev, the conquest of Canaan, along with the defeat of the Amorites, the kingdoms of Og and Bashan, all—all of YHWH's mighty deeds—are celebrated in this hymn of thanksgiving. However, it is verse 23, along with verse 24 that humbles the heart: "who remembered us in our low estate . . . and rescued us from our foes." In addition, the Temple choir punctuates this grateful hymn no less than twenty-one times with the joyful, uplifting, antiphonal refrain: "for his steadfast love endures for ever."

It is one thing to remember the great deeds of any nation's history, or celebrate its defining moments and watershed victories, its art, culture, and civilization; however, it is quite another to kneel before God and thank him for his enduring presence. This is especially so when one is weak and broken, or of low estate and beaten down by foes and bouts of depression, yet in its heart sings: "Thank you, God, for your steadfast love and eternal mercy." Whatever encouragement lies in books, or stares down on us from national monuments, God's grace multiplies and doubles.

Anyone who has ever looked up at Lincoln's face in his memorial, or stared in awe at the figures chiseled into Mt. Rushmore, or wandered the fields of Gettysburg, the Arlington Cemetery, or passed by the white-marbled crosses and Stars of David that over look Omaha Beach, or toured Athens, Rome, Paris, or Edinburgh, Potsdam, Weimar, or Luther's Wartburg, has a sense of appreciation, too deep for words, of the sacrifice and zeal required for the building of a civilization. Yet! More than all that is here! Monuments age and crumble; tapestries mold or dry rot; histories are rewritten to support the peeves of the writer; cemeteries become neglected and their headstones topple. Only one thing endures: God's steadfast love. Thus the Temple priests sang it with fervor, if not a sense of rectitude.

We are creatures of time, place, culture, and heritage—all of which is dear to us, whether embedded in our past, conscious in the present, or as a form of metaphysical reality, governing our future choices for a meaningful life. What the Psalmist reminds us is that all of that is measured vis-à-vis the one, enduring, life-fulfilling promise we have: God's grace. He alone is the abiding constant that underlies and undergirds all else. That is why pride can never be the ultimate standard for the fulfillment of mankind's dreams or of a nation's destiny, or a civilization's contribution to what is good, beautiful, or noble.

∼ ∼ ∼

> By the waters of Babylon, there we sat down and wept, when we remembered Zion. On the willows there we hung up our lyres. . . . How shall we sing the LORD's song in a foreign land?
>
> Psalm 137:1-2, 4

Few lines of Scripture equal these. How spiritually accurate Hölderlin was and still is! Regardless of one's opinion of his views, like Nietzsche's

"Mad Man's Speech," or Rilke's *einmal, und nicht mehr,* his insight bears the truth that our time still needs to hear. We do live poetically on the earth, as all the playwrights—Greek or contemporary, Elizabethan or modern—knew and know.

To be or not to be?

remains a valid question. Cast in poetic form, it enables us to ruminate on our soul's condition before one another and God.

In truth, how beautiful and devastating the Psalmist's words are! Are not the waters of Babylon those ceaseless rivers that run through our hearts; where we hang our harps on life's willow limbs, too sad to sing, yet not too sad to weep when life goes wrong?

The truth is, life doesn't have to "go wrong" for our hearts to mourn a loss or struggle with despair. Life is like that, surrounded by moments of remembrance of joy and sorrow. We never forget the "Jerusalems" of our past, or cease to anticipate their rediscovery at some future time. "You can't go home again," wrote Thomas Wolfe, but your ruminations never die. Your Jerusalem is still there—those long ago, past events of nostalgic or melancholic bliss, or of intense yearnings and passion. Setbacks and defeats are part of life, as well as memories of young love, schooldays, career, and the creating of new hearths. Life requires the investment of God's talents, which he has given us. Not all our investments repay dollar for dollar, but life invites risk, lest we lose both the physical and spiritual capital that God has invested in us.

The lonely in Exile stared into the streams of the Tigris and Euphrates and longed for home again. The home to which they returned caused the elderly among them to weep as they sweated with shovel and trowel in hand and wiped the tears from their eyes, but they built a new Jerusalem, a Second Temple, and completed their Torah and Books of Psalms to sing once again to the Glory of God.

It is all right to weep, to throw oneself down by the waters of Babylon and long for joy again. But the greatness of God resides in the strength he provides when we struggle to our feet, wash the tears from our eyes, and bend our hearts once more to serve and love God and neighbor.

As for the dashing of one's enemies' babies against their city's walls, we must leave that to the time and place of the ancient world, as well as the weeping of God.

> On the day I called, thou didst answer me, . . .
> Though I walk in the midst of trouble [*sarah*], thou
> dost preserve my life.
>
> Psalm 138:3, 7

Trouble comes in many forms. In an age of pop-culture and pop-psychology, we are often urged to "move forward," "adjust our attitude," "leave the past behind," "step up to the next level," "think positive thoughts," "see ourselves already where we want to be," etc. All of these counseling insights are worthy of their aim. We need not denigrate any. Yet, the soul hungers for more. Its memory bank of past woes can't help but jolt our happier moments with its solemn bell of old wounds. We live "in the midst" of these, in the face of recurring and debilitating troubles, not in their absence. Even the most hermetic monk or devout nun cannot escape a restless past, or the shattered hopes they bring to a monastic life. Not even David could, to whom the Psalmist attributes this piece. That is why grace is essential, because it "preserves" our life in spite of Babylon's doleful streams that bring to surface remembered woes.

His was a biblical name, given to him by his mother. Named for one of the Old Testament archangels, his quiet demeanor evinced as much. Hardship had stooped his shoulders—though he was only in his early-forties—tinted his arched eyebrows gray, and snatched patches of pepper-black hair from his head. A cobbler by trade, he had been a student of music before his parents succeeded in sneaking him out of Austria before the *Anschluss* changed all. He never saw them again. It was only after Israel's independence was established that he made it to the Haifa area and later to the kibbutz to which our group was assigned. There he learned of his parents' death and of a sister, living in Poland, unable to immigrate and join him. He didn't even know her address.

By day he made shoes, brogans, and sandals, and stitched cloth bags for gathering fruit and vegetables. He also cut out and assembled shoulder pads for transferring banana bunches from the groves to the tractor carts for hauling back to the kibbutz. Industrious he was, to say the least. By night he sat in the refectory, sipping on a glass of sweet wine, slipping off to his sleeping quarters after dark. He showed an interest in all the members of our group, though three-fourths of the "kids" were German. His eyes masked his story, as well as his smile. I was fortunate one evening to catch him in a mellow mood and asked him, "G, . . . what was it like as a young teenager, wondering where your parents were, and what might happen to you?" He looked up, somewhat shocked, as if I surely understood how painful those years had to have been; then put his hands to his face for a moment. "I was fortunate, that's all," he said. "Now I am here." Later that spring, he made a pair of sandals for me that lasted for fifteen years. I was still wearing them as a young professor teaching courses in philosophy and religion. Sometimes when I showed slides of the kibbutz, it would all come back to me. For G . . . wasn't the only refugee whose home was the kibbutz. Almost half of its residents were survivors of the Diaspora that Hitler sought to destroy. Because evil is so evil, God has his hands full trying to "preserve" us all; but through friends and the sacrifice of loved ones, he saved G . . . and countless more. We must see it that way else we are no better than the minions who do evil's will. We do not have to.

"O God, in the midst of our own troubles, may we never forget the sufferings of others, lest we fail to serve either man or thee. O thou who preservest us, not merely in our times of triumph and success, but in the heart of our spiritual darkness and most anxious hours, to thee, O LORD, may our hearts ever turn in praise and thanksgiving, gratitude and love, whether by day or by night. Amen."

16
The Unsearchable and Immeasurable Depths of God

> O LORD, thou has searched me and known me! . . . Even before a word is on my tongue, lo, O LORD, thou knowest it altogether. . . . Such knowledge is too wonderful for me; it is high, I cannot attain it. . . . Whiter shall I go from thy Spirit? Or whither shall I flee from thy presence? If I ascend to heaven, thou art there! If I make my bed in Sheol, thou art there!
>
> Psalm 139:1, 4, 6–8

If there is one, lone, pinnacle Psalm, Psalm 139 qualifies for the title. It stands shoulder-to-shoulder with Psalms 130, 116, 90, 51, 42, 23, and 8. One might even argue that it towers above them. Why? Because it confirms what every heart knows: that God is inescapable, an innate, inborn presence we can never flee; yet whose wisdom and omniscience is beyond our capacity to comprehend or conceive.

Two schools of theology vie for attention here. The most ancient is Augustine's, whose Neo-Platonic views found strength and joy in the soul's "ascent to God." As his mind scaled the ladder of intellectual ascent, moving from the earthly to the heavenly, and from the mortal to the Eternal, Augustine delighted in contemplating the immeasurable and unsearchable reaches of God. There all wisdom, joy, love, and grace abounded beyond imagination. The other school, represented by Pseudo-Dionysus the Areopagite (late Patristic Period) and Karl Barth of modern times, favored an opposing view. Dionysus doubted that the finite mind of man had anything in common with God. So also believed Barth. For both, fallen humanity may know of God's existence as an *idea* but cannot know God as *God*. Mankind can only know how fallen, miserable, estranged, and alienated they are. However, in Augustine's case, far to the contrary, the heart that longs for God feels loved, wanted, and nearer to God than in Barth's approach. Indeed, the Augustinian way senses God's presence as a reality already within one's heart. No distance separates God from man other than man's indifference to God.

Clearly the Psalmist was "Augustinian," while as a "Barthian" he realized how little his soul comprehended the true mind of God. We can believe both: that God is near, immediately accessible in our souls; while realizing how little we know of God aside from his self-revelation in Scripture. That is what makes God God, creator of heaven and earth, and our only, holy, true, and living savior.

Indeed, it is a pinnacle Psalm. In truth, most hearts are scarcely swayed by theology, as essential as theology is. What mends our hearts and heals our spirits is precisely what the Psalmist experienced in his own depths: that God is ever at hand, ever near, and that even the darkest hours of our darkness are not dark to God. Lo, he is there, our light in the midst of darkness, our joy and our redemption, elements of any religion's theology of wholeness and grace.

***

> Guard me, O LORD, from the hands of the wicked; preserve me from violent men, . . . I know that the LORD maintains the cause of the afflicted, and executes justice for the needy.
>
> Psalm 140:4, 12

The men in the County's Work Detention Center "welcomed" my appearance with silence and, no doubt, some indifference. Being required to endure religious services was part of their unspoken sentence in keeping with the County's long tradition. After all, the South has always prided itself on its "chain gangs" and their amenable behavior, notwithstanding guards and shotguns. Nonetheless, the inmates studied me with doubtful eyes as I entered the facility and, alone, by a makeshift podium, eyed the group myself.

Dressed in khakis, jeans, sweaters, flannel shirts, slippers or brogans, the men sat on the edge of their beds, some slumped forward in chairs turned backwards, so as to rest their arms on the chair-back as they faced me. "Good afternoon!" I greeted them. "Amen!" several black men replied—one with a smile as disarming as a child's. "Let us worship God," I stated, as I turned to Psalm 130: "Out of the depths I cry to thee, O LORD!" Immediately, many identified with the Psalmist's lament and listened quietly as I read the rest of the Psalm. I don't remember what I said, but I delivered an abbreviated version of the sermon I had preached earlier in town. The service ended with the "Lord's Prayer" and the singing of "Blest be the tie that binds." Throughout the service, many black inmates often joined in with an appreciative, "Amen!" Others just sat there. It was hard to read their thoughts. It was the first time I had ever ventured any form of prison ministry, and I walked out feeling empty, saddened by their eyes and demeanor, and confident I had failed miserably.

I would go back several other times, as well as make pastoral visits to the inmates in the town's jail. Most of these men were awaiting trial, their charges ranging anywhere from public drunkenness to assault and battery, petty theft and domestic violence. Many were still angry and wanted "release" more than "redemption." "Preacher, what I need is a lawyer. Not you, sir! No offense!" Still, I'd walk around to the various cells and offer prayer where it was wanted. The cells were cold, narrow, and the bedsprings lacked mattresses. I was too young, or either too naïve, to know whether I was achieving more good than harm. But several months after I ended visits to the Work Detention Center, the black man who had welcomed me with his smile came by my office one afternoon to thank me and to ask for my help in writing a recommendation for him to find work. It is so easy to condemn the "wicked" and the "violent." Indeed, many need to be in prison, isolated from society, restrained lest they hurt others again. Nonetheless, they and we alike need forgiveness and understanding, grace and comfort from those who care. They need our love and efforts to fund rehabilitation, to preach the good news to the evil as well as to the good. For in God's eyes, we are all in need of redemption and grace. Surely, "Amen!" As those humble, incarcerated souls moaned.

> I call upon thee, O LORD; make haste to me! ... Set a guard over my mouth, O LORD, keep watch over the door of my lips! Incline not my heart to any evil, to busy myself with wicked deeds ...
>
> Psalm 141:1, 3–4a

The Mosaic Covenant captures the above in two of its more unforgettable Commandments: "Thou shalt not bear false witness, nor covet anything of thy neighbors." The Buddha addressed the same temptations in his famous "Noble Eightfold Path." Steps Three and Five express his concern equally succinctly. They are known as "Right Speech" and "Right Livelihood."

Both the Ninth Commandment and the Buddha's Third Injunction speak directly to our hearts, unnerving us with their unflinching, cathartic diagnosis: "A loose tongue can destroy your soul, your happiness, your dignity, if not your life. Don't let it happen to you!" It is so easy to violate that truth, especially in an age like ours buffeted by self-indulgence, the absence of restraint, and the loss of civility—both at home and in society. How we want to lash back, rise equally to the level of impatient hyperbole, simmering with discontent.

Lying and gossip are no better. They whittle down the other to compensate for our own jealousies and shortcomings. They mask our dark intentions and compromise our souls. And, how difficult it is to stop both! "O LORD! Help us to seal our lips as well as our thoughts when eager to heap recrimination against others!"

The same follows for the Buddha's Fifth Injunction and the Tenth Commandment. The Buddha wanted his followers to seek careers and livelihoods that minimized or totally reduced the suffering of others. In a contentious world of struggle and greed, his Fifth Step eliminated many work-choices for Buddhists. In Christianity and elsewhere, any career that contributes to the good of the commonweal is considered worthwhile. The Psalmist knew that when we are "busy" tearing down another's life, we ultimately destroy our own. To seek worthy and attainable goals, vocations that honor and glorify society and God, contributes to a life of pleasant gain and proud achievement, versus one of envy and spite, covetousness and discord. To that extent, the Psalms will always speak to our souls, for they bring God's comfort down not only to mend our hearts but to encourage us with truth and goodwill for all our time on earth.

~ ~ ~

> I cry with my voice to the LORD, . . . I pour out my complaint before him, I tell my trouble before him. When my spirit is faint, thou knowest my way!
>
> Psalm 142:1a–3

We have to admire this anonymous man—the Psalmist's editor. He knew so well the pace and limits, the depths and lows that mark our days and, far from unseen, remain visible to God. From nudging our consciences to lifting us up into God's presence, the Psalmist keeps our hearts hopeful and souls embraced by God's transcendent love. We need both: to experience God's Ineffability as well as God's saving grace. Both remind us of how destitute we are without either.

We need God's *transcendence,* his immeasurable "I am that I am," to lift us up to heights to which we cannot go, unless God should bend down to hear our prayer. Luther interpreted it as much as he mulled the limited reaches of fallen humankind's cry.[1] Yet as the Psalmist looked up in hope, his gaze was likewise drawn down to the condition of his soul. That's when he knew he needed *grace,* a love that would not let him go until he yielded his whole heart to God. *Transcendenc*e and *grace* are as much a part of the biblical story as God's *hesed* love and *zedek* longing for mankind's happiest ordering for a just and fruitful life.

If we settle for *transcendence alone,* we can never know whether the transcendent experience is merely a phenomenon of our innate subjectivity, longing to know him whom we can never truly know unless he descends to us, or an actual experience of his indwelling presence as Psalm 139 presents. If we exult in *grace alone*—God's unearned gift (Eph 2:8)—without remembering the passion and sufferings of Jesus, then we

---

1. Luther, *Works,* Vol. 14, 179.

never truly know the God of Scripture, whose ways are not our ways, nor thoughts our thoughts, and to whom alone belongs all glory.

The story of Isaiah's call to prophecy, which occurred in the Temple on the occasion of Uriah's death, combines the two. Isaiah saw the LORD, high and lifted up, as God's train of twinkling stars filled the Temple. "Holy, Holy, Holy, is the LORD of hosts," sang the six-winged seraphim. Then Isaiah received God's call and confessed his miserable status, while a seraph cleansed his lips with the glowing coal of forgiveness (Isa 6:1–9). Transcendence and grace—each is a mirror of the other, revealing while concealing the majesty of God.

As mentioned in the meditation on Psalm 55, what attracted so many Parisians to André's Villemétrie was de Robert himself. Humble, yet imbued with patient longsuffering, he was the magnet that drew the Center's guests. You'd see them walking together along the grand alleyway, or sitting on a ledge of the estate's stone walls, conversing, André listening, often concluding such pastoral "sessions" with a grave, "*Ah, bon!*" Then, in characteristic French style, he'd enfold their hands in his own. "*C'est bon!*" he'd sometimes add. They'd leave knowing, that if André had heard their whispered litany of trouble and disappointment, then surely God had heard them, too. He combined God's inimitable transcendence with Christ's spirit and grace in a ministry of mending disquiet souls.

Now comes the part we have come to expect—that inevitable question that the Psalms put directly to us. When was the last time that we listened with longsuffering to a friend or companion who needed our reassuring, "*Ah, bon!*"? It is never too late to enter the vineyard and help the Master Vintner gather his crop.

∽ ∽ ∽

> Hear my prayer, O LORD; . . . Enter not into judgment with thy servant; for no man living is righteous before thee. . . . Hide not thy face from me, lest I be like those who go down to the Pit.
>
> Psalm 143:1a, 2, 7b

Possidius—Augustine's earliest biographer, life-long friend, and fellow monk—tells us that Augustine died on August 28, 430. His death came ten days after falling ill and isolating himself in one of the Order's cells. As we know by now, the weakened saint ordered the Seven Penitentials to be copied and hung in his room that he might focus his thoughts on them during his declining hours. Possidius further relates that as the hour of his death drew nigh, he—Possidius—and other monks, along with Augustine, were chanting canticles when suddenly the Saint's voice grew weak; then inaudible. Before they could attend to him, he had already slipped beyond their arms into the hands of Another.[2]

Psalm 143 is the last of the Seven Penitential Psalms. Their earliest usage by the Patristic Fathers eludes us, but by Augustine's time, they were revered for reminding all that only God can forgive sin. No man can expiate his own transgressions. His pride is simply too deep and his spirit too weak to overcome his host of sinful commissions and omissions. Psalm 143 emphasizes that reality.

In his own book on the Penitentials, Luther wrote: "The life of a saint is more a taking from God than a giving; more a desiring than a having; more of a becoming than a being pious."[3] He knew such piety, such longing and desiring is a journey, not a destination to be reached this side of God's time. It humbled Luther as it had Augustine, St. Paul as well as the Psalmist. There are things to be desired, the granting of which belongs entirely to God. The forgiveness of sins is at the top of that list. "For no man living can be righteous before Thee."

We cannot know Augustine's last thoughts as he lapsed into the arms of our heavenly Father, but in his Commentary he knew how deeply he needed God: "How straight soever I seem to myself, Thou bringest forth a standard from Thy store-house, Thou fittest me to it, and I am found crooked."[4] Augustine entertained no delusions vis-à-vis his life as a bishop-monk. Yes, he had dedicated well over 50 years of his life to essays, scholarship, letter writing, preaching, teaching, lecturing, and creating such magnificent books as his *Confessions* and *The City of God*. All this he did up to the end, revising his entire massive works during his last few years, and that while attending to the affairs of his church in Hippo and its monastic orders. Never once did he cease to counsel any who came to him. But he knew the depths of his heart, the Pit that yawned ever within to draw him down, the foolishness of pride, and the

---

2. Smith, *Augustine*, 168.
3. Luther, *Works*, 14, 196.
4. Schaff, *Augustine*, 652.

emptiness of self-righteousness. Any good he had ever achieved, lives he had lifted up, souls he had nurtured, or causes he had championed were all to God's credit, not his. As he looked back across the years of his prodigious career, the Psalmist's words of vss. 5–6 especially haunted him— "I remember the days of old, I meditate on all thou hast done . . . I stretch out my hands to thee; my soul thirsts for thee like a parched land." What more was there to say, but to place his heart in God's hands? As he had advised others, did he recall his own words of comfort and release? "Look back then upon the Framer of thy life, the Author of thy substance, of thy righteousness, and of thy salvation."[5] It all belonged to God. Just as our frame, substance, and righteousness belong to God.

"O Heavenly Father, save us also from the Pit, that we may ever love and serve thee and our fellowman. Help us to be humble yet zealous, wise yet caring as Augustine was. Strengthen us also to be faithful as he was, down to the final breath of his soul, as he sang beside his faithful Possidius, surrounded by thy Psalms on his wall. May it be so for us as well! Amen."

~ ~ ~

Deliver me, O LORD, . . . Teach me to do thy will, . . . Let thy good spirit lead me on a level path! For thy name's sake, O LORD, preserve my life!

Psalm 143:9a, 10, 11a

How can we leave this Penitential without acknowledging David's imperatives? Neither Augustine nor Luther could. Let us note all four: *deliver, teach, lead,* and *preserve*! Not even Plato would have dismissed them, if the Psalmist could have handed him a copy. Remember in Plato's "Allegory of the Cave," the imprisoned inmates, chained with their backs to a wall, had only the shadows of objects before them to contemplate and from which to gain knowledge. To reverse this situation, Plato describes how a volunteer descended into the cave, unchained and "dragged," yes, "dragged," a prisoner to the surface. The ascent was difficult and the light blinding at first, but, O the joy of the released man when he beheld the

---

5. Ibid.

light for the first time! What a contrast! There is Augustine with the Penitentials to reassure and enlighten him; while the incarcerated of Plato's cave had only wavering and dim shadows on which to rely! Yet, in each case a savior descended to save the Saint as well as Plato's prisoner.

We need God's light, too! Even if we have to be "dragged" into God's radiant truth and forgiving presence! We are so fearful of losing control of our life. With grim intransigence we hold on, confident that we know what is best for ourselves and even others. Pride in self-sufficiency is difficult to quell. Even Paul had to be knocked down, sent sprawling off his horse before he realized what an unparalleled obsession God had in store for him. O to be delivered; to be taught, led, and preserved by God's hand! What greater satisfaction could life have? "The good I would I cannot do," lamented Paul. "The evil I distain I do! O wretched man that I am!" (Rom 7:19, 24). Paul had no misgivings. That is why the Psalms remain so relevant—reflecting the truth about our lives and souls. Perfectibility lies beyond our power, but not God's love, which he freely bestows on all who cry to him.

∽ ∽ ∽

> O LORD, what is man that thou dost regard him, or the son of man [*ben-ish*] that thou dost think of him? Man is like a breath [*he-vel*], his days are like a passing shadow.... Happy the people whose God is the LORD!
>
> Psalm 144:3–4

It is of interest that in the above text the Psalmist does not use the phrase *beni-ha-atham*, i.e., "the sons of men," or "the sons of Adam." Recall that the latter refers to that universal class of mankind that stands outside the circle of God's chosen ones whom he called in Abraham to be his special envoys for all humankind. Not that God doesn't care for the former, or hear their prayers, though the Post-Exilic community seemed to indicate so. Actually, the *beni-ha-atham* belong to that class of survivors descended from Noah and with whom God did make a covenant, referred to as the "Noachean Covenant." Its sign is the rainbow. We find the Covenant recorded in Genesis 9:1–17. No! But here the Psalmist employs the phrase *ben-ish*, i.e., an individual who stands before God in all his mortal being, not the faceless universal mankind of abstract existence. In other words, he is speaking to you and to me—directly—in all our solitariness and existentiality. It is I; it is you, for whom the LORD has regard, about whom he cares. Yes, you and I, in all our passing vanity, which is what the word *he-vel* means. Yes, we, who are like the dancing shadows on Plato's cave's wall! Here, there, up to the right and down, darting aimlessly in the fire's light! No more than silhouettes, appearing suddenly to disappear forever. What an image he gives us! Yet what a hope! For happy are those whom God regards, from whom YHWH will never turn away, betray, or cease to love.

17

An Epilogue of Praise

> Great is the LORD, and greatly to be praised, and his greatness is unsearchable.... The LORD is gracious and merciful, slow to anger and abounding in steadfast love. The LORD is good to all, and his compassion is over all that he has made.... The LORD is near to all who call upon him, to all who call upon him in truth.
>
> Psalm 145:3, 8–9, 18

There is a time to laugh and a time to lose, a time to reflect and a time to lament, a time to love and a time to grieve, and even a time to prepare for the grave. The Psalmist knew of them all. But throughout his hymns of angst and redemption, fear for his life and the Torah's revival, he knew equally of the soul's need to praise God, to bow in thanksgiving and in silent grace, to bow before the Eternal in contrition and gratitude. Having compiled Five Books of Israel's most poignant prayers, the Psalmist knew it was time to consider an Epilogue. It was time to end his work, to bind the Psalter's prayers to the hearts of his nation, as in the process of editing them, they had bound themselves to his own.

From his multiple collections of hymns, laments, confessions, and temple songs, the Psalmist/editor chose only six brief masterpieces with which to bring his tome of verse to a conclusion. All six are hymns of praise, the final five opening with the signature word: *hal-leh-lu-jah*, yes, "Hallelujah," meaning, "Praise the LORD," and ending with the same.

He knew it was time for a doxology, of canticles of joy. No doubt he chose some from the Temple's repertoire of both current and ancient songs, hymns of gladsome praise sung by Israel's festival-goers, as well as chants intoned by the Temple's choir of roundabout priests. In all likelihood, he created a few simply to fill out the collection. All in all, they were meant to lift up the community, the Assembly of God's weathered souls, to fill their cups of *auld lang syne* with joy and gratitude.

God never meant for our lives to become burdensome or weighed down from exhaustion. It is we who make them that way. For every hour of solemn grief, God's Word provides a rainbow to behold. Abraham found it in Isaac and Sarah; Jacob in Rachel's eyes and Benjamin's smile; Moses on the Mount overlooking the Promised Land; Elijah in the fire in his struggle against the priests of Ba'al; Mary Magdalene in the mist of that first Easter morning; Peter weeping in the arcades of the courtyard, hearing the cock's thrice, garbled crow; Paul, on the brow of the seafaring ship that bore him toward Rome; St. Augustine in Ambrose's Garden, clutching Paul's Letter to the Romans, knowing that, at last, his restless heart had found rest! Or St Anselm in his abbey, replying to Gaunilo's philosophical objections while wrestling with the "fool" in his own heart; or Luther kneeling in penitence on the eve of reading the Psalms. God has a way of bringing joy to his servants' heart, just as he longs to bestow his joy and grace on each of us. It is a fitting way to end each day, to conclude each lament with a doxology of praise: "Praise the LORD!"

"O Heavenly Father, help us also to do so every day! To end our prayers of grief and trouble, fear, remorse, and repeated petitions in a manner that hallows thy name!"

~ ~ ~

> Put not your trust in princes, in a son of man [*ben-atham*], in whom there is no help.... Happy is he whose help is the God of Jacob, ... who keeps faith for ever; ... executes justice for the oppressed; ... gives food to the hungry ... sets the prisoners free; ... opens the eyes of the blind ... lifts up those who are bowed down; watches over the sojourners, ... upholds the widow and the fatherless.
>
> Psalm 146:1–3, 5, 7–9

We find these verses—almost to the letter—preserved equally in Isaiah Chapter 61:1–2, and 58:6. Luke would cite them again in Jesus' reflections on Isaiah's passage in the first sermon he preached in his hometown of Nazareth. After closing the scroll, Jesus announced: "Today this scripture has been fulfilled in your hearing" (Luke 4:21). His hearers were shocked. No, no, no! In their minds, only God can do that! Only God can bring down such liberty, mending, and joy. They were prepared to lynch him. Jesus ignored them, however, and in the few brief years of his third decade fulfilled every hope the verses contained. Indeed, he loved the promises so much he repeated them in his famous Parable of Great Judgment. Matthew recorded every word, every stirring and momentous verse. "For I was hungry and you gave me food, . . . thirsty and you gave me drink, . . . a stranger and you welcomed me, . . . naked and you clothed me, . . . sick and you visited me, . . . in prison and you came to me" (Matt 25:35–36).

Our Psalmist's Epilogue calls us to embrace this mission, too. Both his and Jesus' message is unforgettably clear: *If you want to experience the presence of God, then care for his children, the wretched and the neglected, wherever you find them*: the hungry, the naked, the thirsty, the stranger, the prisoner, the ill, the lonely, and all who are weary of heart.

It may seem strange, if not an anomaly, that the heart experiences its highest joy in reaching out to others, not in seeking consolation for itself. In a world of constant indulgence and an economy of "me first," the Psalmist's call of "Hallelujah" is a summons to celebrate God's care for all humankind. There can be no peace of soul if one's soul exists at the expense of another's. God is not like that, nor was his Son. There would be no salvation if God had withdrawn from the world. Nor can we pray for ourselves without remembering others. Even Nietzsche's Zarathustra had to come out of his cave and mingle with the haughty and ignominious in order to confront the nihilism of his day. If he had remained secluded in his moldering lair, *Thus Spake Zarathustra* would have died in silence, just as the philosopher died in his sister's armchair in her home in Weimar. If you've ever walked through that room, or into its office, and seen Heidegger's letters to Der Führer requesting permission to research Nietzsche's files, while having to sign his requests with: "*Heil Hitler*," then you know how dark the world can become without the light and glory of God to fill it with hope and goodwill. The letters hang framed on the walls for all to see. O Luther! Where were your Penitentials? Your thoughts of Augustine's verses on his wall? Surely Heidegger knew of them, as well as Hölderlin!

Yes, *there are*, and *will be*, times when existence reduces us to weeping, when the providential hand of God seems far removed and only the shadow of his left visible. Since the fall of Adam, such has been the case, along with Achilles' senseless vengeful slaying of Hector, or Cain's pitiless murder of his brother, Abel. The Bible's "mirror" confronts us precisely as we are, reflecting our noble as well as ignoble poses. That is why God's *hesed* love and *zedek* longing for peace and order are so essential to our lives. It is why his grace and favor remain our highest hope; and why his descent down Jacob's ladder in the life of the Only Begotten Jesus transforms our sorrows into happiness and joy.

∽ ∽ ∽

> He determines the number of the stars;
> he gives to all of them their names.
>
> Psalm 147:4

Few verses of the Psalmist's strike us with such immediacy and grandeur. Thanks to modern astronomy, the orbiting Hubble Telescope, and the ceaseless planetary cataloging of the night sky, our universe's stars and galaxies fascinate us today more than ever. Who does not marvel at the whirling spirals of glowing light that constitute the spinning streams of shining stars, pulsating in galaxies millions of light years away? Billions of particles of sparkling dust, floating in spheres of galactic wonder, throbbing with young and dying stars, drifting in pink and yellow clouds boggle the mind and fill it with awe. Of such is the glory of God, who numbers and names them all.

The counting and labeling of the stars of night began long ago. By the time of the Late Bronze Period, if not earlier, the astronomers of Babylon had already mastered mapping the night sky and naming its brightest constellations. Even the Bible records the names of two: Orion (Job 9:31) and the Pleiades (Amos 5:8). The planet Venus is mentioned, too, though often in pejorative terms because of its identification with the worship of Ishtar, whose lustrous orb was Venus.

The beauty of the Psalmist's reference, however, far exceeds any later or earlier disapproval of mankind's naming of the stars. The Psalmist's point underscores the sheer wonder and glory of the universe's existence.

From the aspect of eternity, the gleaming spirals of galaxies and burning stars adumbrate the far-reaching and far-loving hand of God. He loves it all! He rules it all! He created it all! Night and darkness, light and stars, all belong to God. We who stare into his vaulted night, awed by its splendor, are lifted once again into God's grace and glory. Whatever our sorrows, disappointments, or worries, the handwork of God seems to restore an inner order with an invitation hard to refuse! He who rules the endless stars longs equally to love and guide our hearts.

"O God of light and glory, rule our life, our thoughts, our individual journey, that we may ever trust thy providential hand of healing wholeness. What so ever betide our present or future, hold us close to thy love and goodness, until it overflows our souls and, through our lives, flows out to others."

∽ ∽ ∽

> He gives snow like wool; he scatters hoarfrost like ashes. He casts forth his ice like morsels; who can stand before his cold?
>
> Psalm 147:16–17

Our second day in camp, our hosts drove our group from Israel's alluvial slopes into the heart of its ancient hills. We arrived in Jerusalem in the cold of winter, in a February mist of swirling snow. Snow in Jerusalem? Yes, snow! So few of us ever link the two. We passed through a district that was home to varied groups of Hasidic Jews, of whom many had suffered horrific loss under Hitler's reign.

Our bus stopped for a brief reprieve. We were asked not to stare at the Hasidic men, or at their hats, nor curls of beard, nor overcoats, or black shoes. I descended the steps with the rest of the others. I pulled my leather jacket about my chest and tried not to stare. He sends his snow as white as wool, his cleansing symbol of hope and renewal. How good and holy, frightful and humble it felt to be in David's City, God's promised Zion of light and redemption—a fact now of history. We all watched as the snow fell soft, white and fluffy, capping our hats with its wistful wonder. "Purge me with hyssop, and I shall be clean; wash me, and I shall be whiter than snow" (Psalm 51:7).

God has a way of awakening hearts, especially when we least expect it. Once more it is February, and God has gifted the South with snow.

WINTER HYMN[1]

In the deep of winter, when the cold was ripe,
God sent forth a snowflake, soft, angelic white.
How its form and beauty, filled the dark with light!
God created others, downy, soft and light.

Come, behold his handwork, God of frost and ice,
Cleansing all of mankind's, heart of hardened vice.
O the deep of winter, when the time was right,
God sent forth a Savior, to redeem man's life.

∽ ∽ ∽

Praise the LORD! Praise the LORD from the heavens, . . . Praise him, all his angels, . . . sun and moon, . . . all shining stars! Praise him, . . . highest heavens, and you waters . . . monsters and all deeps, fire and hail, snow and frost, . . . mountains and all hills, . . . cattle . . . flying birds . . . kings of earth and all peoples, . . . young men and maidens together, old men and children! Let them praise the LORD, . . . praise for all his saints.

Psalm 148: parri passim

Note the subtle difference between Psalm 147 and the above. One is the converse of the other. In the former, the Psalmist praises God for his creative power and oversight of the universe—from the heights of heaven to the depths of man's soul. Now he turns to us. It is we who must step forward. It is our turn to praise the living God. Even his vast and starry universe is summoned to blend its voice with ours, harmonizing with its elemental sounds, however inaudible or vocal. Notice, too, the scale of the Psalmist's order—from the lofty realm of angels, to the bright and shimmering stars; from the heights of the sun-caped mountains, to the depths of Leviathan's sea; from the storms and winds of the vortex, to the

---

1. By the author, February 12, 2014.

sleet and falling snow; from the beasts and creatures of meadows, to the kings of nations and people: down to the tiniest child. A Ptolemaic order to say the least! All, all are to praise God—we especially, who bear his image and to whom he looks for reciprocity, trust, and love. All reflect God's infinite wonder, regardless of the level of glory they are capable of displaying in their frame or form.

In an age of science versus religion—(according to Hawking, Wilson, and Dawkins)—the Psalmist bids us to soar above such foolish bickering to behold the God who loves us all, whose inimitable splendor throbs in everything, below and above. Here is God, the all in all, the transcendent Creator, whose hand and presence are immanent in all. Not faith versus reason, nor science in conflict with religion, but the one and sole universal God, overruling and ruling all, calling us to trust in him, beholding his grandeur in all we see, hallowing him in all we do, say, and love. That is what the Psalmist mulls in his own time of cultural moil. His was a life seasoned by God's wisdom and God's long and holy history of uplifting Israel when she needed it, descending down to comfort her in times of pain and trouble. This is God, maker of heaven and earth, who cares for all. Will he not care for you and me as well? Remember Jesus' words: "Look at the birds of the air: they neither sow nor reap nor gather into barns, and yet your heavenly Father feeds them. Are you not of more value than they?" (Matt 6:26)

"O God, grasp our hearts to help us see it all, even if only in a mirror dimly! Encourage us that we may serve and care for others, preserve thy works and all thy creatures, praising thy providential hand everywhere."

∿ ∿ ∿

> Let the faithful exult in glory; let them sing for joy . . . Let the high praises of God be in their throats and two-edged swords in their hands, to wreak vengeance on the nations and chastisement on the peoples, to bind their kings with chains and their nobles with fetters of iron.
>
> Psalm 149:5–8

Yes! Israel was still Israel. Surrounded by nations keen to fetter her. Under David, her armies proved invincible, his troops serving him with fervent loyalty. How they danced with sword in hand, to the clang of armor, shield, and spear! These were Israel's valiant men, bound by oath and gallantry, inspired by heroes like Joshua and Caleb, Gideon, Samson, Jonathan, and Jo'ab. Theirs was not the season of global peace; their walls, tents, cities, and campsites had ever to be guarded. It was an era of Israel's *Iliad*, sworn to valor, sword, and God.

This may not be the penultimate song our hearts expected or our souls longed to savor, but faith's reality has always existed in the midst of strife and conflict. It is not ours to fault the Psalmist's editor for his militant flourish, just one poem from the end. If God had not emboldened their armies, filling them with hope and courage, their faith might never have survived the Ba'als of Canaan, or years later, the Babylonian Captivity. Yet, through God's grace they did, God sending them home to rebuild the Second Temple, to reconstruct Jerusalem's walls, and to await Isaiah's Suffering Servant. Their faith lived on, surviving Herod and the Roman occupation, though ending in disbursement throughout the world.

Faith requires preparedness and vigilance, our very best, self-girding of the soul. Something of a Spartan spirit is needed to keep us bold. Courage, sacrifice, and self-restraint are allies of the soul. They keep us wary, our hearts strong. So, the Psalmist consented to David's warriors, hallowing their dancing to tambourine and lyre, even depicting them reclining on couches of well-earned rest and glad repose.

It was a different era, but the soul's condition remains unchanged.

Still, there is something more. Metaphor, allegory, and history always prompt us to search for more. His scroll was running out. Room remained for only two poems, Psalm 149 and 150. For one-hundred-and-forty-eight poems, hymns, and laments, the Psalmist prayed to God, pouring out his nation's cries and crises—individual and collective. But by whose providential power had Jacob, Judah, and Jerusalem managed to endure and strive? Of course, by the hand of God and his fatherly favor! But providence, along with all first and final causes, requires intermediate agents, too. Through whom does God bring such grace if not through our resources, our men, women, and warriors of our common cause? Even Plato's *Republic* recognized the role of guardians to defend Athens from sedition within and foes without. No nation can exist without its army, its troops in enclaves, far away, dedicated to the life and liberty of those at home. The Psalmist did not flinch from his last tribute, which he knew he owed to God and Israel's valiant souls. No epic ode or poem is without its Memorial Day. Nor any nation worth its salt!

That too is part of saving history and God's steadfast grace!

~ ~ ~

Praise the LORD.
Psalm 150

It was time now to bring the Psalter to a close—its hymns of prayer and thanksgiving, remorse and redemption, longing and thirst for God. How to do it? Should the Psalmist create still another ode, or monologue, or soliloquy? Were not Five Books of treasured dicta enough? He must have thought so, for as a choirmaster himself, if not a Temple Singer, the Psalmist laid aside his pen, and picking up his maestro's baton, tapped it on his podium. With rapt attention, he then began to lead the Temple's orchestra in the only biblical symphony we have—Psalm 150. If only its melodies and papyrus sheets of scores had survived! One must seek refuge in synagogues to recapture something of Israel's ancient chords in the voice of the cantor as he sings with sonorous melancholy the forgotten language of God.

But, no! Not here! Certainly, the temptation was real! Instead, the Psalmist chose another means by which to end his Psalter. He wanted God to hear their music, to savor David and Israel's joy. He wanted God to bend his ear, to marvel at the Temple's brass ensemble and its primal strings. He glanced about and tapped his baton. He raised his hands amid the hush; he nodded toward the Temple's Band. He wanted so much to cry aloud, "Now sound the trumpet and the timbrel! Play, you flautists and you pipers. Let me hear the roll of drums! Praise the LORD with clanging cymbals, melodies of harp and horn!" Of course, he kept this to himself, a secret for only God to know. But the thought was there in his soul. Yet, on and on he flailed his baton; back and forth he swung his arms. Softly, swept the hair-strung bows, with fingers trembling on tight-stretched strings. Equally wept each heart within. Then rose the leading cantor, and, glancing toward the Maestro's pose, began to sing, "He-ar, O Yish-ra-el. Adonai, Adonai! Hear, O Israel! The LORD, the LORD is One!"

Would Beethoven have approved of this "Hymn of Joy"? Did it equal Bach's fugues, or Handel's royal arias, or Brahms' "Academic Overture"? Would it have mattered? It was meant for God to hear. Equally, it was meant to preserve David's memory, a legacy for all God's children everywhere, far and near, and for all God's Diaspora, who love and cherish God, including you and me.

18
Postscript: Poetry, Time, and Eternity

Poetry, as a facet of language, has always enjoyed a unique venue, deemed irreplaceable throughout the centuries. It is the language of humankind's depths, of mankind's Spirit, *Geist,* or élan. It flows from his heart like waters from a fountain. Like snow-melting streams that form pleasant brooks, it cascades in his youth over rocks and cliffs to meander more gently through life's meadow years as the song of life bears his heart to the sea.

In religion, poetry rises to its loftiest heights when drawn to ponder the mystery of human existence. "What is man that thou art mindful of him?" captures it all in a single sigh. It is the means by which the human soul relates in *time* to the *eternal* élan that will not let it go. It is in and beyond us—this aesthetic call—to acknowledge an order of transcendence that fills us with awe while soliciting and fathoming our heart's despair. It is inescapable, wherever we turn. We cannot help but address this "call." And the catch to it all is the genre in which we feel commanded to answer. Often nothing less than a soliloquy will do as we have seen in the Psalms. Here it is filled with metaphor and a strange off-stage voice, whispered in monologues of oracular verve. Thus for mankind was poetry born as a language of the soul to converse with God, rendered to God in an ode of spiritual verse.

Over the centuries, mankind's religious poetry has been preserved in numerous Scriptures. Depending on the religion, it has appeared in the guise of provocative legend, along with saga and soulful reflection. Above all it serves as a narrative history, not only of the past but, of man's present plight and cry for redemption. In hymnbooks, it is couched in quatrains and lyrics to be sung by the faithful, or cherished simply by the self when alone. But its prayers introduce its pinnacle feature. After all, mankind's prayers and monologues of his journey require a listener to fathom his story. And who was that listener at first but the self? Then came the sky and the moon and the stars, the rise of the shaman, and the role of one's people, until mankind's soul could soar no higher and burst aflame, like the bush in the wadi that glowed before Moses. "I am that I am!" Man sank to his knees. "Look in your heart. You will find none other," spake the voice with gentle thunder. So man turned to poetry in a voice of his own to honor his heart and the heart of that Other to the sound of his harp and his cadent rich strophes. For how could mere words express the soul's essence that beauty and truth compelled him to utter? Only poetry and metaphor, lyrics and verse seemed qualified to carry his inner voice.

Poetically, aesthetically, man dwells on the earth! How can it be otherwise? For his dwelling on earth is his dwelling in *time*. And what is time's worth or the glory of its hours if all time were equal without the *eternal*, all time mundane and simply mortal? No infinite mystery of beginning or end? No formative principle, Tao, or Companion? No peace or repose at the close of the journey? Only to vanish and fade from memory! Thus were the songs of the *Rig Veda* ignited, the dancing and chants of Samuel's ecstatics (1 Sam 10:9–13), the oracle in white of the Temple of Delphi, and the *Nunc Dimittus* of Simeon and child: "Now may my soul depart in peace" (Luke 2:29).

If for no other reason than our *beingness* alone, the Psalms touch our hearts with God's truth and glory. They lift us to God and the realm of the holy. They cleanse our sad hearts and make glad our own stories. They fill us with hope when our souls sink in sorrow, with courage and resolve to love one another, and with God's mighty strength when our courage falters. And why, just O why is that so, if not for God's *hesed* that restores our soul?

Selected Bibliography

Buber, Martin. *The Eclipse of God*. New York: Harper & Row. Harper Torchbooks, 1957.
Bucke, Emory Stevens. *The Interpreter's Dictionary of the Bible*. Vol. 1, New York: Abingdon, 1962.
Calvin, John. *Commentaries on the Psalms*. Vol. 1. Grand Rapids: Eerdmans, 1963.
———. *Ecclesiastical Advice*. Louisville, KY: Westminster/John Knox, 1991.
Dawkins, Richard. *The God Delusion*. Boston: A Mariner Book. Houghton Mifflin, 2008.
Dillenberger, John, ed. *John Calvin: Selections from His Writings*. Missoula, Mont: Scholars Press, 1975.
———. *Martin Luther: Selections from his Writings*. Garden City, NY: Anchor Books, 1961.
Dostoevsky, Theodore. *Notes From Underground* in Gill and Sherman's *The Fabric of Existentialism*. Englewood Cliffs: Prentice-Hall, 1973.
Forsyth, Peter. *The Soul of Prayer*. Grand Rapids: Wm. B. Eerdmans, 1916.
Goethe, Wolfgang. *Goethe: Selected Poems*. London: Penguin Books, 1964.
Heaney, Seamus. *Opened Ground: Selected Poems 1966-1996*. New York: Farrar, Straus and Giroux, 1998.
Heidegger, Martin. *Being and Time*. New York: Harper & Row, 1962.
———. *Existence and Being*. Boston.:Henry Regnery, Gateway Edition, 1968.
Hartshorne, Charles. *Omnipotence and Other Theological Mistakes*. Albany New York: State University of New York Press, 1984.
Heschel, Abraham. *Man's Quest for God*. New York: Charles Scribner's Sons, 1954.
———. *The Sabbath*. New York: Farrar, Straus and Giroux, 1951.
Homer. *The Iliad*. Translated by Peter James with D.C.H Rieu. London: Penguin Books, 2003.
Jackson, Danny. *The Epic of Gilamesh*. Wauconda, Ill: Bolchazy-Carducci Publishers, 1992.
Jowett, B. *Dialogues of Plato*. 2 vols. New York: Random House, 1937.
Jones, W. T. *A History of Western Philosophy*. New York: Harcourt, Brace, 1952.
Kierkegaard, Søren. *Philosophical Fragments*. Translated by David Swenson. Princeton: Princeton University Press, 1971.
———. *Stages of Life's Way*. Translated by Howard Hong and Edna Hong. Princeton: Princeton University Press, 1988.
Kittel, Rudolf. *Biblia Hebraica*. Bibelanstalt Stuttgart: Ptivileg. Württ. Hergestellt, 1959.
Ludwig, Emil. *Goethe: The History of a Man*. New York: Putnam's Sons, 1928.

Luther, Martin. *Luther's Works. Vol. 14*. Edited by Jaroslav Pelikan. Saint Louis: Concordia, 1958.

Maimonides, Moses. *The Guide For the Perplexed*. Translated by M. Friedlander. New York: Barnes & Noble, 2004.

Marcel, Gabriel. *Being and Having*. Edinbrough: Dacre Press. A & C Black Ldt, 1949.

Nietzsche, Friedrich. *On The Genealogy of Morals*. Translated by Water Kaufmann. Princeton: Princeton University Press, 1969.

Oates, Whitney. Editor. *The Manual of Epictetus* in *The Stoic and Epicurean Philosophers*. New York: Modern Library Giant, 1940.

Pascal, Blaise. *Pensees and the Providential Letters*. New York: Modern Library, 1941.

Rilke, Rainer Maria. *Duino Eelegies*. Translated by Stephen Mitchell. Boston: Shambhala, 1992.

———. *The Notebooks of Malte Laurids Brigge*. Translated by Stephen Mitchell. New York: Vintage Books, 1990.

Russell, Bertrand. *Why I Am Not a Christian*. New York: Simon and Schuster. A Touchstone Book, 1957.

Sartre, Jean-Paul. *Being and Nothingness*. Translated by Hazel Barnes. New York: Philosophical Library, 1956.

Schaff, Philip. *Augustine's Expositions on the Psalms* in *Nicene and Post-Nicene Fathers. Vol. VIII*. Grand Rapids: Wm. B. Eerdmans, 1974.

Smith, Warren. *Augustine*. Atlanta: John Knox, 1980.

Solomon, Robert. *Existentialism*. New York: Modern Library, 1974.

Weingreen, J. *A Practical Grammar for Classical Hebrew*. 2nd Ed. Oxford: Clarendon Press, 1959.

Weiser, Artur. *The Psalms: A Commentary*. Translated by Herbert Hartwell. Philadelphia: Westminster, 1962.

Wilson, Edward. *The Social Conquest of Earth*. New York: Liveright, 2012.